Advance Praise for *Original, Unconventional & Inconvenient*

"Governor Ehrlich's latest is an insightful look at the successes and failures, triumphs and defeats of a very different political leader. You will come away with a better understanding of what the Trump Administration accomplished—and a sense of the array of opposition to his agenda and manner."

—Governor George Allen

"Governor Robert L. Ehrlich's writings on the Donald Trump era's political and rhetorical ups and downs are the most incisive and realistic of our times. Writing from a responsible conservative perspective, his analysis is unimpeded by ideological blinders, writing at one point, in summarizing the tremendous accomplishments of the administration as undermined by conflicts of Trump Republicanism, 'The establishment wants its party back…and Trump's ways certainly turned off many veteran Republicans.'"

—Richard E. Vatz, Ph.D, Professor, Towson University

"Ehrlich knows politics, he knows America, and he knows how things work both in D.C. and outside the Beltway, where the rest of us live. In his columns for the *Western Journal*, he has brought clarity—and a desperately needed civility—back to political discourse, without ever compromising his conservative values. If our nation still stands a century from now, it will be because of the thoughts, words, and deeds of Americans like Gov. Bob Ehrlich."

—George C. Upper III, Editor-in-Chief, *The Western Journal*

"*Original, Unconventional & Inconvenient* is vintage Bob Ehrlich—insightful, powerful, and well-written. It's a must-read for anyone interested in better understanding Donald Trump, his movement, and its impact on our nation and politics."

—Charlie Gerow, Vice Chairman, American Conservative Union

"Bob Ehrlich knows politics—not just from books and articles, but from personal experience. From being out on the stump, and 'in the arena,' and in office. He has a lot to say, to Republicans, Democrats, and Americans at large."

—Jay Nordlinger, Senior Editor, *National Review*

Also by Governor Bob Ehrlich

*Bet You Didn't See That One Coming: Obama, Trump,
and the End of Washington's Regular Order*

ORIGINAL, UNCONVENTIONAL & INCONVENIENT

DONALD J. TRUMP AND HIS MAGA MOVEMENT

GOVERNOR BOB EHRLICH

Post Hill
PRESS

A POST HILL PRESS BOOK
ISBN: 978-1-63758-124-7
ISBN (eBook): 978-1-63758-125-4

Post Hill Press
New York • Nashville
posthillpress.com

Published in the United States of America
1 2 3 4 5 6 7 8 9 10

To my incredible family, with lots of love. No son, husband, father could be more fortunate.

TABLE OF CONTENTS

PREFACE

We all know life can be unpredictable, but I did not envision a fifth tome from yours truly. Truth be told, I believed *Bet You Didn't See That One Coming* would be my last literary effort. Four books and hundreds of book signings over the past eight years had grown a bit stale. I had simply experienced enough of the hustling and travel that is a fact of life for any author interested in hawking his wares.

But the life, times, successes, and tribulations of Donald J. Trump are far too interesting to leave alone. His focus on dominating the daily news cycle was truly unique. Few pundits thought such dominance possible, even for a president of the United States. Yet, the commentators got it wrong, just the way they had since the very moment Donald J. and Melania Trump descended that escalator at Trump Tower on June 16, 2015. Early morning tweets in (prompt) response to detractors of all stripes or simply seeking to promote presidential initiatives constituted "never miss" fodder for the Trump-loving *and* Trump-hating media. Both pro and con pundits were compelled to cover and comment on the latest from Mr. Trump, thereby doing precisely what he wanted them to do. That he reportedly watched the fruits of his labor on the cable news networks is yet one more indication that this president brought a truly unique approach to the job.

Most Americans followed along for the daily ride. They just couldn't help themselves—and it sure beat late night replays of *Sports Center*!

INTRODUCTION: HOW WE GOT HERE: A BRIEF REVIEW

A proposed superhighway to an Americanized version of socialism-lite was put in place by the Obama administration from 2008 until the latter part of 2016, at which point a johnny-come-lately edition of a progressive successor was scheduled to complete the transformation. The presumed "fact" that Hillary Clinton would become the first female president only added to the anticipation. But the celebrity reality show host Donald Trump would appear out of nowhere and spoil the party. Seemed flyover America had a belly full of resentment, contrary to popular belief on both coasts and within the mainstream media. That Mr. Trump would campaign and govern as the second coming of Ronald Reagan (for the most part) added insult to injury—but also may have changed the tone, tenor, and expectations that go hand-in-hand with the country's highest office. Alas, a grievance-filled "Resistance" immediately formed. A frustrated media joined the fray. For these groups, "Trump the President" was unacceptable. He was counterfeit. He could not last. He lacked discipline, intellect, and preparation. His preferred method of communication was Twitter. After all, who (other than he) would conduct government by... tweet? Who (other than he) would so disrespect the long-tenured establishments of both parties? Who (other than he) would duly circumvent the self-appointed gods of our cultural and political values? In response, establishment types from both major parties would spend the next four years (including only the third and fourth presidential impeachments in

U.S. history) attempting to convince us that he simply was not up for the job. Mostly, though, he was not sociologically correct.

Perhaps this last charge best sums up the Left's problem with our 45th president. They (approximately half of the country) saw an "imposter" (Nancy Pelosi's term) with incredibly rough edges who had the temerity to highjack a political party—and then the country. But the other half saw a renegade dealmaker and unapologetic patriot intent on restoring America's mojo—getting America to win again—while restoring the notion that we *should* want to win again!

The Trump presidency will produce volumes of critical histories. Such is the byproduct of an unanticipated political force and the historic movement it generated. But how best to chronicle this president and his highly successful, yet hyper-polarizing presence on the national stage?

My answer, as set out in this book, is to first set the scene for the most important chapters of the Trump era—and then follow with my most relevant, contemporaneous columns from the time period.

Of course, the administration of Donald J. Trump is so chock-full of newsworthy events that picking the most important ones is no easy task. But it is within the following columns that the reader will (hopefully) come to better understand the life and times of Donald J. Trump. These, then, are my most critiqued (and sometimes controversial) opinion pieces, written for those forever attempting to figure out the ways, means, and ends of our 45th president and his merry band of disruptors. I hope you enjoy reading about this most consequential time in America's history as much as I did writing about it.

CHAPTER 1

OUT OF THE BOX

The first two years of the Trump presidency did not disappoint. How could it be otherwise? It was "The Donald" 24/7 per his above-described master plan. "Good" days and "bad" days were often conflated, as well-delivered, Reaganesque speeches were followed by missed high fastballs (Charlottesville); as serious policy pronouncements competed with Twitter wars waged against the likes of Rosie O'Donnell and *The Pope*. Supporters and detractors could agree on only one thing: the Trump era was never boring—its central character would never stand for it.

The most startling (and disquieting) news for those of the "Never Trump" ilk was the "new" Donald J. Trump. The former apolitical casino magnate, celebrity host, and supporter of New York Democrats would campaign and govern as an economic and cultural conservative. Indeed, the Right watched with amazement (and glee) as Obama-era regulations were quickly shelved, historic tax cuts passed, originalist judges confirmed, and the American military unleashed on a rapidly dwindling terrorist caliphate. Uncle Sam's withdrawal from the Paris Climate Agreement, Iranian Nuclear Deal, and Trans-Pacific Partnership signaled a new era of American unilateralism. Even more incredible to some—a pro-charter school, pro-life, pro-gun president actively solicited support from cultural conservatives—and received it. In the end, many of the original dyed-in-the-wool "NeverTrumpers" joined the Trump Train, notwithstanding their continued discomfort with their guy's sometimes cringeworthy, deeply personal style. Still, conservative successes produced a backlash, especially with the specter of a Special Counsel's investigation hanging over a highly ideological administration intent on challenging so many of Washington, D.C.'s most cherished assumptions.

Let's Make a (New) Deal

Washington Examiner
January 24, 2017

Campaign 2016 will generate years of scholarly analysis, as most expert pundits missed their mark by a wide margin. Few foresaw the advent of a Trump "movement," the long-rumored but never quite completed realignment of the white working class, or the stunning demise of the vaulted Clinton Money Machine. This race was more a WWE grudge match than a political campaign—no surprise to millions of wrestling fans who watched the future president of the United States forcibly shave the head of Vince McMahon at Wrestlemania 23.

But "leader of the free world" is not a scripted production. The Oval Office now replaces the rectangular ring. Here, the challenges are quite real. And the bad guys enter not with masks and chairs but with cyberattacks and ballistic missiles.

On the domestic front, the novice politician/businessman faces a difficult yet opportunity-laden challenge: how to marry traditional Republican philosophy (and constituencies) with the non-traditional views of the Trump coalition—and sustain the marriage in the face of a media and cultural elite fully invested in its failure.

The upside lies in a rare opportunity to jumpstart an economy suffering from slow growth and working-class distress—much of it directly related to our overly complex tax code. Both parties recognize 73,954 pages of federal tax law act as a serious drag on economic growth. That it includes a world record high corporate tax rate of 35 percent makes matters worse. Even Mr. Obama recognized the halting impact of such a high business rate—but refused to do anything about it unless the GOP Congress went along with new social spending. No relief for either side was the unsurprising result.

But minority status tends to sharpen one's focus.

Congressional Democrats could choose to participate by exchanging demands for more social spending with another Democratic priority—infrastructure spending. Interestingly, such a strategy may not be a killer for Republicans who have real infrastructure needs at home. The GOP view would *not* be a function of a Keynesian predicate, however: A low unemployment environment and the recent memory of Obama's failed $1.2 trillion stimulus (with all those not quite "shovel ready" projects) is not a formula for GOP enthusiasm, but rather, a realization that aging roads, bridges, tunnels, and airports require periodic repairs and upgrades.

Another potential element concerns a bipartisan desire to "bring the dollars home." Approximately $2.1 trillion in corporate profits is presently parked off-shore. Numerous high-profile corporate inversions have in turn occurred—to the detriment of the U.S. Treasury. The Obama administration's delusory response was to activate the Treasury's regulatory power to punish rather than work with congressional Republicans to fix the problem.

A business savvy Trump administration possesses the wherewithal (and votes) to bring it all together: real reform with fewer brackets and preferences; infrastructure revitalization that meets cost-benefit analysis; a lower corporate tax rate; and a tax holiday whereby repatriated profits would be subject to a reduced rate.

The last comprehensive tax overhaul occurred in 1986 wherein a conservative president, Ronald Reagan, struck a historic deal with the liberal Speaker Tip O'Neil. Senior players such as Jim Baker, Jack Kemp, and Dan Rostenkowski kept the bill on track—especially when the "losing" economic players to the deal screamed bloody murder. Today's political landscape is more complicated. Partisanship is front and center at all times. And social media makes discreet negotiations far more difficult to conduct. One thing has not changed, however: strong presidential leadership is essential to getting to "yes." It's all about the art of the deal—so to speak.

The proliferation of safe House seats on both sides of the aisle has given rise to a hyper-partisan Capitol Hill. Today, any enthusiasm to negotiate with the other side is muted by the likelihood of provoking a primary challenge for the offense of "weakness," "softness," or (on the GOP side) "RINO-ness." Accordingly, big ticket items tend to get accomplished only when the same party controls the House, Senate, and presidency.

With said monopoly power only guaranteed for the next two years, Republican power players would be wise to make its likely once-in-a-generation big ticket deal as balanced, impactful, and bipartisan as possible.

Recent experience is instructive. A Democratic wave propelled Barack Obama into the presidency and Democrats into control of both Houses of Congress in 2008. Two big ticket—but poorly produced—bills were shoved through a deeply divided Congress: the aforementioned stimulus (0 GOP House votes, 3 Senate) and the unnatural disaster popularly known as "Obamacare" (0 GOP votes in either House or Senate).

The respective failure of each initiative contributed mightily to the Republican romp of 2010—and to a realignment that has cost Democrats 63 House seats, 10 Senate seats, and 900 state legislative seats over the last six years.

Moral of the story: big ticket things can get accomplished under monopoly control, but better things get done (and last longer) when there is buy-in from the other side of the aisle.

From Transformation to Displacement

Washington Examiner
February 2, 2017

The unhinged post-election behavior of America's progressives and their media enablers proceeds unabated. Seems the angry reactions of so many cable news pundits during the evening hours of November 8, 2016, have metastasized into daily (if not hourly) attacks on everything Donald J. Trump.

A number of explanations are self-evident. First, the surprising loss of the woman who was pre-ordained to break the proverbial glass ceiling at 1600 Pennsylvania Avenue. Little did the Democratic Left anticipate that nearly half of America's female voters would prefer the alleged rogue billionaire with the supermodel (third) wife. Second, *both* party establishments have been shocked by the animus directed to their respective throats by the self-proclaimed leader of a populist "movement." Mr. Trump's inaugural address only added fuel to this antagonistic attitude toward Washington's powers that be. An enthusiasm for confrontation and very public willingness to indulge petty grievances adds to the list of Trump offenses.

OK, you say, all this is easy to understand. But there must be some other factor—some compelling explanation for the historic inaugural boycotts and unrelenting personal attacks. And you are correct.

Left under-analyzed by the breathless reports of angry millennials and large protest marches is a sense of displacement—not a word you see every day, but nevertheless the appropriate adjective to explain such unrelenting angst.

Websters defines "displace" as "to move from its usual place." The usual place herein is the recently concluded Obama era, a wonderfully progressive time wherein an unapologetically progressive president did all kinds of progressive things to change our cultural and economic values—to "transform" us into the Western European style welfare state Mr. Obama and his acolytes envisioned eight years ago.

And so America moved in the desired direction—which was scheduled to be followed by eight additional years of the same from the newly minted progressive Hillary Clinton. Sixteen years of this "usual place" would have indeed changed America forever.

But a bolt of lightning out of nowhere in the form of Donald J. Trump ended the experiment in the blink of an eye. Suddenly, the progressives' new age agenda was out—replaced by something very different. To wit:

The Obama administration's decision to protect "dreamer" parents through (what the Supreme Court ultimately decided was an unconstitutional) executive order was one step, as was the rapid expansion of the illegal immigrant safe havens better known as sanctuary cities. All this was in turn supposed to lead to the ultimate relaxation of our immigration system itself—the so-called "open borders" resolution. Alas, Mr. Trump's proposed wall, strengthened vetting procedures, and opposition to sanctuary jurisdictions have stopped this utopian vision cold.

Recall Obama's final fastball at Bibi Netanyahu's head in the form of a U.N. step aside so that the world's Israel haters could have at it one more time over the issue of West Bank housing developments. Of course, progressives applauded the unprecedented move. But even the best laid plans can go awry. Trump's unabashed pro-Israel views will end talk of a (forced) two or three state solution. Further, America will once again step forward as Israel's most reliable ally in a world body full of anti-Semitic Jewish state haters. Note that our Sunni allies are no doubt pleased with this dramatic change of direction. Their quiet accommodation with Israel against ISIS and Shiite Iran will be strengthened under Trump's reign.

Contrary to what Mr. Obama famously promised the naive brass at the University of Notre Dame, his administration nevertheless targeted the Catholic hospital-friendly Conscience Clause (during the Obamacare debate) in order to prove its progressive mettle. In fact, Obama's lawyers went all the way to the Supreme Court to argue that religious freedoms do not follow individuals performing secular activities in the marketplace (the "Hobby Lobby" case)—as though American citizens lose their freedom to follow their religious convictions when performing secular activities (such as filling out insurance policies that include abortion coverage) outside of a religious venue.

The Supreme Court rejected such a proposition, but Hillary Clinton campaigned hard on this "women's issue"—her court would have assuredly flipped the vote here. A Hillary-sponsored court would also have been on a clear path to another campaign promise—abortion on demand. But all of this was not to be. Judge Neil M. Gorsuch, President Trump's nomination to replace the late Antonin Scalia, will sustain a five-vote conservative majority for years to come.

Teachers unions viewed the Clinton candidacy as an opportunity to slow the momentum of the school choice movement. After all, hard line defenders of the indefensible never miss an opportunity to take educational options away from poor parents. But Mr. Trump and his choice of education secretary, Betsy DeVos, have far different views. Big time choice is their mantra. Private vouchers are back on the table. It's now "all of the above " when it comes to failing public schools—which means four (or eight) years of heartburn for the Trump-hating education establishment.

The new president is serious about change, progressive anguish notwithstanding. His inaugural address included the following promise: "We are transferring power from Washington, D.C., and giving it back to you, the people." It would be difficult to imagine a more pleasing comment for conservatives; it would be equally difficult to imagine a more disquieting message for the left.

Displacement, indeed.

Like Him or Not, Trump Is Now a Member of the Republican Family

Washington Examiner
July 11, 2017

The aftermath of the special election in Georgia's 6th Congressional District has been predictably brutal. Critical reviews from the progressive hinterlands have littered social media after yet another Trump-era special election defeat for the Democrats.

The ferocity of the criticism speaks to partisan frustration; this district was supposed to be chock-full of suburban Republicans just itching for an opportunity to register their disdain for Trump. But the depth of "Trump trauma" was far less than advertised; a late Trump endorsement may have even helped newly elected Rep. Karen Handel, R-Ga.

For the Democrats, two problematic narratives have emerged:

1. What if the Russian hacking/Trump story continues to go south?; and
2. What if a more moderate message is not a winning message in suburban swing districts?

You can bet each scenario has the attention of Democratic operatives desperately searching for a winning strategy against a supposedly vulnerable Trump. A related and equally interesting high-stakes discussion is playing out on the other side of the aisle. And it has been on my mind since a significant percentage of the "loyal opposition" shifted into resistance mode during the late evening hours of Nov. 8, 2016.

The conversation pertains to a condition (henceforth to be called "family syndrome") that afflicts a subset of Republicans who have never been enthusiastic participants in Team Trump. These are predominately conservatives who supported other GOP candidates in the primaries and were latecomers to the Trump bandwagon.

Post-election, they are generally pleased with Trump policy (especially the promotion of Neil Gorsuch to the Supreme Court), but remain ambivalent (or worse) with just about everything else connected to this president and his unorthodox methods of operation. Most have grown weary of the daily drama that defines the Trump White House.

Yet, the vast majority have stuck with Trump, and it is not merely because of common ground on most issues. They are digging in for the same reason that family can criticize family—but not so much outsiders. Most of you are familiar with the phenomenon.

Truth be told, these Republicans willingly and regularly engage in Trump bashing amongst themselves. They are often reminded (sometimes by Trump himself) that he is no lifelong Republican or movement conservative. And they remain uncomfortable with the edginess, the petty beefs, the daily tweets, and the relentless media bashing.

Nevertheless, the president remains (albeit new) family, and the party leader, after eight agonizing years in the desert. And so Trump trashing generally remains an intramural sport. When outsiders seek to indulge, an instinctive defensiveness is triggered: Wagons are circled, foxholes are dug. It's a doubling down in support of this most unlikely Republican president—yet another fascinating aspect of Trump's unique appeal.

In the real world, this defensiveness plays out in many ways. Often, the offended right-winger seeks to magnify opposition misdeeds. In the case of progressive Democrats, generally (and Hillary Clinton particularly), there is no shortage of such travails. This exercise also tends to minimize Trump's flaws. After all, he's our guy, he's under relentless attack, and now is not the time to talk outside the family (so to speak). Here, marginal supporters ratchet up their emotional capital invested in Trump. This reservoir of support in turn will make it harder to divest when times turn difficult.

In this context, embarrassing episodes such as the recent CNN-sponsored fake news story on alleged links between a Trump confidant and a Russian bank only serve to deepen the reservoir. This will typically be the result when the "Hate Trump Always" members of the media are shown to be wrong, negligent, and sloppy in reporting on Trump.

It's fair to ask how long this protectiveness can last. Persistent, ugly conflict with the mainstream media and our cultural elites could at some point simply exhaust this constituency—or lessen the desire to circle the wagons yet again. Still, with no moderate Democrat on the horizon, it will take a lot of turmoil for GOP partisans to willingly take a pass on Trump.

My fellow Republicans should feel free to test my theory. The next time one of your conservative friends starts to complain about Trump's latest outburst or tweet, tell him that you agree—and that you watched the very same criticism of Trump from Bernie Sanders, Elizabeth Warren, Hillary Clinton, Nancy Pelosi, Chuck Schumer, Debbie Wasserman Schultz, or Keith Ellison on CNN the previous evening. Then, stand aside and watch the sudden change of heart. ("What? They can't talk about the president like that!") This might be followed by an aggressive, possibly even passionate, defense of the same man they were tearing apart just a minute ago.

All of which may give Trump a longer-lasting reign than his multitude of critics could possibly imagine.

Yes, Trump's Presidency Is Still Worth It for Conservatives

Washington Examiner
January 12, 2018

What are we to think and do about misbehaving public figures? Peggy Noonan's Dec. 7 must-read column delved into this question, addressing the Al Franken affair and his half-hearted Senate farewell address. The punchline arrived near the end of her piece, when Noonan quoted approvingly conservative writer Sohrab Ahmari's condemnation of social conservatives who excuse "vulgar populists" because of their right-leaning policy positions.

The latter context was devoted to Alabama's now-defeated Senate candidate Roy Moore—and the omnipresent President Trump.

In truth, the entire column spoke to the Trump era and can be summed up in one question: Are the Reaganesque policy successes and judicial nominations of the Trump administration worth three (or seven) additional years of small-minded Twitter wars, off-the-cuff policy pronouncements, and occasional bad taste one-liners?

Ahmari's (and it appears, Noonan's) conclusion seems to be this: No amount of good news is worth abetting an "insufficient" and "inadequate" leader's refusal to abide by behavioral norms ("standards") expected of our commander in chief.

Noonan concludes with a sound admonition: "Don't let your fears—even wholly legitimate ones—drive you." Certainly good advice, but other compelling notions could have been added to her disquieting analysis.

Here are three for your consideration.

The first hearkens back to the romantic notion of the "will of the people," in this case, a free people who had a full opportunity to weigh Trump's personal and professional shortcomings and nevertheless voted him into office. Here, nullification is not an option. Free and fair elections must never be discounted in a democracy.

A second (indelicate) notion is more of a reality check on what giving up the ship would produce. Indeed, a hint of what could be in store for the country under Democratic control is supplied by "resistance" behavior over the past few months: 58 House votes for a groundless impeachment, embarrassing amnesia regarding past pronouncements in support of moving our embassy to Jerusalem, and over-the-top-reactions to a tax bill that returns billions of dollars to American taxpayers.

It is accordingly easy to see how Trump's abdication would empower really bad behavior by those who desire a return to former President Barack Obama's slow economic growth, timid foreign policy, and open-borders regime. Alas, many of us are unwilling to pay such an exorbitant price simply because we are at times uncomfortable with this president's disquieting behavior.

The third consideration is Washington's continuing astonishment at Trump's unapologetic jettisoning of principles that have guided presidents in recent years—especially the Obama years. To wit, Trump expects our NATO allies to pay their dues, in full and on time. He has (successfully) pressured the United Nations to cut spending. He will no longer inform our enemies of arrival and departure times for U.S. troops on the battlefield. He will support democratic uprisings against autocratic, anti-American regimes. He does not believe "Gitmo" merely fuels the fire of those who have hated us for decades. And he does not feel an obligation to accede to multilateral agreements (e.g., Iran, Paris) that do not benefit the domestic or foreign policy interests of the U.S.

Some may recall a guy named Reagan issued similar challenges to a resistant establishment. His tenure worked out pretty well.

I understand Ms. Noonan's high-ground disregard for a "win at any cost" rationalization of the Trump presidency. But periodic discomfort and sometimes frustration with the egocentric ways of this president does not compel me to indulge a "give it up in order to start anew" mindset.

The Obama-era damage to our economy and culture still burns too brightly. And Trump's administration holds forth great promise on issues such as taxes, education reform, foreign policy, Internet deregulation, and a number of other areas whose importance people underestimate.

Obama's disregard for the rule of law and enthusiastic fomenting of identity politics are things I do not miss and do not wish to revisit. So, with due respect to one of the country's most thoughtful writers, I'll put up with the tweets. I'll countenance the over-the-top salesmanship. I'll pray for more decorum and less vitriol.

But I'll pass on unilateral disarmament. The stakes are far too high to give people who are presently going about the business of giving socialism another test run the keys to the car yet again.

CHAPTER 2

SURVIVAL MODE: LEAD-UP TO THE 2018 MID-TERMS

Every political leader (let alone president) knows of the intense daily analysis and accompanying criticism that goes with the job. But the unprecedented animus directed at Mr. Trump and his administration was indeed extreme.

Each and every week since the beginning of the Trump era, the public was told to expect the imminent demise of DJT. Every new item of breaking news was guaranteed to be **THE event—THE faux pas— THE mistake** that would bring the Trump administration to its knees, once and for all. Alas, similar to Mark Twain, reports of Mr. Trump's demise were always premature and "greatly exaggerated." Some media reports were just plain wrong, the byproduct of lazy, hostile reporters from a "Never Trump" media. Others failed to generate the kind of impact that would have brought down any other American politician you care to name, with the exception of Bill Clinton (circa 1992 of course). Indeed, Donald J. Trump was a survivor. How else to explain political survival despite early "birther" movement sympathies; accusations that Ted Cruz's father was involved in the JFK assassination; criticisms of a Gold Star Mom; the Access Hollywood tape; rape allegations by columnist E. Jean Carroll; "I could stand in the middle of 5th Avenue and shoot somebody and I would not lose any voters"; Charlottesville; Robert Mueller's special counsel investigation; Michael Cohen's grand jury and congressional testimony; and more Twitter battles than space allows.

Then there were the outright discredited "fake news" (to borrow a phrase)—allegations sure to appear above the fold in America's leading newspapers—before discreditation down the road. The multitude of black eyes suffered by the Fourth Estate included but in no way was limited to false reports that Mr. Trump had removed MLK's bust from the Oval Office; that aide Anthony Scaramucci was involved with Russia; that attorney Michael Cohen was "told to lie" by Trump; that Trump attended a meeting with a Russian spy at Trump Tower; that Don Jr. took a mysterious pre–Trump Tower meeting phone call; that Don Jr. possessed stolen WikiLeaks emails prior to public release; that senior Trump campaign officials had repeated contact with senior Russians; that Mueller's subpoena to Deutsche Bank personally targeted Trump; that Russians had hacked into the U.S. energy grid; and that the CIA had removed a valuable agent from its Moscow office because the president was not capable of handling sensitive information.

A Trump fake news hall of fame to be sure, but not one to cool the jets of a relentless media engaged in unending conspiracy theories. Here, CNN contributor (and Watergate demigod) Carl Bernstein best exemplified the media's obsession with a multi-year string of "Trump is worse than Watergate" comments, reproduced below courtesy of political pundit Drew Holder:

December 2016	Trump's "lies are worse than Nixon's"
February 2017	Trump's attacks on media "more treacherous than Nixon's"
May 2017	Firing Comey is potentially "more dangerous" situation than Watergate

November 2017	[If Trump colluded with Russia] it's "worse than Watergate"
February 2018	Trump response to Russia investigation "eerily similar" to Nixon's leading up to Saturday Night Massacre
August 2018	Trump presidency "is worse than Watergate"
October 2019	Watergate Journalist Compares Trump and Nixon, says "We Are Watching a Coverup"
November 2019	Trump has at every turn "served the interests of Russia, a hostile foreign power"
September 2020	Trump COVID-19 tapes are…"worse than Watergate…called 'homicidal negligence'"

But the "Trump is worse than (fill-in-the-blank)" was only one theme of the media's crusade. Another was devoted to degrading Trump supporters in the heartland. Distilled down for mass consumption purposes, the indictment read: Trump supporters do not know better; the women are as bad as the men; and what do you expect from the great unwashed between the coasts?

These deplorables were the focus of particular media invective in the aftermath of two gun-related mass shootings (one in El Paso, Texas, and the other in Dayton, Ohio) during the summer of 2019. The usual suspects adopted their usual response: calls for additional gun control from the left and demands for concealed carry and enforcement of existing gun laws on the right. But a major difference this time was the occupant of the Oval Office. Unlike the doctrinaire anti-gunner Barack Obama or the pro-gunner George W. Bush, herein was a politician who had leaned left on guns while in New York but who had adopted the NRA line while campaigning for president. This flexibility immediately manifested itself in the aftermath of the two horrific events wherein Mr. Trump took to Twitter in order to call for additional background checks on gun sales and the implementation of "red flag" statutes—both a flashpoint for pro-gunners around the country. The response drew the ire of numerous pro-gun advocates, but the NRA held its fire. The organization understood the importance of having a friend in the White House. Still, the media jumped into the fray with gusto, suspecting they finally had the opportunity to exploit a rare breach between the president and his gun-loving base.

All this and more set the stage for major GOP losses in the 2018 midterms. In the end, the GOP lost 40 House seats—half to self-proclaimed "moderate" suburban Democrats riding the tide of suburban female opposition to the president. Remarkably, however, the advent of the 2020 presidential election cycle saw many leading Democrats enthusiastically embrace an uber-left platform—most spectacularly, a "Green New Deal" initiative that generated early, unwelcome headlines for those newly elected purple seat members. After all, these newbie politicians had just finished reassuring voters of their commitment to a "new" Democratic party that would be more empathetic to the concerns of working-class voters (who had deserted Mrs. Clinton in droves). But the promised new dawn was immediately clouded over by a loud, ascendant progressive base. Just how hard of a leftward tilt, you say? Well, check out these once unheard-of headlines:

- "Bernie Sanders hires undocumented immigrant to help run 2020 campaign"
- "Elizabeth Warren floats reparations before discussing America's ugly history of racism"
- "Trump blasts Dems for blocking bill to stop infanticide"
- "Stacy Abrams claims voter suppression is legal in the United States right now"
- "Pelosi joins forces with Mexican officials at the border to celebrate international bridge ceremony"
- "Democratic governor signs bill allowing state to potentially bypass electoral college"
- "Harris push for legalized prostitution gains ground"
- "College students harass border patrol agents, liken them to KKK"
- Multiple Democrats replace POW flag with transgender pride flags outside their offices

Such new era storylines were not simply a reaction to Mr. Trump and his administration. Newly empowered progressives sought to target any and all institutions that stood in the way of a remade America; that is, any obstacle to the consolidation of power within a supercharged administrative state. To wit: former FBI deputy director Andrew McCabe admitted to discussions with senior DOJ officials regarding the removal of the president from office under the 25th amendment, while Democrats began a dual-frontal assault on the Electoral College by either constitutional amendment (requiring a two-thirds vote by the House and Senate and ratification by 38 states) or the newly knighted "National Popular Vote Interstate Compact" (which awards a state's electoral votes to the candidate with the most votes nationwide). Note that the second option may be closer to reality than one might suspect. As of July 2020, it has been enacted into law in 16 jurisdictions possessing 196 electoral votes. The Electoral College would be effectively repealed once that number reaches 271. In a similar vein, congressional Democrats and presidential hopefuls began talk up a "court packing" proposal to expand the number of seats on the Supreme Court in light of a persistent five-seat conservative majority—then six with the addition of Amy Coney Barrett. And, yes, FDR is no doubt smiling down upon this new iteration of his failed New Deal–era ploy to accomplish the same goal.

The hard-left turn was accompanied by a barrage of (count 'em) six House committee investigations into the personal, political, and business life of the president and his family. A tidal wave of subpoenas, interview requests, and document requests would guarantee a busy two years for an overburdened White House Counsel operation still recovering from the two-plus year Mueller investigation. Yet, the velocity of the inquiries (together with the underwhelming findings of the Mueller report) only added to the widespread perception that the congressional "resistance" hated too much; that the unreserved ire focused on all things Trump risked turning off Independents and middle-of-the-road (let alone conservative) voters unimpressed with the Democrats' newfound enthusiasm for 24/7 investigatory hearings and socialism-lite policy. Had not the unexpected fall of the midwestern "blue wall" in 2016 taught the Democrats anything?

Perhaps a short-lived vignette from a back-bench member of Congress provides the best context. On March 3, 2019, in the midst of a congressional showdown over southern border funding, a series of powerful tornadoes swept through Lee County, Alabama. The fast-moving storms killed 23 and caused widespread property damage. Shortly thereafter, the president signed a major disaster declaration for the county. Nearly a week later, the Trumps left D.C. to tour the tornado-ravaged area.

Nothing out of the ordinary here. Presidents and governors typically tour storm-damaged areas in order to reassure victims and their families that the government is there to help. Everyone understands such visits are expected—even required.

But this was the social media–driven Trump era. There was no *normal*. Every action, every movement was hyper-analyzed and usually to the detriment of Mr. Trump. And so the president's visit to rural Alabama was made the focus of a tweet by Democrat Congressman Ted Lieu of California:

> *Can you feel the urgency?*
> *Is this why @realdonaldtrump is going to Alabama? Because*
> *we need to build a wall along Alabama's southern border?*
> *Oh wait, I just looked at the map…*

What was intended to be a quickie, drive-by strike against the president's insistence on a border wall turned into political embarrassment, as it became apparent Congressman Lieu had no knowledge of the death and destruction left behind by Mother Nature.

Republicans Need to Play Obamacare Repeal Right or Face Disaster in 2018

Washington Examiner
July 20, 2017

It's a shame Senate Republicans are having such a difficult time getting their act together on health care. After all, "Obamacare: Reality Sucks" is playing all over the country right now, to dreadful reviews for familiar reasons.

Major carriers continue to flee Obamacare exchanges en masse, its co-ops continue to go belly-up (only four of the original 23 remain in business), and its networks continue to shrink. Without a massive influx of subsidies, the program's demise is no longer "if," but "when." And our old friend, Professor Jonathan Gruber, is nowhere to be found.

Yet, despite all of this unraveling, recent polls reflect newfound support for the embattled program. The reform that contributed mightily to historic Democratic losses in the House and Senate is suddenly, if not popular, at least not so unpopular.

Alas, the public does not appreciate confusion when it comes to their health care. They understand Obamacare has fatal flaws, but what of the "replace" part of "repeal and replace?" Here, the GOP Senate's bumbling and stumbling is embarrassing; its credibility diminishes by the second.

Meanwhile, Democrats have doubled down on defense of Obamacare. It seems that even four election cycles (and the loss of more than 1,000 seats in local, state, and federal legislatures) of voter retribution has failed to dampen progressive enthusiasm for President Barack Obama's signature health care reform. This devotion to Obamacare is in one sense not surprising, since the law represents a tangible first step toward their ultimate goal: single-payer, government-sponsored health care.

At times, a sampling of Democrats will admit to Obamacare's deficiencies, but usually in the context of condemning cold-blooded Republicans who turned the taxpayer faucet off just when Obamacare's subsidies were most needed. (Note that this narrative ignores the ugly irony that the intended beneficiaries of additional taxpayer largesse are the big, bad insurance carriers who require subsidies in order to keep offering plans that are otherwise unprofitable.)

It is now eight years later, and decision time draws near. A "replace" bill will have profound consequences for our health care delivery system. Accordingly, this is the time and place when real political leaders earn their money—and their legacies.

The Left smell a paper tiger. They know many Republicans like to talk the talk at Lincoln Day Dinners; that throwing spitballs from the bleachers is the easiest thing to do in politics.

But it's a different ballgame when real votes bring real consequences to real people. Suddenly, your "safe seat" is competitive because the Democrats have run a million dollars of "mediscare" commercials against you.

The bottom line: Democrats do not believe enough Republicans have the chutzpah to make tough votes, that the GOP lacks the courage to eliminate goodies previously awarded to the voters—especially when a government entitlement program is at issue.

Something close to the Senate health care draft can counter this narrative, especially one that includes the modernization that transitions Medicaid to per capita block grants and returns all enrollees to the traditional (approximately) 50/50 federal/state match rate that existed prior to Obamacare. Recall many governors of both parties bought into Obamacare in order to access Washington's "free money" for new able-bodied enrollees, a win-win for fans of the welfare state, and a "success" that has resulted in one in four Americans now covered by the program.

But their "victory" has helped further expose Medicaid's subpar service regime. The number of participating physicians has dropped as reimbursements are cut, while Medicaid spending continues to exert immense pressure on federal and state budget deficits. Indeed, Medicaid spending now represents 10 percent of the entire federal budget.

The Senate draft is therefore a rare opportunity to control what amounts to an open-ended federal entitlement. This is a big deal.

A decent compromise on Obamacare's community rating mandate is another step in the right direction. As discussed in previous columns, expanded pricing options as a function of age more accurately reflect market costs even with the inclusion of pre-existing disclaimers.

A potentially winning Republican narrative emerges: able-bodied, non-poor men are given the opportunity and (responsibility) to purchase an insurance policy that best suits their circumstances. The vast majority of this healthy subgroup will be covered by inexpensive, high-deductible catastrophic policies while people who have experienced more problematic health histories (those with pre-existing conditions) will continue to have access to affordable health coverage.

Note the Senate draft does not contain the House repeal of Obamacare's taxes—presumably to mute the Democrats' mantra of "tax cuts for the rich and service cuts to the poor." This will of course not diminish Democratic fondness for class warfare rhetoric, but it does free up dollars to meet GOP moderates' demands for additional spending on out-of-pocket costs and the opioid epidemic (albeit not enough to date).

The end game is fully in the GOP's court. Few of its supporters will be satisfied with a failed attempt at "repeal and wait for two years." Rather, the choice is clear: either lead or be exposed, either wilt or show the voters that a federal entitlement can be reformed, either pass a bill that lowers premiums or expect a "what for?" from voters come November 2018.

How wonderful it would be if the GOP chose to compete—pass a bill, celebrate health care choice—and then went out and won the 2018 mid-terms on a "can do" platform.

One can dream, right?

Talking Past Each Other on Gun Control

National Review
April 26, 2018

Parkland happened. Again, America watched in horror as children fled from a murderous school rampage. Immediately, the usual fingers were pointed at the usual suspects. The media coverage was wall-to-wall. But what followed was different from the aftermath of other school shootings. A national town hall was scheduled, a day of protest drew hundreds of thousands around the country, and calls for gun control filled the airwaves. Kids took the lead, at least in the eyes of the general public. A movement seemed poised to effect change.

More than two months down the road, one wonders if that change has really materialized. It seems more likely to me that, despite relentless media coverage of Parkland's student activists, the respective sides have simply dug in again. What follows is a distillation of conversations I've had with gun-control advocates of various stripes over the past month. See if it sounds familiar.

> **Gun-control advocate**: The time has arrived. America is ready for change. School shootings have finally become intolerable. Even Fox News devoted serious coverage to our Washington rally.

> **Me**: The testimony of the Parkland students and families was heart-wrenching. Every parent—every human being—can only attempt to imagine their pain.

> **Advocate**: Empathy is one thing, but Parkland was a tipping point. The message is, "No more mass shootings, whatever it takes."

> **Me**: I agree with the "no more." But guns weren't the sole cause of this shooting. The FBI and local police were grossly negligent—multiple warnings over many years were missed or ignored, and the armed officer on the scene chose not to enter the school and engage the shooter.

Advocate: Police inaction and incompetence are legitimate concerns, but far less important than controlling weapons of war. .

Me: Not so fast. Did you catch what went down at Great Mills High School in southern Maryland 34 days after Parkland? There, a bad guy with a gun was confronted by a good guy with a gun. The shooter killed himself after being shot by a school resource officer. No obsessive cable-news coverage followed. No rallies were scheduled. It was a one-day story. The facts did not fit the chosen media narrative.

Advocate: A classic right-wing response. It seems there are never enough guns to please your side. But this time, even red-state America is paying attention. Public opinion is turning. The NRA is on the wrong side of history.

Me: Most gun owners have no problem with reasonable restrictions on bump stocks and other commonsense measures to keep guns out of the hands of felons, the mentally ill, and otherwise irresponsible individuals. For example, Senator Rubio has introduced a bill that would require the FBI to notify local law enforcement whenever a "prohibited" person is rejected from an attempted gun purchase. That seems sensible.

Advocate: We are not interested in "small ball" changes. The problem is guns. There are too many of them, and there's too little regulation. It's time to act.

Me: But so many well-intentioned gun-control measures inevitably penalize the law-abiding. Recall that criminals are forbidden from possessing firearms in the first place. Any law that requires a felon to register a firearm or submit to a background check or other legal process is unenforceable; the government cannot require prohibited persons to incriminate themselves.

Advocate: That is a good debate point but ignores the gun culture that defines us. America is no longer a rural society—the Wild West has come and gone. Most countries (and cultures) do not glorify gun ownership. Some have successfully confiscated private weapons, including assault weapons. These societies suffer far fewer gun-related accidents and deaths.

Me: What is an assault weapon?

Advocate: It's…a semi-automatic dressed up with combat accoutrements.

Me: At the end of the day, a semi-automatic is a semi-automatic—and there are tens of millions of them in this country. If you want to ban all of them, just say so.

Advocate: I'm saying so.

Me: What about Justice Stevens' recent call to repeal the Second Amendment?

Advocate: He shouldn't have written that. We know your side will run with it as "proof" of our agenda, and the NRA will raise money from it.

Me: Still, isn't it fair to say many progressives would at the very least support national gun registration?

Advocate: What can I say? We wish America looked more like Sweden.

Me: America is not Sweden. You cannot redo culture (try as you might). Gun ownership has always been a central tenet of our culture, symbolic of freedom *from* government.

Advocate: As I said, the Wild West is history. Dodge City is a suburb. The threat of homeland invasion is non-existent. Yet our urban areas are suffering from a gun epidemic!

Me: No, our urban areas are suffering from a *crime* epidemic!

Advocate: You just don't get it. More guns equal more death!

Me: No, *you* don't get it. More guns equal less crime.

Advocate: Whatever. 2018 will be a turning point. Democrats will run on an unabashedly anti-gun platform. The merchants of death will be demonized at every opportunity. Our base is enthused. We will win.

Me: Good luck with that. Proposals like a national gun registry are non-starters with the vast majority of Americans.

Advocate: I would feel so much better if the government knew the whereabouts of every firearm in this country.

Me: This is going to be a long year…

Don't Throw Stones at Barking Dogs

National Review
May 15, 2018

A favorite Churchill quote has been on my mind lately: "You will never reach your destination if you stop and throw stones at every dog that barks."

The reasonable takeaway for political warriors is that you should refrain from hating the opposition because such vitriol can distract you from your own purposes. Of course, that lesson is much more easily understood than it is internalized in the rough-and-tumble world of Trump-era politics, but both sides of the political divide could stand to take it to heart.

On the right, it would be wise for President Trump to somehow re-strain himself from tweeting aggressive rejoinders to each and every move by Special Counsel Robert Mueller and his team. Similarly, Trump's protectors in Congress would do well to resist the lure of nightly appearances on Fox News. Fighting Mueller's fire with fire might incite the base and provide grist for nightly GOP opinion journalists, but it won't move the White House closer to Rudy Giuliani's stated goal of completing the Russia investigation as soon as possible. The president's occasional propensity to misstate facts and/or overreact in response to criticism does not help his cause in this case, either.

I understand that this advice runs counter to Trump's stated preference for an overwhelming show of force in response to criticism. Yet it would be prudent for a president with a special counsel breathing down his neck (and opponents eagerly waiting to begin impeachment proceedings) to be more flexible at times—especially if he intends to allow Mueller's investigation to run its natural course.

To be sure, however, the president's hyper-aggressive responses to the multitude of dogs barking at him pale in comparison to the Left's incessant attacks on just about any idea or individual associated with him. Over-the-top appeals to emotion are part of the progressive Left's DNA;

you can see their striking appeal on just about any college campus these days. But they're also an extension of Chicago mayor and former Obama chief of staff Rahm Emanuel's widely quoted quip that "you never want a serious crisis to go to waste."

Alas, the modern Left never misses an opportunity to indulge.

Some of you may recall the vitriol pouring forth from the lips of Democratic leaders at the funeral of former U.S. senator Paul Wellstone in 2002. Here, what was supposed to be a solemn ceremony for a departed politician shamelessly degenerated into a campaign-style rally. GOP leaders were jeered and liberal icons were cheered. Even the left-leaning media reported the bitter partisanship as a bridge too far. The voters saw it the same way, electing Republican Norm Coleman over Walter Mondale in the race for Wellstone's seat. A private Democratic poll confirmed that the circus backfired on the Democrats nationally as well. Maybe the rule should be "no stones" allowed at a funeral.

The anti-gun/anti-NRA agendas on display at various events held to honor victims of mass shootings are a more recent case in point (e.g., CNN's post-Parkland national town hall). But real dogs are never enough—today's "resistance" persistently pursues bogus dogs. For context, recall the following counterfeit reports by media and politicians alike:

- On Trump's Inauguration Day, a *Time* reporter erroneously tweeted that a bust of Martin Luther King had been removed from the Oval Office. Social-media reaction was brutal—until the reporter corrected his error.
- A week into the new administration, the *Washington Post* reported "mass resignations" at the State Department. Social-media reaction was again vicious—until it became clear that the four departures the *Post* was referring to were pro forma resignations of the kind traditionally submitted at the beginning of a new administration.
- Late last year, ABC's Brian Ross reported that the president had directed Michael Flynn to contact the Russians *prior* to the election. A later clarification (Trump's instruction had been

given *after* the election) could not save Ross from a four-week suspension without pay.

- On December 8, 2017, CNN breathlessly reported that candidate Trump and son Donald Trump Jr. had been given access to hacked documents from WikiLeaks prior to their publication online, before it was shown that said access had been offered *after* the documents' publication.

- One day later, the *Washington Post* famously misrepresented a sold-out Trump rally by publishing a photo of an empty arena… hours prior to attendees' being allowed to enter.

One may ask why the media feel the need to go after the president with false or exaggerated stories when his administration produces more than its share of genuinely rich targets. The answer, of course, takes us from Emanuel's cynicism back to Churchill's admonition. You see, emotional opportunism of the variety seen at Wellstone's funeral tends to cause the aggrieved to lose focus, retreating into ultra-partisanship and the delusions it can engender. Recall Hillary Clinton's effort to "expand the map" two weeks prior to Election Day, when she thought victory was assured. The media bought it. Emotions were at a fever pitch. Clinton was on a roll, and cocky. All she could see was a basket of "deplorables" on the other side. She couldn't lose—and then she did. A loss of focus, indeed.

Time to Take Obamacare Off Life Support and Let It Go

LifeZette
August 29, 2018

President Donald Trump sucks so much oxygen out of the daily news cycle that it is easy to forget other mightily important issues. One such qualifier is health care reform—presently relegated to the back burner as Bob Mueller and Stormy Daniels dominate the national headlines.

But it would be a mistake to conclude that the GOP's failed Affordable Care Act (Obamacare) repeal effort is the most recent—or important—development within the health care narrative. Facts on the ground reveal a far more promising environment.

The Trump administration, congressional Republicans, and judicial decisions have helped mitigate Obamacare-inflicted damage while incrementally replacing it with more consumer-friendly, real-world solutions.

To wit:

1.) **Corridor payments.** Recall how congressional conservatives resisted attempts to throw additional taxpayer dollars into failing Obamacare exchanges, even taking the Obama administration to court in order to forestall unauthorized spending by the executive branch.

   As expected, insurers sued for their promised cut of the money. (These taxpayer dollars had been dangled as bait by the Obama administration in order to secure the industry's political support for Obamacare.) Ultimately, the Federal Circuit ruled Congress lawfully withheld risk corridor funding.

   At least in this case, the time-tested Washington, D.C., practice of repeatedly subsidizing failure while hoping the taxpayers look the other way was thwarted. Score one for fiscal restraint and the rule of law.

2.) **Lighter options.** The Obama administration rejected the concept of shorter-term, more flexible ("mandate light") plans that may have appealed to consumers uninterested in Obamacare's expensive exchange plans.

   Even Obama's three-month cheaper option did not exempt consumers from the individual mandate penalty. Obama needed everyone in his exchanges for his health care math to work.

But now the Trump administration has proposed an extension of the lower-cost option, but without the added burden of the mandate (now zeroed out by the Trump tax cut and reform bill) and other Obamacare-mandated benefits such as prescription drug coverage.

The new rule allows for extensions of up to 36 months. The primary beneficiaries will be non-poor (unsubsidized) working and lower-middle class consumers who are hurt by higher premiums, higher deductibles, and carrier flight from the exchanges.

Opponents complain the option will attract younger, healthier enrollees, further pressuring the already-underwater exchanges. But such is the byproduct if government is to expand affordable choice within the health care marketplace.

3.) **IPAB.** Included in the 2017 tax reform bill was repeal of the much maligned Independent Payment Advisory Board (IPAB). You may recall this beauty was designed to foist price controls on Medicare reimbursement. Much criticism was directed at its powerful, unelected governing body.

Obamacare's drafters made it especially difficult to appeal its decisions. Thanks to Trump, IPAB is now gone and forgotten.

4.) **Association health plans.** Another pressure point concerns association health plans (AHPs). Obamacare forced businesses with 50 or more employees to provide heavily mandated coverages that many employees did not need or want.

One unfortunate byproduct was a conversion of full-time employees to part-time employees. Other employers simply dropped their health care coverage. Enter the Trump administration's new rule expanding the scope of association plans.

Experts project that between 4 million and 5 million people over the next four years will leave the individual and small group markets for new AHPs. Such plans are popular with many Republicans, as they allow small businesses and the self-employed to band together and thereby achieve economies of scale.

Accordingly, they feature choices at less expense, but fewer benefits as compared to Obamacare plans. Here again, fewer mandates and cheaper options will entice younger people and further destabilize Obamacare's exchange plans.

5.) **Health savings accounts.** This increasingly popular option accomplishes two policy goals: First, it maximizes health care freedom; and, second, it encourages health care consumers to consider the real, unsubsidized price of care as part of the purchasing process.

There were approximately 22 million HSAs in America at the end of 2017, up 11 percent from 2016. Each new account nudges U.S. health care consumers away from our price-distorting third-party payer delivery model and toward marketplace-pricing freedom to choose. Not a bad deal.

The bottom line: Obamacare was flawed from the jump. Its presumptions were cynical, especially its reliance on mandates to force younger, healthier people to pick up the health care tab for older, sicker people.

Obamacare sought to rearrange an entire insurance market rather than focus on a critical need: How to secure affordable insurance for the non-Medicaid qualifying working poor and working class. It was a one-size-fits-all, mandate-heavy political compromise with too many moving parts.

To boot, even Obamacare's much ballyhooed pre-existing condition disclaimers have proven flawed.

Recent studies reveal how insurers that offer high-quality coverage for the very sick—including those who receive tax subsidies—do so at a loss. Accordingly, as more expensive older folks continue to sign up, the carriers are forced to raise prices or leave the market.

The foregoing does not lend itself to a 10-second sound bite. Insurance issues can be complex and confusing. Nevertheless, Republicans are proceeding on numerous fronts to further downsize Obamacare's decaying infrastructure.

In the process, they must better explain their policy initiatives to an audience that does not understand what Obamacare did, let alone what it looks like today. While they're at it, reformers must maintain their moral and political obligation to the underserved by "replacing" Obamacare with options that provide the near-poor access to affordable care.

It's no easy task—but is still desperately needed.

Trump's "Big Stuff" and "Little Stuff" and How to Know the Difference

LifeZette
September 7, 2018

Recent headlines constitute a microcosm of the Trump era: reports of sustained economic growth, new records in a long-running bull market, an 18-year-high in consumer confidence, real progress on NAFTA renegotiation (if we can still call it by its "old" acronym), and an Iranian economy careening toward collapse, thanks to Trump's punishing U.S. sanctions (and the promise of additional sanctions come November).

All of these are substantive accomplishments. All are familiar items on a to-do list regularly updated by a White House administration and conservative media serious about keeping an accurate score.

And then there is the other side of the president's world: an unprecedented revocation of a former CIA chief's security clearance, the Manafort verdict, the Cohen plea deal, needless controversy over how long the White House flag remained at half-mast in honor of the late Sen. John McCain (R-Ariz.), new revelations of administration infighting in a Bob Woodward exposé, and never-ending, withering criticism directed at the once-favored son, Attorney General Jeff Sessions.

The contrast is startling. It's the big stuff against the small stuff; needlessly complicated stuff; personal stuff; issues we-do-not-usually-have-to-worry-about stuff.

The big stuff improves economic outcomes for millions of people, empowers job creators, makes the country stronger, and reassures many heretofore forgotten folks in flyover America that Washington, D.C., is truly listening to their concerns—and acting!

The president's big stuff is typically accompanied by elements of populism and nationalism—and that's OK. Many Americans had had enough of "you didn't build that" and associated Obama-era apologies for our wealth and well-established cultural values. To boot, a long record of big-stuff success is also the way a politician secures his or her re-election, a chicken in every pot (or healthy 401[k]), as the case may be …

As noted, the small stuff is by definition far less substantive than the big stuff. In a hyperpolarized culture, however, it generates as much or more media attention. Indeed, there is a reason cable television ratings remain sky high during the Trump era.

Here, less substantive includes an endless number of mini-dramas and subplots. Most particularly, there is the omnipresent Russia collusion narrative, a storyline that somehow continues to receive daily attention despite its abject failure to produce any corroborating evidence over the past two years.

The apparently limitless jurisdiction of special counsel Robert Mueller and his team of happy Democratic contributors/prosecutors/investigators may indeed continue to produce sensational headlines about former Trump associates, including indictments and prosecutions for misdeeds that have nothing to do with Russia and were allegedly committed many years ago.

One wonders whether the left-leaning cable networks could continue in business without Mueller's operation, but I digress.

The small stuff extends to self-imposed wounds, from Stormy pay-offs to missed fastballs (e.g., post-Charlottesville, post–Putin summit, post–McCain passing). These were and are relatively easy occasions to note the obvious: Skinhead racists are evil, Putin is not to be trusted, McCain is a certified American hero.

How many times a week am I approached on the street by a like-minded Trump supporter and queried as to why such tweets continue when they so often trump (excuse the pun) important and often positive accomplishments of this president? Answer: More than I care to count.

Parenthetically, it is the small stuff that is so often the predicate for the seemingly daily condemnations from GOP establishment types. You know, those who remain in denial concerning the results of Nov. 8, 2016.

For this subgroup, Trump is the archetypical killjoy. He questions their assumptions. He challenges their status quo. He stubbornly refuses to adopt traditional behaviors associated with POTUS, and he does so with an abrasive confidence (arrogance to many) that is truly unique.

I do not pretend my answer satisfies the typical questioner. It generally acknowledges that the query is legitimate because positive news should never get stepped on. But I hasten to add a caveat:

It just may be that such regular order is simply not possible with this president, that his disruptor ways will always swamp (pun intended) accepted rules of political communication, that large swaths of working-class America happily identify with this rejection of the status quo, and that to adopt a more recognized process would simply not be… Donald J. Trump.

This final observation is important. Today's culture alternatively describes my takeaway as "it is what it is." The Trump world version is closer to "what you see is what you get"—traditionally that for which the general public clamors—and, by the way, what helped take down that once impregnable blue wall. The modus operandi almost assuredly will not change.

Alas, many on the Left—and more than a few on the Right—will never accept this reality.

Tuesday's Election Will Show if Left's 'Hate America' Strategy Worked

LifeZette
October 31, 2018

Many opinion pundits are focused intently these days on what the correct temperature is for a mutually respectful national political conversation.

To wit, the Right blames recent incendiary comments by former Secretary of State Hillary Clinton, Rep. Maxine Waters (D-Calif.), and a host of left-leaning talking heads for the ugly and very public confrontations lately perpetrated on Trump administration officials and GOP members of Congress by progressive activists.

In turn, the Left (and many of its acolytes in the mainstream media) blame President Donald Trump for the coarse, hyper-personalized tenor of today's public dialogue and say he is responsible for the pipe bombs sent to high-profile Trump enemies. Some are adding this past weekend's synagogue murders in Pittsburgh to the indictment of the president.

Typical of such skirmishes, each claims to be the "wronged" party—and is aggressively taking its case to the voting public in the most emotional terms possible. The goal, of course, is to emerge the winner in the 2018 midterms.

Recent over-the-top invective notwithstanding, here are a few observations for consideration.

Toxicity in the pursuit of power is a familiar narrative. Recall your high school civics class, wherein you learned how Thomas Jefferson and Alexander Hamilton hired surrogates to attack one another in that era's newspapers.

There was also the lesson about how Aaron Burr later shot and killed Founding Father Hamilton in a duel, how Union General and then President Ulysses Grant was portrayed as a habitual drunkard on the campaign trail, how John F. Kennedy's Catholicism led to ugly innuendo regarding his "true allegiance," and how five U.S. presidents were assassinated by political opponents.

The deep and abiding social chasms that accompanied the civil rights and anti-war movements of the 1950s and 1960s (along with the assassinations of Bobby Kennedy and Martin Luther King) also apply here.

You get the point. Democracy is never pretty. The worst among free people have often resorted to the most vicious modus operandi (and actions) when fighting over political power.

In modern times, left-leaning activists tend to act out because it's what they do. Campus demonstrations organized by leftist professors and administrators and large boisterous marches on Washington are so…1960s. And, yes, such demonstrations were at times violent and disruptive.

Equally reminiscent of that era is the specter of Hollywood actors and comedians jumping on the progressive bandwagon (think Jane Fonda, Dick Gregory) in order to agitate for political change.

The bottom line: Loud and very public social activism is more associated with progressive causes for a reason. The Left has always used its influence venues (academia, Hollywood, the press) to further its agenda. Today's resistance fully understands its considerable assets and acts accordingly.

There is nevertheless something fundamentally different about the messaging from today's resistance movement. I (and many other observers) discern something unique within today's unremittingly contentious culture, and it's not simply the visceral reaction to the ways and means of one Donald J. Trump.

The focus seems to be on the country itself. Even the culturally divisive social movements of bygone eras retained a sense of recognition (to some extent celebration) regarding the great American tradition of dissent.

For example, flag burners claimed theirs was a constitutionally protected form of expression and what was more American than good old-fashioned political speech? Herein was a sense that America's innate goodness was being perverted by an indefensible war, or the denial of civil rights to minorities and women.

In contrast, a growing segment of today's progressives reject the centrality of the American experience, of our alleged goodness, and greatness (yes, exceptionalism). These folks have a more attenuated adherence to traditional American values and allegiances.

Further, they tend to shy away from reflexive support for U.S. history with or without its well-chronicled warts. This modus operandi is far different from the past, and is perhaps best captured by New York Gov. Andrew Cuomo's recent comment that "America was never that great."

The governor (and likely 2020 presidential aspirant) follows this critique with the usual hyperbolic narrative: Our storied American experience in pluralism, capitalism, and religious freedom has proven to be more of a flawed journey into imperialism, nativism, and racism.

This once career-ending remark proved to be a short-lived story. Remarkably, leading progressives (including members of Congress) are daily taking to the stump in order to denounce a sadly "-ic" and "-ism" ridden America. Here, it's not the familiar struggle to better a flawed America, but rather America, flawed.

That this revisionist narrative has found a comfortable home on the new Left is without doubt.

Whether it is a winning message in a presidential election cycle is a far different matter.

In light of the progressive tenor of the 2020 Democratic field, however, we will likely witness this hypothesis put to the test.

CHAPTER 3

DISRUPTOR

What was so discombobulating on the left was so satisfying (and obvious) to Trump supporters on the right. For many of his supporters, it was all about Trump's willingness to challenge Washington, D.C.'s most cherished bipartisan assumptions. This was not disruption for disruption's sake (as so many on the left and right sought to argue), but rather a genuine desire to take down the established ways and means of the people who had run Washington, D.C., forever—often to less than stellar results—sometimes to downright disastrous results. A not-too-subtle Trumpian subtitle read: "Why not challenge assumptions—and change practices—that have not inured to the benefit of America's working class for so many years…what do we have to lose?"

Herein was the foundation of Trump's sustained appeal throughout the heartland. While watching this populist message gain momentum around the country, I compiled a list of the many sacred assumptions the president had dared question, herein reproduced for your review. In true Trumpian form, he would ask:

WHY?

- A porous southern border?
- A ten-year war in Iraq?
- An eighteen-year war in Afghanistan?
- Taxpayer dollars to the PLO?
- Unilateral economic disarmament under the Paris Accords?
- Deadbeat NATO allies?
- Bogus national monument designations?
- A planeload of shakedown cash to the terror-sponsoring ayatollahs in Iran?
- A "One China" policy?
- Campus speech codes?

AND, WHY NOT:

- Originalist judges?
- The Congressional Review Act?
- Border enforcement?
- A wall?
- Tariffs to leverage Mexico's border enforcement?
- 4 percent growth?
- Energy independence?
- Call out Germany's assistance with a Russian pipeline?
- Move our embassy to Jerusalem?
- Recognize the Golan Heights as part of Israel?
- Engage Sunni states in bilateral peace deals with Israel?
- Voter photo ID?
- Call out the Fed on high interest rate hikes?
- Tariffs to leverage the Chinese in trade negotiations?
- School choice?
- Due process under Title IX?
- American nationalism?
- A military parade?
- "America First?"
- Merry Christmas?

These are just a sampling of the often-uncomfortable questions asked during the Trump era, as a host of Washington, D.C.'s sacred cows unexpectedly found themselves in Trump's crosshairs. Suddenly, "It's the way we have always done it" became an unacceptable response. Veteran bureaucrats pushed back as best they could, but this was no longer the Obama administration—the Lois Lerners of the world were nowhere to be found. To boot, the relentless Mr. Trump kept on lobbying, agitating, cajoling, and of course tweeting. Comfort zones were few and far between for those who found themselves caught between the president's priorities and a resentful, angry, dysfunctional Washington elite.

So Which Part of "Disrupter-in-Chief" Did You Expect to Play Nice?

LifeZette

August 7, 2018

I'm often asked why the Trump era is so messy, so acrimonious. One obvious (and well-analyzed) reason is the extreme disappointment—frustration—anger felt by the American Left, especially by those who readily identify with the resistance.

Indeed, the daily vitriol directed at the president is high-octane, relentless. But the remainder of my answer is more rhetorical in nature: "What part of 'disrupter' did you expect to be pleasant?"

This response focuses on an often-neglected point: Disrupters are often uninvited, unappreciated guests. They have little respect for tradition. They revel in upsetting the apple cart, personal feelings be damned.

But it's not just "feelings" in their crosshairs—it's also assumptions and accepted premises, the traditional rules of the road valued by establishments everywhere.

Suffice it to say no modern politician (let alone president) has gone about the business of challenging so many assumptions and accepted premises in so brief a period of time.

For context, try on these familiar D.C. storylines:

NATO. This bastion of the Western alliance has traditionally been immune from substantive criticism—until Trump inconveniently pointed out how a number of member states were failing to meet their promised level of defense spending. He also questioned the continued validity of ("one in, all in") Article V, just in case his initial shot across the bow was ignored.

More recently, the president took Germany to task for its heretofore virtually unpublicized and internationally undebated building of an energy pipeline with the Russians, while falling behind with respect to its NATO commitment. The foreign policy establishment condemned the intemperate Trump. Our embarrassed allies were none too amused.

Tariffs. Generations of free-market Republicans have been conditioned to champion free trade—even when reciprocity is not so forthcoming or when unfair trade practices (state subsidization, material stealing of intellectual property) accompany the trading regime.

Indeed, a traditional Republican president would never countenance talk of a "trade war," but then along comes Trump with his "America First" salesmanship and "Why not a trade war?" tweet.

To no one's surprise, said tweet caused heartburn at the U.S. Chamber of Commerce and the *Wall Street Journal*, and with free-trade advocates everywhere.

It remains to be seen how long the most serious trade skirmish (with China) will last, and there is no doubt some Trump (midwestern) constituencies have been hurt by trade reprisals.

Still, friends and foes alike should suffer no illusions about the president's intent to challenge long-honored and well-established trade practices and procedures.

North Korea. Treading lightly with the nuclear-armed hermit state has produced nothing but decades of bipartisan foreign-policy failure. Hand-wringing on both sides of the aisle has in fact only encouraged the communist regime to engage in further provocations, including, but not limited to, a 2017 missile launch over Japan.

Still, under no circumstances would the establishments of either major political party entertain the idea of insulting the unpredictable, nuclear-armed dictator, Kim Jong-un.

But that is precisely what Trump did. And his "Little Rocket Man" and "My button is bigger than your button" rhetoric resulted in…a summit…and now the first halting steps on the long road to a denuclearized Korean peninsula.

Any progress on this genuinely worrisome front has to be the most shocking foreign policy development to date. Talk about throwing away the diplomatic rule book…

The FBI. My earliest television memories are of Sunday nights spent with Efrem Zimbalist Jr. and the television program *The FBI*. They were the good guys. They placed themselves in harm's way to protect us.

They were the best of the best. The G-Men engaged in the business of taking down the Mafia, drug cartels, and bank robbers. My experience as a member of Congress and as governor of Maryland only strengthened my fandom. My interactions with the agency were always professional, always focused on the job at hand. Love those guys.

Now fast-forward to the Peter Strzok and Lisa Page email saga. Include Strzok's recent appearances before Congress. Throw in former FBI Director James Comey's politically motivated feck-lessness and that phony dossier (paid for by Hillary Clinton's 2016 campaign and the Democratic National Committee).

The dossier was used as a predicate to conduct a counterintel-ligence operation into the Trump presidential campaign. The result is a big political mess and major black eye for the once revered, post-Hoover FBI.

In response, the president openly criticizes the leadership of the agency for its political manipulations during the 2016 campaign. This, of course, is unheard-of behavior…but right out of Trump's anti-establishment playbook. You recognize the fearless response: Hit back, hard and fast, even when the intended target can help prosecute you.

Growth. Perhaps the least provocative challenge issued by the Great Disrupter was to question the progressive Left's retreat to 2 percent annual growth as the "new normal."

This was the target adopted by President Barack Obama while he went about the business of apologizing to the world for America's mass consumption economy.

Many conservative politicians and pundits took Trump and his allies to task for this limited horizons narrative. But leave it to the consummate salesman to throw out the "four-word"—4 percent annual growth—as reachable and sustainable. Note: establish-ment economists were eerily silent as the U.S. growth rate surged to 4.1 percent in the second quarter.

Beware of traditional assumptions and premises in the Trump era.

How Trump's Surprising Election Triggered the Left's Spectacular Self-Destruction

Western Journal
June 21, 2019

One of the goofier inventions of the campus speech code police is the so-called "trigger warning." Your college kid can fill you in on how such warnings are often included on campus syllabi, ostensibly to help sensitive undergraduates better acclimate to troubling—disquieting—disturbing course material.

Once warned, they are then presumably better prepared to deal with troubling events, and not so easily "triggered" into negative moods or behavior. To boot, some schools allow their students to recuse themselves from classes covering material students adjudicate as upsetting!

For example, Irish youngsters might be forewarned about the Great Potato Famine, African American kids about slavery and Jim Crow, Russian kids about Stalin and the gulags, Jewish kids about Hitler and the death camps.

A reasonable person may at this point ask how every previous generation of students was able to digest (and learn from) horrific chapters in human history without reliance on trigger warnings.

A related query may inquire as to how the "Greatest Generation" defeated the Axis powers (and saved the world) without the aid of such a construct.

It is fun and rather easy to poke fun at such pseudo-instruction. After all, most students will graduate into the real world where they will soon forget such "lessons."

Still, I must admit to one instance where a trigger warning could have proved useful; where its issuance could have saved many from consternation and derangement—even psychosis.

I refer, of course, to the celebration scheduled for the evening of Nov. 8, 2016. No trigger warning had been issued prior to that night because most of the country thought none would be required. Had not the national news media reported just a week earlier that Hillary Clinton and the Democratic National Committee were "expanding the map," spending money in supposedly safe red House seats given the expected size and scope of Clinton's landslide?

But the pundits got it wrong. The evening's events brought the reality of President-Elect Donald J. Trump, who arrived with no forewarning.

For half of the country watching in stunned happiness, the new president was a breath of fresh air. They had voted for the disruptor, and the promised disruption began immediately. There would henceforth be no regular order in Washington, D.C. The new sheriff would operate outside establishment norms, often engaging foes and friends alike in a direct, hyper-aggressive way.

To this, the great unwashed said, "Hallelujah!" They had finally been given a leader willing to challenge the orthodoxies of both political parties.

The other half of the country was woefully unprepared for this sudden turn of events, but nevertheless began its "resistance" in short order. For them, the president-elect was coarse, abnormal, and dangerous. They accordingly opposed him with all their might.

And it is here where the unplanned triggering continues to gain momentum. How else to describe a political opposition that has moved so quickly, so decisively, so resolutely left? Indeed, the shift is unprecedented in its scope and depth.

For those continually attempting to catch their breath due to the daily assaults on moderate sensibilities, check this out:

Illegal Immigration

A decade ago, New York Senate candidate Hillary Clinton opposed drivers' licenses for illegal aliens. Four years later, the certifiably progressive Barack Obama assured the country (in a State of the Union speech) he wished to work with "[both parties] to protect our borders, enforce our laws and address the millions of undocumented workers who are now living in the shadows."

Three months ago, New York senator and presidential candidate Kirsten Gillibrand proclaimed, "There is no such thing as an illegal human." She followed up this astounding statement with a promise to provide Social Security benefits to illegal aliens. Neither statement generated public condemnation from her fellow Democratic competitors.

Abortion

In 2008, Clinton repeated her previously-expressed view that abortion should be "safe, legal, and rare, and by rare, I mean rare." Today, almost all the Democrats running for the presidency seek to make abortion free and available up to the very moment of delivery.

Such a stance was once thought tantamount to political suicide but is now deemed "moderate" after a March 2019 interview by Virginia Gov. Ralph Northam described a hypothetical wherein he appeared to support infanticide in cases where a baby is delivered deformed or likely not to survive birth.

To no one's surprise, this same field of candidates is equally supportive of full taxpayer funding of the procedure. Even Joe Biden has gotten on board by rescinding his decades-long support for the funding compromise known as the Hyde Amendment (no federal funds for abortion with exceptions for rape, incest, and life of the mother).

Full disclosure: the triggering of such uber pro-choice positions may have as much to do with the recent promotion of Brett Kavanagh to the Supreme Court as it does with the president. Kavanagh is widely viewed as the likely fifth vote to overturn *Roe v. Wade*.

Health Care

Again, the reader does not need to travel so far back in time to appreciate how far today's progressives have evolved on the issue of government-financed health care. Recall President Obama's first term decision to forego a push for single-payer health care when the Democrats controlled both chambers of Congress.

Conventional wisdom at the time dictated a piecemeal approach (precisely how we arrived at Obamacare) because too many suburban Democrats saw government-run health care as a sure political loser.

The president (correctly) concluded that he lacked the votes to proceed further down that dangerous path. Yet the post-Obama Democratic party is all in on "Medicare for All," including numerous presidential hopefuls who have expressed their support for ending private health insurance in America.

Interestingly, former Vice President Biden has yet to opine on what "MFA" means to him, but recent moves by "Amtrak Joe" (he is now supportive of a plan to provide Medicare to illegal aliens who have not paid into the system) suggest he may end up closer to Bernie Sanders than those people he used to chat up on the train to Washington, D.C.

Green New Deal

The ultimate result of all the Trump-inspired triggering is, of course, the well-publicized "Green New Deal." Nothing speaks to the ongoing progressive stampede better than a program all about pie-in-the-sky goals, especially the targeted elimination of cows and air travel.

Less than enthusiastic reaction to the proposal by the 80 percent of the population that lives between the coasts has some presidential candidates backtracking a bit into "aspirational mode."

But the fact that this proposal continues to be viewed in positive political terms speaks to a deep and ever-widening gulf between a motivated progressive political base and everybody else.

I could go on, but the evidence is clear. Trump's surprising election triggered a progressive Democratic tide that has the base now rushing full-bore to the proverbial cliffs. There does not appear to be anyone in a position to stop him. Trigger warnings be damned.

The Common Thread Between Reagan and Trump

Western Journal
July 31, 2019

That much of the D.C. establishment and their enablers in the media relentlessly pillory our 45th president is a matter of record. The president's core supporters receive much the same treatment as the caricature of gum-chewing, flip-flop wearing, gun-toting white rednecks (yes, the "deplorables") is daily weaponized by the fourth estate.

But it is far too easy to simply dismiss the president's appeal as a product of working class–generated grievance/resentment politics.

In fact, much of what the president and his supporters bring to the table is similar to what Ronald Reagan and his movement once had, albeit in vastly different eras. The respective personalities are of course quite different. Where Reagan was the smooth-talking, unthreatening nice guy actor-turned-politician, Trump relishes the image of the tough guy, plain-speaking dealmaker who can as easily fire as hire.

Still, the similarities between the two presidents on substantive issues are striking. Each passed historic, growth-oriented tax packages, implemented light-touch regulation, advocated traditionally conservative social views, sought out originalist judges, and were (are) unapologetic proponents of American exceptionalism.

This last point makes it easy to imagine "The Gipper" hosting the very same July 4 show of military hardware recently hosted by the president on the National Mall. Similarly, it takes little imagination to guess how a previous generation's anti-Reagan media would have reported the day's events. You can bet pejoratives such as "fascist" and "dictator" would have dominated the coverage.

Today's Trump-crazed and highly polarized culture makes it easy to forget the vicious reviews and slanders hurled at Reagan during his campaigns and as president. You will recognize the indictments: intellectual lightweight, lazy, dangerous, warmonger, racist. Per everybody's favorite catcher, Yogi Berra, [the Trump era] is "déjà vu all over again."

Back to the two presidents' respective views of America. Both assured us America's best days lie ahead. Both stressed an opportunity society, regardless of sex, creed, or color. Both were willing to leave high-stakes foreign policy summits empty-handed, each declaring no deal was better than a bad deal.

There is another similarity between the two presidents that will not generate much analysis but is nevertheless true. Both took on comfortable, intellectually arrogant monopolies that do not take kindly to disruptors who refuse to play by the rules. Both enjoyed rabid base support as a result.

Indeed, their respective cores became ever more enthusiastic when outrageous charges were lodged. This base of support knew (knows) that whether the target is Reagan, Trump, or Pence, America's secular cultural elites will relentlessly seek to vilify, especially when traditional social views are at issue.

You can check it out for yourself. Nancy Reagan was hounded for her old-fashioned commonsensical ways, particularly her anti-drug culture campaign ("Just say no"), in much the same way as Pence is today on account of his strong Christian convictions.

One more point. When the bi-coastal value-makers do their number on Trump as they did on Reagan—and politically correct corporate America falls in line (as just went down with Nike and Kaepernick)—the middle American fault line is dug even deeper. But few comment on it. There are no bumper stickers to reflect it. The *New York Times* and CNN either will not or are unable to recognize it. Many House Democrats do not even pretend to understand it.

But you'd better believe that today's relentless attacks on its conservative sensibilities cause flyover America to buy ever more shovels.

Here then are the (knowing) silent looks, the closed-door conversations, the secret handshakes, and millions of $25 checks made out to "Trump re-elect," often from people who do not have $25 to spare. These plain ole regular folks are simply tired of progressivism's tolerance for identity politics, socialism-lite, and open borders.

Of course, the only cathartic event that truly counts occurs on the second Tuesday of November, every four years. It was on one such day that a past generation's deplorables gave Reagan a 49-state win, another one when that seemingly impenetrable midwestern blue wall came tumbling down…

Led by the so-called "squad," the works and deeds of today's ultra-aggressive progressives, who embarrassingly intimidate less radical (let alone moderate) Democrats, are again driving large numbers of the great unwashed to the edge.

All in all, it is a most positive development for Donald J. Trump.

Polls Won't Tell the Whole Story in 2020

Western Journal
January 9, 2020

History shows that the vast majority of public opinion polls taken during the campaign of 2016 underweighted the strength of candidate Donald J. Trump.

The phenomenon was exacerbated by the anti-Trump, left-leaning media, whose worst moments may have been typified by the following headline in the Oct. 24, 2016, *Washington Post*: "Donald Trump's chances of winning are approaching zero."

This and other similar polling results constituted daily fodder for the Hillary sycophants and lefty pundits who sought to reassure the country candidate Trump could never win. Indeed, the looks on the faces of the assembled at the Javits Center in New York City on the evening of Nov. 8, 2016, show that they, too, believed those polls.

Now fast-forward to the present wherein weekly polling shows top-tier Democratic contenders either leading or within the margin of error in match-ups against the president in the highly competitive, all-important states of Pennsylvania, Michigan, Wisconsin, and Florida.

With a national approval rating that never exceeds 50 percent, the president can rest assured 2020's campaign polls will again reflect a dangerous vulnerability—to the delight of Trump haters everywhere.

I was reminded of this narrative while reading about the president's impressive cash haul ($46 million) during the final quarter of 2019. Call it the "Deplorables strike back" syndrome.

You know the theory: The opposition piles on your guy so much that you feel compelled to defend—really act out—in response to the endless piling on. In this case, the reflective defense is to write a check. Here, the full-speed "gotta get it done before Christmas" impeachment sham led to an awful lot of people deciding to reach for their checkbooks.

To boot, in addition to the re-election campaign's $46 million raised, the GOP's "WinRed" joint fundraising platform (included are the Republican National Committee, every state Republican Party and most House and Senate campaigns) brought in $101 million in the second half of 2019, most of it since the day of the party line impeachment vote and most of it in small-dollar denominations.

Other acts of conservative resistance are also at play during the Trump era, and they are often far more subtle than writing a check.

It can be as simple as a secret fist pump or a knowing glance with a fellow conservative whenever the Left oversteps its bounds—a daily occurrence in this era of progressive lunacy.

It can also be that angry feeling you get when you read about a restaurant requesting (contrary to our freedoms) Trump staffers leave the premises, or when you watch many of the Democratic presidential contenders express their support for *free* health care for illegal aliens, or see those same candidates enthusiastically manifest their intent to eliminate high-paying, blue-collar energy jobs in natural gas and coal, or when *your* religious values (especially Christian values) are regularly dismissed as "phobic" at best, mere "dogma" at worst.

But it is not the oft-demonized deplorables alone who react so negatively to the daily assaults on their belief and value systems. Today's progressives fail to comprehend the impact of their over-the-top policies on moderates as well.

Yes—those all-important middle of the roaders. The ones who may not belong to the NRA but understand how fast-thinking, gun-toting good people saved a whole lot of lives in a Texas church a few weeks ago; the ones who oppose discrimination but believe that only girls should be allowed to compete in female athletic contests; the ones who support *Roe v. Wade* but oppose late-term abortion and most certainly afterbirth abortion.

Recall these are the voters supposedly up for grabs—the unhappy folks (who voted for the disruptor/outsider) that progressives only three years ago promised to engage in dialogue.

Those conversations never did take place. Far from it. Anti-Trump rage replaced the scheduled "listening tours." The party's leaders instead made a sharp left turn—further left than ever before. So far left that Joe Biden and Pete Buttigieg are now said to be the "moderate" alternatives to Bernie Sanders and Elizabeth Warren.

As a result, you can expect more than a few of these important "gettables" to break for Mr. Trump at the end of the day.

The message here is a simple one. The next time you see or hear that the president is four points down in Pennsylvania, do yourself a favor. Read it as "lean Trump"—at least you will be the one living in the real world.

Trump's SOTU Was about Showing He's Gotten Results—In Nov., That's What Will Matter

Western Journal
February 5, 2020

President Trump's State of the Union address included a long list of policy successes, much to the chagrin of official Washington.

You see, it is a rare instance in our politics wherein the voters revisit the results of a policy dispute, so overwhelming is the weight and volume of the 24/7 news cycle.

But revisitation is urgent for the informed voter. Who was right and who was wrong should count. Credibility should be a function of how well recommendations and positions turned out. How better to weigh the merits of a candidate or party?

Think about recent national policy debates for context.

Immigration

Remarkably, last summer's siege at the southern border was alleged to be nothing more than a made-up narrative offered up by an anti-immigrant president.

Here, you will recall House Democrats' and left-leaning cable networks' relentless criticism of an "invented" crisis.

But the disturbing reports on the evening news painted a very different picture: Images of chaos and confusion and criminality and questions about the well-being of migrant children. The bottom line was unsettling: caravans of Central American migrants proceeding through an uninterested Mexico and expecting easy entry into an unprepared America.

But the president acted with resolve. Administration policy changed so that migrants were made to wait in Mexico until their immigration court hearing date. Simultaneously, the president went full-court press (after a protracted court battle) to find the funds required to expand the physical barrier on the southern border. The combination of additional manpower, policy changes and a relentless commitment to additional fencing has helped quell the situation—and put an end (at least for now) to the seemingly unending migrant trains.

In the end, the media's "no crisis" narrative was proven to be just plain wrong. Illegal crossings are down 75 percent from the spring. Will our media miscreants fess up during the forthcoming campaign? I'll take the "under" on that one.

Tax Cuts

The Trump tax cuts and accompanying regulatory reforms were passed with the usual cries of outrage from the left. Speaker Nancy Pelosi opined that the tax overhaul was "the end of the world" and "Armageddon."

Not to be outdone, former Treasury Secretary Larry Summers predicted 10,000 people would die annually as a result of the bill. The usual suspects (the *Washington Post*, the *New York Times*, the *Los Angeles Times*, CNN, MSNBC) all piled on in due course.

But that was then. Two years later, the American economic co-lossus is extraordinarily strong. 401(k)s are riding a bull market and, best of all, the economic data reflect historically low unemployment for African Americans and Hispanics and real wage growth for working- and middle-class Americans. Such are the irrefutable facts of the Trump economy.

Iran

The ineffectual—many would say indulgent—policies of Mr. Obama vis-a-vis the world's leading sponsor of terror is part of the histori-cal record.

How else to characterize an administration that provided only benign support to the Iranian street protests of 2009, gifted the mullahs three planeloads of cash valued at $1.7 billion, and signed on to a highly prob-lematic nuclear accord that enabled Tehran to aggressively strengthen its ballistic missile program. The world was rewarded with aggressive Iranian proxy armies in Yemen, Syria, Lebanon, and Iraq.

Fortunately, the election of 2016 brought an end to American ac-quiescence, as the U.S. withdrew from the flawed nuclear accord. Then Mr. Trump imposed punishing new sanctions on the regime, which led to Iranian adventurism and provocations against Saudi and Western interests in the region.

Still, sanctions have left the Iranian economy in tatters; growth contracted by nearly 10 percent in 2019. Further sanctions as a result of the recent tit-for-tat military operations and the downing of a Ukrainian civilian airliner have now been imposed. The Iranian street is again up in arms. And France, Germany, and Great Britain have signaled their opposition to renewed Iranian nuclear development. Just what the doctor ordered as the Trump administration attempts to secure regime change without war.

Trade

OK, most of us understand that in the real world, administration-imposed tariffs have hurt some American manufacturers, while helping others.

The same can be said for our farmers. Despite these short-term mixed results, the fact remains that an American administration has now done *something* after decades of failed bipartisan negotiation with the Chinese. That the president was willing to place his political base (agriculture, small manufacturers) at risk in order to move the seemingly intractable Chinese off the dime speaks to the unique and often high-risk but necessary approach of Mr. Trump and his senior advisors.

The free-trade D.C. establishment will continue to take the president to task for his protectionist-first (read: tariffs) ways, but a Chinese government credibly charged with unfair state subsidization, currency manipulation, and theft of intellectual property has now taken a significant step towards engagement with its largest trading partner. Sure beats the familiar—and demonstrably failed—status quo.

Post-impeachment, expect the Trump re-election campaign to remind voters about "bottom lines." They still count.

In 2020 Predictions, Democrats, and the Media Are Overplaying Their Hand

Western Journal
June 12, 2020

Recent national polls reflect anywhere from a three- to 11-point lead for former Vice President Joe Biden over President Donald Trump in the race for the presidency.

The mainstream media are accordingly gleeful. Any bad Trump news is good news for them. Indeed, one would think the race is all but over, that a Biden coronation is simply a matter of time. Such is the state of today's journalism.

My response is to refrain from the defensive "polls don't vote; people do" or the even worse "six months is a lifetime in politics" or even the more interesting "only state polls matter."

While accurate, these responses always sound so defensive and *weak*. I would add to this list of unsatisfying excuses the economic devastation caused by the coronavirus and the ongoing civil unrest from the murder of George Floyd.

I offer four reasons why I believe it is more likely than not Joe Biden will maintain basement residency come Nov. 4.

Reason one is a phenomenon familiar to followers of the post-Clinton Democratic Party. It is the progressive tendency to overplay your hand and not think long-term.

For context, think back to Minnesota Sen. Paul Wellstone's funeral in 2002.

That event was transformed into a party campaign event by overtly partisan speakers, where Republican Sen. Trent Lott's appearance was greeted by loud boos. Such bad form did not go over well with the voters. Former Vice President Walter Mondale shockingly lost the seat in the 2002 election partly due to the poor reviews that followed.

A few years later, "Occupy Wall Street" had a brief run in many of our nation's major cities.

The movement's grievances included a long list of progressive agenda items, but none greater than "economic inequality"—a problem the movement attempted to remedy by erecting mini-encampments along busy urban thoroughfares.

But deplorable and dangerous sanitary conditions spelled their doom long before they could carry their case to the people.

Then came Obamacare, the gift that kept on giving to Republicans for four election cycles. You may have forgotten the botched debut, but you will never forget the empty promises: "You'll be able to keep your health care plan" and "you can keep your doctor."

Today, much of what remains of the original Obamacare is the wholesale expansion of Medicaid, an entitlement that has now expanded far beyond its original target group of poor women with children.

More recently, the election of uber-progressives to the House generated a so-called "Green New Deal," a platform that would have scared away a majority of Democrats not so long ago.

While a number of vulnerable members quietly walked the program back to "aspirational" status, it remains a focal point to the johnny-come-lately progressive Joe Biden.

Now comes a new campaign designed to defund law enforcement in the aftermath of the horrific George Floyd killing. That the poorest minority communities would be the most endangered has somehow been lost in the ongoing debate.

No surprise here: bad ideas often flourish in the aftermath of chaos.

Reason two concerns the incremental reopening of the economy.

It may be that the worst of our self-imposed economic catastrophe has passed. Unemployment claims have stabilized. Businesses of all sizes are again opening their doors. The Dow has rallied (but remains subject to wild fluctuations). And the medical headlines reflect diminishing COVID-19 hospitalizations and deaths in addition to possible new therapies and vaccines.

Coming in third on the list of reasons for optimism are three special election results you may have missed.

The flipping (from "D" to "R") of California's 25th Congressional District is a very big deal. It is the first time in 22 years that deep blue California witnessed such a shift.

And this achievement comes after Democrats changed the rules to allow in-person voting (at a strong Democratic precinct) after early mail-in returns revealed trouble was a-brewing—a stunt that failed to stop the GOP's Mike Garcia from registering a 10-point win in a district Hillary Clinton won by seven points in 2016.

Another special election saw the GOP's Tom Tiffany keep Wisconsin's 7th Congressional seat in Republican hands despite an influx of Democratic dollars. And then there was the local Staunton, Virginia, race in which three incumbent Democratic Council members were defeated in a city that had twice voted for Barack Obama.

The final observation is the most intriguing and yet the one most difficult to wrap one's head around.

I refer to the anomaly that so often accompanies public polling of Donald J. Trump. Recall the now-infamous *Washington Post* headline from Oct. 24, 2016: "Donald Trump's chances of winning are approaching zero."

Similar headlines were backed up with national polls reflecting a comfortable (often double-digit) win for the former first lady. Such strong poll numbers so close to Election Day prompted the Democratic National Committee to "expand the map," thereby infusing new dollars into relatively safe GOP districts in anticipation of stealing seats in the wake of a Clinton landslide.

But the polls were wrong. Trump easily led the Electoral College while Clinton won the popular vote by two points. Trump had again overperformed on Election Day—a trend first observed during the bitterly contested Republican primaries.

This underperforming phenomenon is a matter of fact. What is open to conjecture in this case is the reason for the consistent underestimating of Trump's voting support in the polls.

Democrats cite embarrassment as the primary rationale for the less-than-forthcoming responses to pollsters. Conversely, Trump enthusiasts point to the media-created stigma attached to anything Trump (think of the MAGA hat). The thought is why bother to get into an argument with one's spouse, neighbor, relative, co-worker, doctor, or even a stranger when you have the ultimate power: the vote.

One point is difficult to dismiss: the 2016 victory of Donald Trump represented flyover America's dissatisfaction with both party establishments and politics as usual in Washington, D.C. Another Trump victory would further extend that message.

CHAPTER 4

THE PROGRESSIVES: MCGOVERN REVISITED?

A disbelieving, Trump-bashing base was at least partially responsible for the consistent Democratic overreach. But this iteration of America's labor/left party was about far more than Trump loathing and a now discredited Trump-Russia collusion narrative. These haters had little use for traditional liberalism, middle class values, and condition-less support for free speech. It did not look to the legacies of Truman, Kennedy, or (Bill) Clinton for motivation - or an electoral roadmap. And no homage was paid to free markets, laissez-faire capitalism, American exceptionalism, or national sovereignty. In fact, just the opposite.

These Democrats were younger, secular, green, pro-choice, pro-labor, pro–open borders, and all about LGBTQ rights. The young warriors had been incubated and hatched in expensive crucibles of progressive thought, otherwise known as American colleges and universities. They accordingly manifested disdain for American history, and more generally, Western civilization. In this world, Columbus Day was not to be celebrated, but rather protested as the turning point wherein Western culture began its long and murderous run of attrition over indigenous peoples.

The lurch leftward reminded me of conversations I had with veteran, moderate Democrats after Republicans had secured a House majority in the election of 1994. These blue dog dinosaurs, soon to be wiped out of their suburban southern and western districts, bemoaned the constant chatter within the Democratic Caucus that attributed the Democrats' historic midterm wipeout (a 54-seat net loss) to the fact that *they were not liberal enough*. Still, post-2016 election (public) comments from numerous Democrats spoke to the need to listen to America's working class—to *really* understand why those same white ethnic (and often union) Democrats who had voted twice for Barack Obama would now reject them for Donald Trump of all people!

Alas, it soon became apparent they didn't mean it. In their heart of hearts, the Democratic base had rejected a *pretend* progressive. After all, had not Mrs. Clinton voted for war, represented Wall Street interests, and opposed drivers' licenses for illegal aliens? Gosh…she had even opposed gay marriage for most of her adult life. No, Democratic activists interpreted the loss as a (albeit disguised) call to arms for America's labor—left party to finally go all the way; to finally disassociate itself from establishment liberals and their private sector labor allies who had never shared the progressive preference for gun control, abortion on demand, and secular social mores. Suddenly, "Democratic Socialism" was no longer a pejorative, but rather a rallying cry.

This then was a bold new challenge to a proud but rapidly changing old party. Even reliable old workhorses such as Bloomberg and Lieberman would be told their time was up—that the party had moved on. And the old liberal lion-bashing did not end there. For these old guys and their ilk, age was the least of their alleged shortcomings. (Biden would after all be 78 at the beginning of his presidency.) It was rather skin color that made them less qualified to lead. You see, it was a new time and movement ready to brandish its appeal to urban minorities, gays, millennials, feminists, and unionists that had been turned on by Bernie Sanders' brand of old-time, classical populism in 2016. The contrast with the values of the newly minted conservative Trump and his culturally conservative deplorables could not have been more dramatic.

Happy Graduation!

National Review
April 12, 2018

Springtime means rebirth, baseball, and…new stories about how 99.89 percent of college-graduation speakers are certified lefties. Those of us with opposing viewpoints are left with few options; most of us just suck it up, grin, and sit there—although the grinning part is becoming more of a challenge. You see, our side of the aisle is not so easily agitated into social-protest mode. Still, it would be refreshing to hear at least one college president come clean in his commencement remarks. Just put it all out there for (progressive) mass consumption. To wit:

> Hello, everyone…Happy Graduation!

> Four years of relentless indoctrination is now complete. Most of you no longer trust markets, capitalism, or your parents. You are now officially social-justice warriors; you truly "Feel the Bern." Accordingly, our job is done. But before you leave for the real world—a hate-filled place without safe spaces, speech codes, Play-Doh, warm cookies, and coloring books to help you "recuperate" from dissenting points of view—a few words of review, and caution.

> In the good-news department, our annual giving goal of $1 billion was easily surpassed last year. The school's endowment is now $59 billion, which means only a 6.5 percent tuition-rate increase for next year! For this good fortune, I can only thank the deity that I am forbidden

to mention by name under threat of ACLU lawsuit. So thanks to this unnamed deity for maintaining such high demand for our elite degree among so many of your status-seeking but naïve parents.

More good news: We are excited to announce the construction of what our faculty is calling "Fascist City." This complex will consist of a number of poorly constructed buildings that our students will be encouraged to destroy whenever a conservative speaker arrives on campus. In this way, our young activists can meet and riot at a central location with no fear of police brutality. Further, our faculty have agreed to purchase and supply bricks (for throwing) free of charge. I also want to thank the newly salaried student government of our very own campus political party, "Bernie's Young Socialists," for contributing fire-resistant protest signs (so they may be repurposed). One can never be too environmentally conscious when protesting "the man"!

Let me put your mind at ease with what seems on the surface to be a perplexing proposition—the task of having to rebuild a new "city" every few weeks. Fortunately, we have borrowed an idea from our brothers and sisters at other elite schools and decided to charge the College Republicans for all such damages. This seems abundantly fair to me. After all, we would never be forced to incur such costs were it not for the entitled country clubbers who insist on inviting racist, nativist, homophobic speakers to our sanctuary campus. Mark my words, such behavior has no place at a liberal-arts institution!

I also wish to compliment the faculty on the completion of their "micro-aggression syllabus" program. You will recall that this endeavor is the result of our negotiations following the "Young Irish Progressive" group's violent takeover of my office in October after they discovered that our history department had failed to include trigger warnings on textbooks about the great potato famine. Please note that these culturally insensitive professors were temporarily reassigned to reeducation camps located on the outskirts of Berkeley, Calif.

In a similar vein, I was proud to watch our enthusiastic young activists burn campus buildings until I agreed to add "cultural-appropriation warnings" on our daily food menus. Henceforth, our Italian-American students will be forewarned of "Pizza Fridays"; Mexican-American students, of "Taco Tuesdays"; German-American students, of "Sauerkraut Sundays." We believe that all of our students should be able to enjoy their meals with the knowledge that we are protecting the heritage of their cultural foodstuff.

Of course, there will always be problem children, insensitive types (see above) who insist that airport passenger lounges switch out CNN for FOX, or that public squares continue to exhibit historical monuments of our racist Founders—as though history were important to understand. We will continue to root out these miscreants and redirect them to where they belong: Liberty University.

Recall that these are also the problem children who demand "counter" trigger warnings whenever Bill & Hillary Clinton are the focus of academic study. Seems that these young scholars need to be gingerly forewarned whenever course materials touch on Whitewater, Webb Hubbell, Susan MacDougall, Vince Foster, suddenly "found" Rose Law firm billing records, the definition of "is," cattle futures, "bimbo eruptions," the White House Travel Office, Monica Lewinsky, Lois Lerner, Marc Rich, impeachment hearings, Janet Reno, a Russian "reset," Benghazi, the Clinton Foundation, accidental tarmac meetings, Uranium One, accidentally sledgehammered cellphones, or erased emails.

Let the word go out: our faculty will not stand for such right-wing mockery. True Millennials they are not!

Of course, we are happy to continue accepting the children of the entitled at exorbitant tuition rates. After all, somebody has to assuage your father's alpha male, corporate guilt. Might as well be us!

Now, have a great summer…with the "resistance"!

The Left's Views on "Wealth Equality" Aren't about Compassion, They're about Envy

Western Journal
March 15, 2019

You may have read about Redskins owner Dan Snyder's recent purchase of a superyacht. Yes, there are such beasts—presumably larger and more luxurious than your average yacht. This one certainly qualifies: it includes a certified IMAX movie theater, a helipad, four VIP suites, and a gym. Sticker price: $100 million.

Predictably, rhetorical spitballs came raining down from the bleachers (or end zone, if you will). Said reviews were not the usual "cultural appropriation/insensitive" indictment lodged by those for whom "Redskins" remains a racist term. Rather, this was all about Snyder's alleged conspicuous consumption. How dare he purchase a luxury good of such high value!

The first political spitball was thrown from (you guessed it) senator and presidential candidate Elizabeth Warren. The lady from Massachusetts used the news to promote her proposed 2 percent surcharge on personal fortunes over $50 million. For those of you new to class warfare economics, this would be an additional tariff tacked onto taxes previously paid.

Just in case the voters misread the specific retributive nature of her point, Warren observed that the additional revenue could be used to fund "yacht-less Americans struggling with student loans." The forlorn yacht-less would then presumably get onboard (excuse the pun) with the Warren for president effort.

A majority of Americans might be sympathetic to the proposed surcharge. Some would especially enjoy shoving it to the yacht-owning crowd. After all, the additional revenue would just be chump change to the super-duper rich. Guys like Snyder wouldn't miss it, right?

This is the redistributionist mindset: tax those that have for as much as you can—for as long as you can—in as many ways as you can—and damn the consequences. It's only fair...

Others have a different takeaway. Theirs is not a Pavlovian antipathy toward wealth—even super wealth, where legally earned. These then are the capitalists, ever-ready to pursue success and the money that comes with it. Such marketeers help to create and perpetuate the formerly popular American dream: that innovation and hard work will lead to ever-increasing standards of living; that upward mobility will guarantee you a better life than your parents and grandparents.

Few believed there was anything inherently immoral about the ultimate goal. Back in the day, this narrative was passed from generation to generation and even taught on our college campuses!

Back to the emotion-based ways and means of the readily offended. They are resentful of great wealth and the lifestyle it affords. Per this worldview, nobody "deserves" to make over a certain amount of annual income. In the estimation of progressivism's super-charged but never contemplative leader, Alexandria Ocasio-Cortez, that number is approximately $10 million. The magic threshold may be more or less in the views of other progressives, but the point remains: it is government's moral obligation to step in and confiscate at a particular but ever-changing and arbitrary price point. Market capitalism must recede to considerations of equity and fairness. Get used to it.

Far from the madding D.C. crowd, there is a distinctly different reaction to such views. I refer to the well-demonstrated elevated levels of "wealth flight" from high- to low-tax states. Indeed, the reality of transient wealth is precisely why blue state governors were dead-set against the recently passed federal tax reform bill's capping of the state deduction at $10,000.

Suddenly, the true burden of confiscatory state taxes was illuminated for all to see. It was not a pretty sight. The bottom line: exorbitant taxes encourage the wealthy to exit (their state or even their country) stage left. Gaping budget shortfalls often follow—as does lots of finger pointing.

A final note on basic economic lessons circa 1990. Those of you of a certain age will recall the budget reconciliation act of that year contained a so-called luxury tax on yachts, private planes, and expensive cars. The proposal was accompanied by the typical class warfare rhetoric we see today and reflected above. But the initiative failed miserably, causing widespread layoffs in the yacht industry in particular. Here, working-class/laborer types who were intended to be the political beneficiaries of the tax ended up paying the steepest price. A Democratic Congress was forced to repeal the wildly unpopular tax in 1993. The laws of supply and demand had yet again been honored.

Of course, all of the foregoing is Economics 101 for those who pay attention to such things. If, however, you are not into the "crush 'em/bury 'em" economic angst of the Left or the basic market economics of the Right, try this one on for size: it's nobody's business what Dan Snyder does with his money. Can I hear an "Amen!"

Socialism Is for Dummies

Western Journal
May 7, 2019

You may have read recent polls reflecting on American millennials' infatuation with socialism. Yep—50 percent of millennials and their younger contemporaries in "Gen Z" claim they would prefer to live in a socialist country, while a similar percentage express support for "The Green New Deal."

No real surprise here. These disquieting numbers have been consistent over the past half-decade, reflecting the highly successful political indoctrination your kids receive at our institutions of "higher" learning.

In response, those of us who live in the real world may seek to lash out—write a check to Trump re-elect or immerse yourself in talk radio and Fox News for the evening. Both are reasonable responses.

Still, before you get yourself too worked up, it might be constructive (and instructive) to consider the history of socialism's persistent appeal despite its legacy of failure. Such a step back from the precipice will save you much personal angst—fewer mood swings—even as you watch the entertaining likes of Mayor Bill DeBlasio demand a moratorium on hot dogs and glass/steel buildings—in New York City!

Students of history are familiar with the propensity of Western elitists to be charmed by foreign dictators and their regimes. A most brutal chapter here was the American left's well-chronicled infatuation with Soviet-style communism, wherein many of America's leading reporters and intellectuals (Anna Louise Strong, Waldo Frank, Walter Duranty) wrote approvingly of Stalinist-era collectivism.

High-profile visits to the alleged socialist utopia buttressed the case for the regime. Some fellow travelers remained enamored with the totalitarian dictatorship even after the likes of Aleksandr Solzhenitsyn and his fellow refuseniks began to report the horrific truth.

The Left's interest in autocratic regimes of more recent vintage is equally well-documented. Hollywood actors, labor leaders, well-known academics, and politicians have picked up the torch in the latter decades of the 20th century. For context, recall Sen. Sanders' positive reviews for the Soviet Union's youth and cultural programs—an observation offered upon return from his 1988 honeymoon in that same workers' paradise.

More recently, a long list of celebrity types manifested their enthusiasm for Fidel's island experiment in brutal state control. Here, a familiar takeaway looms: a new iteration of socialism is always going to be the next big thing. It is can't miss stuff—attainable if only the public could shake off its bourgeois blinders in time to see.

This last point is important. The intellectual left's enthusiasm for centralized control carries a mandatory caveat: "If not this time, surely the next." It is history's most dangerous self-fulfilling prophecy. Indeed, generations of progressive apologists have nothing on those long-suffering Red Sox fans who saw a World Series within their grasp every year—for over 100 years.

Yet, inevitably, the gruesome reviews would begin to filter out: a corrupt Soviet Union would implode, broke and drunk; David Ortega's Nicaraguan revolution would fizzle; those Castro boys would build their very own Gulag, this time 90 miles from our shores; tanks would roll through Tiananmen Square—and over democracy protestors—25 years after Mao's murderous cultural revolution; African strongmen would come and go, often with tens of thousands of corpses in their wake; and who could forget Pol Pot's bloody killing fields in Cambodia? Socialist body counts are indeed never-ending.

Still, the dream continues—and not just in campus faculty lounges around the country. Here, a new rationalization has emerged in recent years, popularized by the likes of Congresswoman Alexandria Ocasio-Cortez and her peers.

It's all about Scandinavia, most particularly Sweden—in the way that the country has figured it out—or done socialism "right." You may even hear about Sweden's benign brand of socialism from progressive Democrats running for president this year.

But, as they say in Vegas, not so fast. Even this dressed up and oversold "socialism lite" falls short of the mark. You see, Sweden in the 1990s began to reverse course after an up-close and personal view of centralized control.

Today, democratic Sweden qualifies as a mixed bag, including a large social safety net (universal health care, free education) combined with a deregulatory, market-oriented, free-trade brand of capitalism. Such is not what American progressives have in mind!

As for our impressionable young people force-fed a steady brand of economic mush on campus, an old Churchill critique best sums it up: "The inherent vice of capitalism is the unequal sharing of blessings; the inherent virtue of socialism is the equal sharing of miseries."

Maybe a free week-long stay at "Club Med Venezuela" would wise up American youth, or make them less enthusiastic about "feeling the Bern" in 2020. Just a thought.

America Will Never Become a Socialist Nation

Western Journal
October 9, 2019

Every week I think, "This is it, there is no way they will go further down that road." And then they do. And I think the same thought all over again. What is that old definition of insanity?

"They" of course are the progressives running for president. Their goal is likely unreachable (more on that below) but fascinating to study: demonize anything and everything Donald J. Trump in order to (1.) remove or defeat him; and (2.) jump-start a wholesale transformation of America.

If you think the characterization unfair, check out the recent quote from Saikat Chakrabarti, former chief of staff to Rep. Alexandria Ocasio-Cortez: "The interesting thing about the Green New Deal is it wasn't originally a climate thing at all…. Do you guys think of it as a climate thing?… Because we really think of it as a how-do-you-change-the-entire-economy-thing."

I believe him.

Indeed, it is difficult to imagine otherwise as the progressive intelligentsia (coastal elites, Hollywood, college professors and administrators, the mainstream media) follow Captain James T. Kirk's admonition to "explore strange new worlds…to boldly go where no man has gone before."

Come to think of it, some men (and women) have experienced that world—socialist-inspired body counts in the hundreds of millions speak to it.

Still, today's iteration of American socialists promise a better path—you know, a more benign flavor—like Sweden.

And so, in the lead-up to the 2020 election, escalation is the name of the game—and it appears that no democratic-capitalist value is safe. To wit:

- Health care: **Why not** tax the 1 percent to fund an American version of single-payer, otherwise known as "Medicare for all"? (Estimated cost: $32 trillion over 10 years)
- Climate change: **Why not** eliminate fossil fuels (and cows and airplanes) and replace them with a "Green New Deal"? (Estimated cost: $51–93 trillion over the next ten years = $600,000 per household)
- Homelessness? **Why not** tax the 1 percent to finance a national rent cap? (Estimated cost: I will not hazard a guess; basic economics teaches that such a policy would crumble America's inner cities)
- High tuition costs? **Why not** tax the 1 percent to finance "college for all"? (Estimated cost: $470 billion over 10 years including, of course, those who will not go to college)

But these are merely the big-ticket items being proffered to the American people. A closer look at the "down-ballot" initiatives offered by the leading Democratic contenders includes major tax hikes, some type of national firearms registration, deconstruction of our southern border wall, a narrowing of religious liberties—and perhaps most important of all—the gradual denigration of free speech to which we are well on our way.

With respect to this last item, perhaps you missed the latest missive from the "New York Commission on Human Rights" whereby this branch of the thought police announced that public utterance of the phrase "illegal alien" could result in a fine of up to $250,000. That is no typo. The assault on the English language proceeds apace.

Make no mistake, the activist left has figured out it is far easier to control speech (in order to control thought) than to win competitive elections.

Now that I have wrecked your day, let me bring you back to a better place. Little if any of the foregoing will occur—with the possible exception of additional speech obstacles (the bad guys have made too much progress on campus for a return to normalcy anytime soon).

Accordingly, you can make book that ten years from now, cows will still roam the countryside. Fuel-efficient jets will still take to the skies. American health care will still be the best in the world. American farmers will still feed the world. American manufacturing will still be wildly innovative—and more environmentally friendly than ever.

And American capitalism will still stand—despite the best efforts of the above-cited elitists to the contrary.

How do I (we) know this? Because widespread demonstrations in Hong Kong continue, against all odds. Because Venezuelans continue to escape socialism's death grip. Because North Korea still has a GDP the size of a couple of Vermont counties. Because Brazil is turning to market capitalism after horrific decades of state control. Because "superpower" Russia has a third world economy.

But most of all, because the average American will not happily or easily give up his or her freedoms. There are just too many people in flyover America who will not indulge such encroachment. And no amount of pie-in-the-sky faux aspirational nonsense from the alphabet soup cable news networks will change it.

America's deplorables will simply say, "No."

You can take it to the bank.

Feel better now?

Competing Revolutions—The Progressive Left vs. the Deplorables

Western Journal
October 23, 2019

There are two very different revolutions taking place in America today, but only one of them generates much media attention.

One is impossible to miss: the unrelenting campaign to remake American values and culture. This not-so-subtle revolution is daily instigated by the usual suspects: Hollywood celebrities, the mainstream media, college professors and administrators, and public-sector unions. An ever-vigilant social justice media police aggressively monitors the effort.

Sad to say that great strides have been made by these committed activists. More on the substance of the movement below.

There is an equally impactful campaign afoot on the other side of the philosophical aisle, but this one is much more understated. It concerns the single most important issue that propelled candidate Trump into the presidency.

I refer of course to judicial selection—most particularly, but not exclusively, the selection of justices to the Supreme Court. Here, post-election polls revealed what few in the dominant media thought remotely possible: overwhelming numbers of evangelical voters turning out to support the thrice-married, former casino magnate, reality television show personality on the basis of judgeships alone.

Indeed, few observers believed that Trump's oft-repeated promise to appoint only "originalist" judges to the federal bench would have any impact, much less a material impact.

They were wrong.

Back to the not-so-quiet revolution—the one that not even Barack Obama could have imagined a mere four years ago. You read that right. Obama only thought he defined the left flank of the progressive movement in America. Events soon revealed that he too was wrong.

How wrong? Well, check out presidential aspirant Beto O'Rourke's recent promise to repeal organized religion's tax exemption whenever and wherever a denomination opposes same-sex marriage; or the specter of every Democratic contender promising to extend health care benefits to illegal aliens; or the progressive push to eliminate the Electoral College, or pack the Supreme Court, or end the natural gas revolution that is leading to American energy independence; or, most important, the sight of so many leading Democrats running toward, rather than away, from socialism.

Obama never dared to walk or even flirt with these once-unthinkable positions!

The problem, of course, is that so many of these extreme positions are dead on arrival come Election Day—especially in flyover America where all of those millions of undesirable deplorables tend to gather, live, and vote.

Alas, this inconvenient fact of life has led some of the sharper progressive minds to look to the courts in order to impose new cultural values on all those good-for-nothing rednecks.

But what if those same courts became dominated by those who would seek to interpret the law rather than legislate it? That would be a BIG problem indeed—and one that could lead to all kinds of emotional upheaval (see, e.g., the Brett Kavanaugh hearings). All of which brings us back to the aforementioned quiet revolution.

For the American left, the earth began to move in the wake of Trump's first two Supreme Court nominations—Neil Gorsuch and Brett Kavanaugh. Both are young and originalist in orientation; both hold "pro-life" views; and both tend to vote with the Court's conservative majority most of the time. Accordingly, progressive activists from coast to coast are at DEFCON 5.

Less attention is paid to lower court appellate judges, but here too, the movement is very real and decidedly to the right. An early Trump administration decision to marginalize candidate ratings offered by the left-leaning American Bar Association in favor of vetting by the conservative Federalist Society made it crystal clear where this administration intended to go.

The numbers say it all. As of Oct. 15, 152 Article 2 judges have been confirmed by the U.S. Senate. Of these, 43 have been appointed to U.S. Courts of Appeals and 105 to the District Courts.

Notably, the average age of Trump's circuit court selections is 49 years old, younger than judges selected by the previous five presidents. A long-term majority of originalist jurists is now within reach, just what movement conservatives have long wanted and progressives have long dreaded.

For the latter, repeated losses at the ballot box and in the courts do not a revolution make. These folks are plenty unhappy about both developments. As a result, you can bet plenty more incidents of acting out will occur in the lead-up to November 2020.

Five Things the Left Refuses to Get

Western Journal
November 4, 2019

Here are five observations to keep in mind the next time someone attempts to convince you progressivism is America's future.

Charter Schools

What in the 1990s was an experiment begun by African American women in Wisconsin has progressed into a slam-dunk winner for tens of thousands of (primarily) minority students. The startling academic success achieved by some of America's poorest students makes the case.

Despite this undeniable progress, progressive leaders such as New York City Mayor Bill DeBlasio continue their daily assault against these semi-autonomous schools. Such strident opposition is all about placating powerful teachers unions that enjoy an outsized presence in Democratic primaries. Alas, the fate of these unique public schools will be determined at the ballot box next November. In the meantime, it will serve

Republican interests to aggressively market their strong support of charters in minority communities. Parents of kids lucky enough to attend these schools must be reminded who has their best interests at heart.

Religious Freedom

I'm not sure when it all began, but it is now clear that progressive leaders will continue to demonize religious belief and practice anytime and anywhere such traditions conflict with progressive social mores. The process is by now familiar: progressive talking heads employ their omnipresent speech patrols to dismiss the expression of religious values as "hate speech."

They then double down by contending that such speech is not protected under the First Amendment. That this interpretation of free speech is simply incorrect is beside the point. A relentless shaming of those who seek to stand by religious conviction follows and is often enough to convince the "offender" to back down. Yet, the public censure does not change the offender's opinion.

This is precisely where the difficult-to-measure support for Donald J. Trump comes into play—a point misunderstood by progressives who believe that relentless shaming is enough. It is not.

In fact, while public opinion polls are unable to measure the quiet resistance of those who resent the present-day campaign waged against religious institutions and values, the aggrieved practitioners nevertheless remain registered, highly motivated voters. And they now have added impetus to show up next November.

The Rich

The Left's favorite target from time immemorial. Always a crowd favorite, too, especially among young progressive millennials propagandized into the supposedly evil twins of wealth and privilege. Indeed, entire destructive political philosophies (communism, socialism) have been built on the notions of class envy and the evil rich.

There are American-centric problems with this worldview, however, and they are not going to disappear easily. The first concerns that initial (shocked) reaction when a fresh-out-of-college graduate receives his or her first paycheck. The typical response ranges from mild agitation to not-so-mild outrage as the private sector newbie realizes he or she has never been taught the economics of taxation—or the cost of bureaucracy—in college. Many of you will identify with this life-altering moment, as more than one Republican has been born as a result.

For some, the second life-altering realization occurs at a point down the career path—wherein hard work has resulted in higher income and, in some cases, business ownership. The vast majority of folks who reach this point will never "feel the Bern"; they are proud of what they have accomplished and want to keep it.

Here, the expectation that one is supposed to feel guilty about hard-earned success and wealth is viewed as silly, even un-American. Moreover, these good folks often wish to grow their wealth—and then pass it on to their kids. Not the type of moral you are likely to hear at an Elizabeth Warren campaign rally.

Trump Voters

No new ground here, just more recent evidence that the new Left does not understand—or does not care to understand—what drives the president's appeal between the coasts. I refer, of course, to former Vice President Biden's assertion that the real reason people support the president is "because of the tax cut…they like him because he's a racist…."

The Democratic frontrunner added that those not motivated by prejudice are simply "people…who are afraid."

If you discern a "three-fer" here, go to the head of the class. Recall how President Barack Obama famously dismissed working-class voters as "bitter, they cling to guns or religion or antipathy to people who aren't like them or anti-immigrant sentiment or anti-trade sentiment," circa 2008. Then, of course, came Hillary Clinton's equally infamous "irredeemable deplorables" indictment of America's working-class eight years later.

The attitudes expressed herein reflect what so many working people now realize: progressive elites are willing to write off millions of blue-collar, church-going, gun-owning voters. All the post-election happy talk about starting a conversation with this demographic is now by the boards, replaced by familiar allegations/taunts of racism, nativism, misogynism—and just about any other-ism you care to name.

As a result, FDR continues to spin in his grave. I'm pretty sure JFK has joined him.

Immigration

Today's progressives openly court illegal aliens—and count such courting as high political virtue. Activists challenge border walls they supported only a few years ago. They further advocate for the elimination of the federal department charged with tracking and capturing criminal illegal immigrants in the country. To boot, in some jurisdictions, locally elected progressives have sought to give illegals the right to vote.

That all this new ground has been covered in the three short years since the end of the Obama administration is startling and speaks to how dramatically the leadership of the Democratic Party has moved further left.

But, yet again, it does not mean working-class Democrats (let alone Republicans and independents) have followed suit. Just the opposite in fact.

In flyover country, the voice of millions of legal immigrants who chose to follow the law (sometimes patiently waiting years to become a citizen), is heard—loud and clear—as are the calls for an orderly and fair process at the border.

The bottom line: going 0 for 5 with regard to the things that really count in middle America will be a heavy lift for Democrats attempting to win a national election.

Five More Things the Left Refuses to Get

Western Journal
November 21, 2019

This is the second installment of "Five Things the Left Refuses to Get."

Religion

Not so long ago, pundits believed the emergence of the "Christian right" would be a divisive obstacle to future GOP unity. Today, the polar opposite is true: faith-based conservative denominations are an integral part of the Trump coalition. Here, Vice President Mike Pence is the field general, while Senate Majority Leader Mitch McConnell serves as ground commander in charge of federal judgeships.

Alas, today's faith "problem" is on the left, as working- and middle-class ethnic Catholics increasingly find themselves in the crosshairs of even respected Democratic leaders.

The most recent example herein was California Sen. Dianne Feinstein's characterization of Notre Dame Law Professor Amy Coney Barrett's Catholicism as dogma ("the dogma lives loudly within you"). The charge was not well received in Catholic America. But that 2017 incident will pale in comparison if a re-elected President Trump nominates that same Judge Barrett to the high court.

The mother of seven is highly respected in conservative circles. She is supposedly on the short list. Her nomination will be seen as a sixth conservative vote—and would no doubt set off wild protests and renewed promises to pack the court on the left. That the opposition would focus on her Catholic faith and convictions is without doubt. The expected ugliness would further engender resentment among faith-based deplorables—not a good result for Democratic moderates attempting a comeback in middle America.

Wall Street

Indictments of Wall Street and the business investment sector have always been raw meat in progressive circles. The left has long castigated large investment banks for their periodic scandals and extraordinary profits.

Still, a quiet, capitalist revolution has been brewing for the last three decades; and it has to do with the growing prominence of the defined contribution retirement vehicle—better known as the 401(k).

As of 2018, Americans have an estimated $5.3 trillion in these tax-advantaged savings accounts, as well as $993 billion in "403(b) plans" (for non-profit institutions); $323 billion in "457 plans" (for governmental employers); and $580 billion in "TSP plans" (for federal employees). It is accordingly accurate to say that for an ever-increasing number of middle- and working-class Americans, what is good for the market is good for America.

Yet, you will have to search long and hard in the progressive media to find recognition—let alone praise—for this market-driven success story. Their war against Wall Street will never abate. Capitalism's detractors have invested far too much in a class warfare narrative to ever change.

Race

Progressives want white people to feel guilty about being white, and black people who are insufficiently "woke" to feel even worse. This racial self-animus is relatively new to our culture, so context will help. Recall the manner in which the alphabet soup cable networks covered House GOP members walking out en masse in order to protest Chairman Adam Schiff's closed-door Ukraine interrogations.

The referenced reviews were exceptionally harsh, but it was the media's contempt for the members' race and gender that caught my attention. That the most cynical comments were delivered by white liberals is illustrative. The not-too-subtle takeaway: Republican whiteness and maleness are sufficient to invalidate the party's message. No additional evidence is required. For these opinion-makers, Dr. King's historic admonition of character over race is *so* 1960s.

Similarly, some of you may recall former presidential candidate and U.S. Sen. Kirsten Gillibrand's preachy "white privilege" instruction to a white working-class mother in economically depressed Youngstown, Ohio. What sounded so woke to her campaign advisors was not so well received in the real world, however. Her presidential effort disbanded shortly thereafter.

Fatherlessness

To be fair, not every lefty buys into the "fatherlessness is a racist issue" mantra. The most prominent exception is President Obama, who on numerous public occasions has recognized how the proliferation of fatherless children contributes to generational poverty. Still, what then-Senate staffer Daniel Patrick Moynihan identified as a foundational contributor to a long list of social ills (in 1968) has today become code for racism for some left-leaning intellectuals.

The charge is weak; the plague of social ills associated with fatherless kids (the empirical evidence is overwhelming) recognizes no racial bounds. In other words, white and Hispanic families have not been spared the fatherless epidemic. Yet, it is a problem generally ignored by most political and community leaders out of fear. Our culture suffers as a result.

Progressives who wish to utilize this issue as a white racism/privilege play be forewarned. You will find it difficult to trot out the over-used "dog whistle" analogy here. The statistics—and common sense—make a difficult opponent indeed.

Nationalism

Lately, much has been made about the "rebirth" of American nationalism. (Rich Lowry's new book *The Case for Nationalism* is an excellent read in this space.)

The reasons for all the Trump-era attention on the American experience are clear: (1.) The left is investing ever-increasing invective toward the concept of American exceptionalism while (2.) no president since Reagan has invested more in championing the noble American experiment in democracy, pluralism, and market capitalism.

Regarding the former, progressives no longer feel the need to hide their hostility for the American story—and its Founders. The new narrative (taught in far too many public school systems around the country) focuses on racism, nativism, misogynism, and ethnocentrism—regardless of historic progress in racial/gender equality and wealth accumulation.

The bottom line quickly bubbles to the surface: America is inherently (permanently) racist and therefore fundamentally flawed; only a complete cultural transformation can rectify our countless shortcomings.

The latter could not disagree more. A (still) silent majority senses a rejuvenated patriotism in the Trump era, not such a strange takeaway for what remains a free, vibrant, and wealth-generating country.

Most important, these regular ole folks are able to calibrate the moral stain of slavery and inequality AND the brilliance of the Founding Fathers. They expect their political leaders to do likewise. Those wannabes who fail are inevitably sentenced to the dustbin of history as no candidate has ever (or will ever) won the presidency on an "America is evil" platform. Americans of all colors have simply sacrificed too much in blood and treasure to think otherwise.

Liberals and Conservatives Must Fight against the Left's War on Free Speech

Western Journal
February 20, 2019

Millions of baby boomers came of age during the latter stages of the tumultuous 1960s. Accordingly, we (yours truly was born in 1957) have some remembrance of "I have a dream," the 1968 Democratic Convention in Chicago, Kent State, and the Dr. King and Bobby Kennedy assassinations. These culture-changing events marked a difficult time in our history, as cities burned and college campuses erupted in violent protests. Large demonstrations were commonplace, as many Americans demanded to be heard on civil rights, women's rights, and the war in Vietnam.

Some on the right recoiled at the form and substance of the civil disobedience. Their resulting uneasiness would provide the emotional fuel for a former vice president (Richard Nixon) in his successful campaign for the presidency in 1968.

Much of the era's tension was focused on the lawlessness—the riots—the looting. Notably, few contested the **right** of free Americans to protest; to speak "truth to power" per the contemporary vernacular.

Now fast-forward to the new millennium, especially to the eight-year experiment in progressive activism known as the Obama administration. Here, the empowered Left achieved a modicum of big government-driven (apparent) policy successes, including a huge Keynesian stimulus and, of course, Obamacare. But it charted a far different path on the issue of speech. Startlingly, it used the tools of government to suppress dissent—often in the most illiberal ways.

Check it out:

- The campus-based war on speech is now the topic of daily analysis. Heretofore unheard of strictures such as speech codes and trigger warnings are now part of the college experience. To boot, conservative speakers are regularly shouted down and often subject to abuse on the very campuses that not so long ago gave birth to the free speech movement. Some schools charge outrageous security fees to conservative speakers in order to discourage their attendance.
- Progressives justify this abhorrent behavior as a "just" response to "hate speech": a mightily subjective catchphrase that regularly gets attached to political positions at odds with the progressives' no judgment/race privilege paradigm. Today, it's *always* a home game for the vocabulary cops.
- The obligation of non-profits to protect the identities of contributors has its roots in the civil rights movement. Few could argue with the (civil rights era) policy consideration behind such a privacy requirement: the NAACP needed to keep the identities of its contributors private—for their safety. Yet today, progressives (and

their sponsors in Congress) are actively involved in attempts to un-redact names of contributors to conservative causes. Despite the threat to their safety, primary targets have been groups supporting traditional marriage and, of course, any group connected to the Koch brothers. The latest challenge is a Koch case presently in the Ninth Circuit. Geez…wonder how that one will turn out?

– Recall Lois Lerner's weaponizing of the IRS—one of the most underappreciated threats to our democracy in our time, including her "missing" emails and decision to take the "Fifth" when forced to testify in front of Congress. You may also recollect President Obama's lighthearted dismissal of the entire slow walk charade. Often lost in the hand-wringing are all those right-leaning non-profits that were not certified in time to participate in time for Election 2012…Suppression, indeed.

– The Left's game plan extends to conservative talk radio through administrative initiatives such as the "locality rule," "fairness doctrine," and the Obama administration's "community advisory boards"—all focused on silencing national conservative radio. These concepts are further emboldened by George Soros et al.'s ongoing campaign to pressure sponsors of conservative radio/TV shows to withdraw their advertising dollars.

– Progressives have likewise proven resourceful when it comes to the flip side—finding unique ways to force the unwitting to fund *their* speech.

To wit:

– My congressional tenure spawned the era wherein liberal Democrats regularly agitated for more aggressive underwriting of so-called sub-prime (high risk) mortgage loans. You recall those heady days. Both parties participated in the charade, but the Left transformed home ownership into a civil right. No credit history? No problem. Bad credit history? No problem. Little or no income? No problem. Of course, it all came crashing down when large Wall Street investment banks rolled all those toxic loans into securities that were then sold to buyers around the world. A historic market crash ensued. A major recession followed, as did the Obama Justice Department's lawsuits against those same Wall Street bankers. Said lawsuits, in turn, led to settlements, which led to opportunities for Eric Holder to redirect a portion of said settlements to "community organizing groups." You know, the same ones (such as "A.C.O.R.N.") that helped create the easy mortgage era in the first place.

—   Another way progressives have sought to compel subsidization of leftist speech is to require dues from non-union members. You may recall Wisconsin as a flash point over this hotly contested issue. Alas, the Supreme Court held the practice unconstitutional (in *Janus vs. AFSCME Council 31*) this past year. As a result, millions of laborers are no longer compelled to fund political speech they often vehemently oppose. Three cheers for freedom!

Liberals and conservatives should band together in the fight for true free speech. Enough of the easily and often offended progressive Left. Remember the '60s!

FBI's Treatment of Flynn a Wake-Up Call to All Americans

Western Journal
May 11, 2020

I awakened last Thursday to good news: justice had finally been afforded to Gen. Michael Flynn.

Finally, I thought, enough of the facts had been brought to light that even haters would surely see how poorly the 33-year veteran, three-star general had been treated.

I hoped that even the administration's considerable number of detractors could see that the blemish of Flynn's less than forthcoming discussions with Vice President Pence and non-material and FBI-encouraged false statements did not justify the FBI's plan to destroy him.

And then reality hit me square in the face: apologists for the Obama Justice Department would never let this matter go.

The setting here is the James Comey–generated entrapment of an incoming national security advisor. We now know it was a setup because the FBI possessed the transcripts of Gen. Flynn's (wholly appropriate) conversations with Russian Ambassador Sergey Kislyak and that Comey had previously bragged about his perjury trap on tape—going so far as to say he would never have entertained such a plan when operating under a Bush or Obama White House.

Last week, we found out that FBI agents Peter Strzok and Joe Pientka proceeded to interview Flynn in an attempt to—per the notes of agent Bill Priestap—gain "[t]ruth/Admission or to get him to lie, so we can prosecute him or get him fired."

The public was previously informed that despite this general (and plainly illegal) motive, the interviewing agents concluded that Flynn did *not* lie to them. Recall this conclusion was reached despite their successful ploy to discourage Flynn from bringing an attorney with him.

Most of all, we are now beginning to learn the rest of the story because a lioness of an attorney named Sidney Powell called out all the culpable miscreants of the Obama era in her successful representation of a man who could not afford to pay her. The government, completely abandoning the professional disinterest that is supposed to be their hallmark, had made sure that Michael Flynn was broken in more ways than one.

The most distressing single government act that has recently come to light is the extensive editing of the so-called "FP-302" report (raw interview notes) by Peter Strzok. Indeed, last week's texts show that Strzok edited Pientka's report to such an extent that he told FBI attorney Lisa Page that he was "trying not to completely re-write it." Even worse, the texts reflect that Page contributed edits as well—despite not being present at the interview.

Back to my naïve reaction. In retrospect, it was silly of me to think that those on the other side of the partisan divide would for a split second issue a mea culpa for attempting to destroy the reputation of an American patriot.

Indeed, the dagger to my unfulfilled hope was supplied by none other than the person under whom all the shenanigans took place. Yes, the former law professor Barack Obama, who said in reaction to the DOJ's decision to drop the case:

> The fact that there is no precedent that anybody can find for someone who has been charged with perjury just getting off scot-free. That's the kind of stuff where you begin to get worried that basic—not just institutional norms—but our basic understanding of rule of law is at risk.

Note that the former president did not even get the alleged crime right: Flynn was charged with making "false statements" to the FBI, not perjury.

Left unsaid by most of the outraged left-wing partisans on the cable news networks is an inconvenient legal requirement. To wit: the Department of Justice is compelled to drop prosecutions once it concludes it has little or no chance to prove guilt beyond a reasonable doubt. Here, the accumulating evidence made for a damning case of government entrapment.

The rightful decision to drop the case does not alter the ugly chain of events that placed Flynn in the government's crosshairs. He had the bad timing to join a campaign and incoming administration during Justice Department investigations. He was made a target because he was part of the team that was not supposed to win the election. He subsequently resigned his position in disgrace and then pleaded guilty because prosecutors threatened to put his son in prison. His defense costs broke him. He lost his home.

In this case, it should not matter whether you bleed blue or red, whether you see Mike Flynn as a flawed man who was not straight with the vice president or as an American hero. It matters because if such a nightmare can be foisted upon a three-star general, imagine what could happen to you.

"Not in America," all good Democrats and Republicans should say in unison. Every one of us deserves better—and each one of us must demand as much going forward.

CHAPTER 5

THE DEPLORABLES: NOT TIRED OF WINNING—JUST TIRED OF GETTING SCREWED

It was a theme repeated time and again; first on the 2016 campaign trail and then as a "can do" president. It was also a classic Trumpian sound-bite that spoke volumes about how the celebrity-turned-politician saw the world. For Mr. Trump, everything is a competition—a contest to determine winners and losers. And what better metaphor for this world-view than his number one television show, *The Apprentice*, where contestants either won or were **fired**? There would be no participation trophies awarded on this reality show; those who failed to convince Mr. Trump they were winners were unceremoniously let go, shown the elevator, and promptly escorted from the building—all with camera following in order to record the departing loser's angst.

That Mr. Trump was able to carry over the "winner" theme in his pitch to a beaten-down middle America most certainly surprised the political class, tied as they were to traditional Washington assumptions. The drumbeat for something different hit home: America had been "losing" (especially to China) for too long; the working class was falling behind; the American Dream was at risk; and a bottom line, get-it-done Queens developer had arrived just in time to turn it all around. Here, the contrast with President Obama's delusory comments on the future of American manufacturing ("There is no magic wand to bring those jobs back") was stark. But it was the tale of a broken Manhattan ice rink that best provided context for the "winners get it done" moniker of Mr. Trump.

Longtime residents of New York City will recall the circa mid-1980s tale of the Wollman Skating Rink, a well-known but problem-plagued Manhattan venue with a history of famously failed fixes. Repeated city efforts at repairs never seemed to work. It appeared nobody in charge could get the operation up and running. That is, until Mr. Trump appeared on the scene. In his familiar style, Mr. Trump told the *New York Times*, "I don't want my name attached to losers...so far the Wollman Rink has been one of the great losers. I'll make it a winner." The task was more daunting than you might think. The city had already wasted $13 million in past attempts and had recently announced it needed two additional years and millions more dollars to get the job done. Trump promised he could get the rink up and running in less than six months. Stunningly, he accomplished the task in four, and far below budget. A big payday of positive press followed, but something far more important had occurred. Trump had been successful wherein the local government had repeatedly failed. He had "won." What better metaphor for a future campaign predicated on the charge "America was losing" and that only he (Trump) knew how to fix it? Why, he might even Make America Great Again!

A cousin to "not tired of winning" was "let's stop getting screwed." Here, the consistently repeated indictment was that many trade deals—arms agreements—and multilateral treaties had unfairly burdened the world's sole superpower, especially its increasingly alienated working class. In response, a chorus of opposition sprang up from the very same bureaucrats who had negotiated the deals. Here was one reason (of many) why so many GOP establishment types and NeverTrumpers viewed Mr. Trump as (at best) an acquired taste. You see, full acceptance was always going to be a high bar for those who saw their most cherished policy assumptions and constructs reduced to "Let's make a (better) deal"— and there could *always* be a better deal. Still, the fact that Mr. Trump's methods produced positive results made some accommodation with this crowd possible.

A case in point was candidate (and later President) Trump's repeated pledge to embarrass our allies into footing more of the bill for the deployment of American military forces around the world. Mr. Trump's complaints were not limited to deadbeat NATO allies either, as he often pointed to widely disbursed American naval assets as essential to keeping shipping lanes (such as in the Gulf of Hormuz) open to international traffic. Here, the president would point out how countries that enjoyed the protection of forward-based U.S. troops around the world often failed to pay their "fair share" of the upkeep. America had for decades picked up the tab for supposedly Western-friendly regimes even when those same governments had gone out of their way to oppose U.S. policy in other respects. (Think of Germany's willingness to assist Russia with a controversial pipeline designed to transport Russian gas to Western Europe.) Of course, the substance of the charge was often accurate. But no American president had dared frame the issue in such coarse terms. (The *Wall Street Journal* editorialized unamusingly that the president was in the habit of using our military like a "mercenary outfit"—a view shared by neo-cons and liberals alike.) But an awful lot of right-thinking conservatives bought into the "getting used" critique, especially when employed against the likes of an increasingly malign China. What was an embarrassing ploy for the American foreign policy establishment was to Mr. Trump a negotiating tactic weaponized to cut the best deal for the American taxpayer. To each his own, but still difficult to swallow for the Foggy Bottom crowd!

Takeaways from the NFL's Kneeling Era

Baltimore Sun
January 4, 2018

The NFL's recent attempt to assuage its players through an $89 million contribution over seven years to social justice causes is succeeding. Fewer players (down to 20 in Week 16) are choosing to kneel, sit, or stay in the locker room during the National Anthem. The powers that be are no doubt breathing a sigh of relief after a tumultuous early season.

But before the image of kneeling players, booing fans, and the worst PR season in league history fades from memory, a few takeaways are in order.

There remains a percentage of fans for whom the kneeling continues to mark an emotional turning point. Not that these fans have gone off into the night or lost all interest in America's most popular game. It is more about emotional attachment or, in this case, detachment. For this group, distaste for protesting players continues to translate into fewer games attended, fewer jerseys purchased, fewer hours spent in front of the big screen in the man cave.

One result of all the controversy is an uber-patriotic NFL. Pro-military themes that had in previous seasons (2011–2015) been paid for by the Department of Defense are now all the rage. It's called back-fill from a league that has seen how even a deeply divided America will not countenance (real or perceived) disrespect shown to those who serve. A memorable case in point: a few weeks ago, during a Sunday night game I barely recall, I listened to commentator and former Cincinnati Bengal Cris Collinsworth remind his viewers the kneeling was never about flag and country. But such an emphatic point raises the question of what it really is/was about?

Answer #1: The pig sock–wearing, Che Guevara–adoring, unemployed Colin Kaepernick was (originally) quite emphatic regarding his condemnation of the men and women in blue. The associated indictment of an alleged campaign of police brutality against African American communities was raised as part of a narrative—notwithstanding the absence of hard evidence to back up the charge. (Here, exceptions do not prove the rule.) This is a part of the story Mr. Collinsworth failed to add. But it was an element of the original messaging—a theme that is as offensive to many fans as an anti-military message. Yet, this storyline has lost some vigor over the past two months. Perhaps a rash of highly publicized, horrific murders of police officers has made this charge a bit too inconvenient for the moment.

Answer #2: More recently, the rhetoric has centered on a more social justice–oriented platform—a serious and legitimate point—albeit messily presented. To wit: African American kids who face daunting life obstacles—not least of which are often dysfunctional public schools located in our most depressed communities. Lack of economic opportunity follows, as does a laundry list of associated cultural ills—fatherlessness, homelessness, domestic violence, and addiction. As a result, far too many "savable" kids get swallowed up in our brutal criminal justice system. Any attention (and, more importantly, time and resources) that is productively directed to these persistent problems is welcome. Herein is also a test of good intentions: players who give back and participate in these communities are part of the solution—and should be appropriately recognized.

Besides the aforementioned cash payment, the NFL is also considering going back to its pre-2009 practice (in prime time games) of playing the anthem prior to player introductions. But fans are now accustomed to seeing the players stand on the sidelines while the song that reflects our national pride is performed. The proposed move is too cute by half. A sideline sans players would only serve to remind us of why they were absent.

What to think about Commissioner Roger Goodell? The hostility that greets him each and every time he approaches the NFL draft podium to announce early round picks says it all. The explanation proceeds that his business acumen (most particularly in negotiating big TV contracts) is top shelf. Of course, such skill translates into mega dollars for the owners. This is the only explanation for the league's apparent willingness to pay the man such an exorbitant salary (up to $40 million per year with incentives). It is unclear whether his previous demand for lifetime health care was met. In any case, there will be no Obamacare for this guy, social justice notwithstanding. Do you think he ever bothers to consider why he is held in such contempt by the fans?

As I have opined on previous occasions, the shield (and sport) will likely survive despite television-induced over-saturation, injuries to star players, concussions, bad officiating, indecipherable rules, exorbitant ticket prices, league parity, arrogant owners, tone-deaf players, turned-off fans, and a private-jet-loving commissioner.

Such is the pull of our favorite sport.

Five Things the Left Doesn't Get about Trump's "Deplorables"

LifeZette
July 13, 2018

We are now more than a year and a half down the analytical road chock-full of books, columns, and scholarly reviews devoted to explaining the ways and means of President Donald J. Trump and his merry band of "deplorables."

The most simplistic of these analyses can be watched ad nauseam on the cable news networks daily, if not hourly. Here, the pundits retained by these bastions of progressivism sound a now-familiar refrain first uttered by former Obama aide Van ("It's a white-out") Jones on election night 2016.

Translation: these unsophisticated, low-IQ voters are primarily latter-day racists of various stripes who found their voice in one Donald J. Trump. The narrative further proceeds along the line of "Don't be fooled—they may no longer wear hoods, but we know what they really think."

Left unaddressed is the question of how it is that secretive racists voted for Barack Obama twice—to elect him to the White House in

2008 and re-elect him in 2012—before revealing their David Duke true colors.

A similar ethnic animus toward illegal aliens is said to animate deplorables, aka the "America Firsters." Here, their alleged nativism is reflected in a hostility toward immigrants—especially illegal immigrants—and most particularly illegal immigrants with brown or black skin.

You may recall Obama's dismissive description of this group. ("They cling to guns or religion or antipathy toward people who aren't like them.") Alas, progressives view this subspecies of deplorables with as much contempt as that reserved for overt racists.

To be fair, not all members of the Left's resistance believe the foregoing descriptions cover every one of the 63 million deplorables who cast a vote for Trump. Plenty of vitriol is reserved for white middle- and upper-middle-class conservatives (and perhaps the greatest animosity is aimed toward black traitors to the liberal cause) —who desire lower taxes, less regulation, and generational wealth.

Such is the wish list of the truly "greedy," per progressive philosophy.

But what do deplorables think of themselves? What belief system sets them apart as members of Trump's army, or, as per retiring Tennessee Republican Sen. Bob Corker, sycophants devoted to a dangerous cult of personality?

My interactions over the past few years lead me to five primary attributes:

1.) **A "rigged" system**: An unusual charge coming from a Manhattan real-estate mogul and casino owner hit home with millions of heartlanders who have worked hard all their lives but have relatively little to show for their efforts. They accordingly see their American Dream at risk.

Trump and Sen. Bernie Sanders (I-Vt.) harped on this theme, with both stressing how the Washington, D.C., establishments of both parties were engaged in the power exercise of picking winners and losers—subsidizing the former and letting the latter wither away.

The resulting charge of "rigged" was successfully used by both men. On the political front, Bernie was forced to run a race in a truly rigged Democratic presidential-primary process, while the Trump campaign had to overcome unprecedented partisan shenanigans at the highest level of the FBI and Department of Justice (DOJ).

Recently discovered emails from senior DOJ employees have only added kerosene to the rigged indictment perspective. Interesting that what was once seen as typical Trumpian, over-the-top rhetoric about how the "swamp" conducts business has now gained serious, credible momentum on the right and left.

2.) **A confident leader**: Trump conveys a sense of confident control at all times. His supporters eat it up. His detractors see a charlatan, a con man, all salesmanship and no substance. Regardless of where you might fall in this paradigm, it's difficult to recall a president who appears more sure of himself.

This sense of confidence also describes the deplorables' attitude toward the president. Their confidence in America's (and their families') future is energized by Trump's relentless self-promotion and appeals to American pride and nationalism.

This aspect of the president's personality drives lefty elites and their media sponsors wild, but it has clearly kept his base energized, as polls reflect consistently strong job approval ratings among those who voted for Trump in 2016.

3.) **Disrupters Inc.**: There's that word again. The country has seen how Trump relishes the disrupter tag. The deplorables see themselves in a similar light; they are increasingly distrustful of establishment institutions, including but not limited to the media, Hollywood, and the heretofore untouchable FBI.

Accordingly, they tend to indulge Trump's more extreme disrupter inclinations (immigration orders, tariffs, family separation policies) even where they would normally profess concerns. A logical question emerges: Can daily disruption over the course of four years wear a movement out? A logical query in light of the president's relentless, frenetic style.

4.) **A deep reservoir**: Trump seems to thrive amid seeming chaos. This modus operandi is unique; even (some) supporters have a difficult time accepting the comings and goings—hirings and firings—tweets and retweets that define life in the Trump White House.

It goes without saying that his approach to the most important job in the world would have led to a quick demise for any other politician. But not so much this president, as deplorables are not disquieted by chaos.

Indeed, they see it not as chaos, but as an "active president," a positive term once reserved by liberals. The enthusiasm quotient apparent from Trump's first day in the White House has not dissipated. Here, Trump supporters attach a gigantic benefit of the doubt to their president and his policy initiatives, even when he reverses field overnight. Few democratically elected leaders have ever enjoyed such sustained flexibility.

5.) **Digging in**: This one is self-evident to those on the Right and all but invisible to the resistance. To wit: every boycott, restaurant demonstration, "c"-word/"f"-word incident, or organized traffic disruption perpetrated on behalf of the resistance produces an equal, opposite reaction among the deplorables.

In this case, vicious attacks build emotional attachment as deplorables just dig deeper in their support of Trump. Anyone who doubts this proposition should check the repeated undercounting of Trump support by professional pollsters over the past three years.

How to Engage the Resistance without Losing Your Mind or Your Integrity

LifeZette
July 15, 2018

You are the typical right-of-center voter. You experienced eight years of frustration under former President Barack Obama. You still get night sweats thinking about Attorney General Eric Holder's Department of Justice, national security advisor Susan Rice, and Supreme Court Justices Sonia Sotomayor and Elena Kagan. Let's not forget "You didn't build that," either.

You were understandably excited for campaign 2016, and why not? An attractive GOP field was filled with successful governors and senators. There was the equally exciting opportunity to end the Clinton dynasty for good. You were ready to support any of the major GOP candidates—even the interloper reality TV star with the salesman's pitch and disregard for comity. A third Obama term was impossible to fathom.

And then, on Nov. 8, 2016, your wish came true. The looks on the faces of the alphabet-soup cable news anchors said it all. Some were angry, others cried, more than a few talked not of an opposition but of a new "resistance."

You enjoyed watching the establishment melt down on your TV screen that night.

Many made phone calls and sent emails and texts to friends. "Can you believe it?!" were the first four words in the vast majority of these.

Eighteen months down the road, you are generally pleased with this president, despite misgivings about daily process. You wonder about the modus operandi of the Trump White House, while reassuring yourself that this state of things appears to be how this president operates. Different strokes for different folks (or leader of the free world, in this case). In any event, you support the Reaganesque policy calls enough to let the less important things slide.

But the recent protests regarding immigration and Supreme Court nominee Brett Kavanaugh present a new challenge. How to deal with the Left's unhinged behavior? The reports are shameful: a restaurant refusing service to Sarah Huckabee Sanders; a member of Congress urging ugly public confrontation; entertainment celebrities going full-throttle potty mouth; feminists urging pro-choice women to withhold sex from their boyfriends and husbands in protest of *Roe v. Wade's* hanging in the balance.

You digest the daily shenanigans and get angry. How to strike back at the lefties and their invective?

The problem is that folks like us do not respond in kind. Right-leaning folks simply do not do boycotts. Young Republicans do not invade their university president's office. And the thought of shouting down an opposing opinion is anathema to true conservatives. Still, you want to engage. The future of our culture—and country—is at stake.

One option is to replicate the Left's playbook. I'm not advocating stopping traffic in midtown Manhattan or protesting the next left-winger appearing at Liberty University. But what about that old favorite, the boycott? Why not apply it to Hollywood? Just say "no" to flicks with Robert De Niro, Rob Reiner, Leonardo DiCaprio, Meryl Streep, et al.

The plan sounds good, but the downside immediately comes to mind: One's entertainment viewing options quickly boil down to Clint Eastwood, Gary Sinise, Jon Voight, and Bruce Willis. Love those guys, but how many times can one person watch *Dirty Harry*?

OK, what about television? We know the "idiot box" is filled with not-so-subtle lefties plying their progressive views. This means no more Jimmy Kimmel, Samantha Bee, Seth Meyers, and Jimmy Fallon. That's easy; you don't watch them, anyway.

What about ESPN? That will be difficult, especially with young athletes in the house. How about the NFL?

Your viewing is already reduced due to last year's anthem protests. But it's hard to go cold turkey in late fall.

The NBA? Major figures (LeBron, Curry, Popovich) are famously on the anti-Trump bandwagon. But those late spring playoff games are pretty exciting...

Suffice it to say that the list of potential boycotts from the worlds of sports and entertainment would be lengthy. Most right-wingers would quickly add the *New York Times*, the *Washington Post*, NBC, CBS, ABC, CNN, public broadcasting, Facebook, Google, Starbucks, Broadway, the music industry, and academia to the list.

Sooner rather than later, your life could be limited to Fox, the *Wall Street Journal*, *Field & Stream*, Chick-fil-A, and Franklin Graham gatherings. Some of you may already be in this place, and I do not begrudge you your opinion. But for the rest of us, there has to be another way to engage the resistance.

My suggestion: reject the boycott option (subject to the usual exception of Jane Fonda movies). Rather, double down on the people, institutions, and causes that reflect your values. You will feel better putting your money where your mouth (and heart) is. And it never hurts to eat more chicken sandwiches.

Thoughts on Kaepernick, Nike, and America's Former Favorite Sport

LifeZette
September 14, 2018

Bob Casciola, a former college coach at Princeton, University of Connecticut, and Dartmouth and former president of the National Football Foundation and College Football Hall of Fame, published a book in August—*First and Forever*—in defense of our great American institution.

The book chronicles the lives of former college players (yours truly included) whose lives have undergone dramatic changes as a direct result of the opportunities afforded by football.

I, of course, wanted to support the book and accordingly placed a brief post on my Facebook page. Almost immediately, a number of negative responses were received along the lines of "Sorry, Bob, we are done with the NFL." I was startled, as nowhere in my post did I mention pro football.

As noted above, the book is not about pro football, it's about…football. Alas, I edited my original post to clarify that fact. My immediate takeaway: the NFL's public relations problems are far from over. See, for example, police unions in South Florida recently decided to boycott Miami Dolphins games in response to a number of Dolphins players kneeling prior to an exhibition game.

(And yes, I use the vintage term—"exhibition game"—to describe these rip-off games wherein NFL owners charge full price for what amounts to boring scrimmages—half-empty stadiums speak to this annual phenomenon.)

Now add to the mix Nike's regrettable decision to include Colin Kaepernick in its new ad campaign. My initial reaction upon hearing the news was one of anger and frustration.

Anger because there are so many other players who would fit the job description of groundbreaking, principled football players (Jim Brown, Pat Tillman). Now compare these names to a second-string quarterback barely hanging on in the NFL.

Frustration because the attempted narrative is continuously misapplied. All will remember a hyperdefensive NFL wrapping itself in patriotic themes (especially the flag) in the immediate aftermath of last season's kneeling protests.

It seemed every pregame ceremony would include a gigantic American flag covering the entire field. The NFL wanted its fans to know it just loves those who volunteer to go into harm's way in order to protect our freedoms. All of which is a wonderful notion, but not germane to Kaepernick's protest.

Recall Kaepernick's original comments. His protest was not about military action overseas, nor even the very legitimate issue of criminal justice reform. Rather, these actions and words were directed at the police, the men and women in blue who also protect us from the world's miscreants. Kaepernick's decision to wear "pig" socks to a San Francisco 49ers practice said it all. Funny how that incident is rarely recalled in today's media reporting.

Interested folks on both sides of the Kaepernick divide should take the next step—attempt to figure out if the substance of his complaint is valid. Two thoughts come to mind.

One concerns the fact that police can and do commit negligent acts; that there have been highly publicized cases wherein deadly force was used inappropriately against African American men.

In a couple of these cases, police have been wrongfully exonerated. It is important to note the foregoing does not include Michael Brown in Ferguson, Missouri, or Freddie Gray in Baltimore, Maryland. The evidence in both cases did not justify prosecution/conviction of the police officers involved, street legends to the contrary notwithstanding.

Still, a cautionary note to those of us who tend reflexively to support the police in these difficult cases: the damage inflicted on the public trust in lower income, predominately minority communities by a handful of such cases is immeasurable.

The second concerns Kaepernick's central thesis, that there exists an organized campaign of police brutality targeting minority communities, especially African American men. But the facts do not support the indictment.

In fact, the advent of de-escalation training techniques and additional mental health intervention teams have resulted in a decline in shootings of unarmed African American men. For those who care to delve deeper into the facts, check out the excellent statistical analysis compiled by the *Washington Post* over the past three years.

Upon further review (so to speak), this conclusion is not terribly surprising. Black and Hispanic officers are heavily represented in urban police departments. Some are majority-minority departments. It would indeed be startling if the facts reflected a concerted campaign of police violence by minority police officers against…minority communities.

Many of you have grown tired of Kaepernick, kneeling players, and the disingenuous actions of the NFL. Still, sometimes it's refreshing to revisit facts as opposed to popular narratives, either Right or Left.

I will leave it to you, the fans, to decide your preferred football days: A) Friday. B) Saturday. C) Sunday. At present, options A and B carry far less baggage.

The "Other Deplorables" the Media Can't Even Fathom

Western Journal
February 22, 2019

Pundits and pollsters are focused on a familiar demographic landscape. On the left, an emerging progressive coalition of millennials, minorities, and upper-income professionals has the media intelligentsia counting down the days until the president is either impeached, indicted, or loses re-election. On the right, the new shiny thing remains those lovable deplorables comfortably situated between the coasts.

I do not take issue with a portion of the analysis. The objective evidence reflects stark voting disparities between the generations, races, classes, and sexes.

Still, not every Trump voter is so easily identified—or dismissed. There is, in fact, a rather large subgroup of deplorables (both men and women) that receives little attention. I should know. I'm a dues-paying member of this group. I'm talking about professional deplorables; graduate degree–holding deplorables; business deplorables. Indeed, these are Trump supporters that many on the left are unable to fathom.

No books have been devoted to the emergence of this subgroup; no television specials seek to explain the pathology of their voting behavior. Why the cold media shoulder, you ask? Maybe this group is simply too inconvenient for the media to wrap its collective brain around. Indeed, if they ever observed a hybrid car bumper with an elite university logo on one end and a MAGA sticker on the other, they might have a conniption.

Further complications arise when one or more mandatory attributes are missing. For example, some uber-Trump supporters are highly educated women who voted for Trump notwithstanding his "colorful" private life. They simply liked the idea of keeping more of their hard-earned dollars. Others had grown weary of an increasingly PC culture. Some may have been incredulous that Trump seemed alone in wondering why trade deals were so consistently one-sided against the United States. Still others desired an end to the Obama-era's world apology tours. Interestingly, I have yet to find a woman who voted for Trump because a husband or boyfriend told her to do so. Many, in fact, got a chuckle out of Hillary Clinton's now-famous diagnosis of rampant misogynistic voting instructions.

Other counterintuitive attributes abound. Many of these deplorables do not hunt, fish, belong to the NRA, or watch WWF. Most could not pick Dwayne (The Rock) Johnson out of a crowd.

All of which prompts the question of why educated, upwardly mobile professionals could pull a lever for Trump. Don't they watch CNN?!

The answer is not especially complicated, but difficult for many elitists to comprehend. You see, these deplorables discern in Trump an unvarnished willingness to challenge harshly the cherished assumptions and otherwise unchallenged hierarchy of values of the Washington establishment—and they like it. They like it not in the sense of a desire to destroy the ways and means of official Washington, but as a way to redirect policy toward growth—opportunity—security—and American interests first.

For context, check out the following alleged faux pas committed by the president, supposed missteps condemned by the establishments of both parties—but well received by voters in flyover America.

> **Paris Accords**: Despite strong rhetorical support for its environmental agenda, a Democratic president and Congress could not muster sufficient votes to pass any item on the green lobby's

agenda. Trump exposed the bluff, quickly pulling America out of the oversold Paris Agreement. No "Yellow Vest" protests here.

Energy independence: A favorite rhetorical goal from establishment candidates of both parties. It sounds so promising on the stump. That is, until the Trump administration's all-in support for a shale revolution that has brought America, in fact, appreciably closer to this long-promised goal.

Border security: Both parties claim to support it. Fifteen to 20 million illegal aliens later, and they still support it. Then, along comes Trump with a line (wall) in the sand. Unlike Obama and his Syrian "line," this president appears to mean it.

Trade: Both parties claim to support "free but fair" trade, another popular campaign slogan, but meaningless without context. Alas, Trump has removed the U.S. from the Trans-Pacific Partnership (for now), renegotiated a modernized NAFTA, and is presently engaged in high-stakes negotiations over tariffs and intellectual property protections with a country (China) that has been an open and notoriously bad (trade) actor over many decades.

U.S. embassy move to Jerusalem: Possibly the most empty bipartisan promise offered by the two establishments. Presidents of both parties participated in this charade for decades. You recall the modus operandi. Make the easy campaign promise in order to generate Jewish votes up front. Then never follow up, in order to placate the permanent foreign policy establishment. Such was the real politic calculus until Trump showed up and finally pulled the trigger.

North Korea: We do not know if any real progress will be made with the hermit state. But we do know this: every U.S. president (and both parties) has wrung his hands and looked the other way as the Korean peninsula has grown more dangerous year after year...until Trump decided to play one-upmanship with Kim Jong Un. Reminder: you can't be a Trump summit-hater if you sat on your hands and did nothing for the last 70 years!

Title IX: Loss of due process rights in Title IX campus sexual assault hearings had even the left-leaning ABA expressing concern. Courts followed as dozens of wrongly accused students began to receive monetary damage awards. Trump's Department of Education appears serious about restoring a more level playing field in these difficult cases.

Merry Christmas: Sure to offend the easily offended...which is the point. The president reminds us that our pluralistic society does not require the suppression of religious expression—a point no longer being taught on our college campuses.

My point here is not to argue that every Trump disruptor move has been successful, and certainly the accompanying rhetoric can be inconsistent and coarse. It's just that so many have been unexpected, daring—sometimes even reckless—but always with an eye toward challenging Washington assumptions that (in many cases) have not inured to America's benefit over the years.

Radical, yes. Different, you betcha. Entertaining, always.

The Deplorables vs. the Progressives— Whose Version of America Will Win?

Western Journal
April 22, 2019

Barack Obama was a master at it—but in limited circumstances. Alas, it was the pre-Trump era, seemingly light years ago to activists on the uber-left. Today it is utilized on a more regular basis, whenever the latest progressive full court press against accepted social norms is on the receiving end of cultural pushback.

I refer, of course, to the "that's not us" mantra. You have become familiar with the context. Progressives advocate on behalf of the latest and greatest social justice cause: sanctuary cities—no border "walls"—voting rights for illegal aliens—elimination of ICE—"free" college tuition—"free" health care—reparations—"trans" anything—court packing—and whatever is the next frontier identified as requiring change of societal attitudes.

Yet when the committed opposition answers, the response is instantly seen as illegitimate and immediately transformed into indictments of "white privilege"—"toxic masculinity"—"white nationalism."

The resulting cultural battle lines could not be more transparent. All of the socially abhorrent beliefs of Trump's irredeemable deplorables on one side aligned against a new progressive program and value system on the other.

In this fight, the Trump folks and their Neanderthal attitudes are guaranteed to fall woefully short. After all, what they represent is certainly "not us." CNN just told me so!

The rhetoric is powerful. "Not us" is an emotional appeal to the great American traditions of tolerance, pluralism, freedom—the melting pot at its very best.

Now, some of you may be confused at this point because progressivism hardly celebrates America and its grand traditions these days. It more typically seeks to degrade the American experience as an exercise in greedy materialism/destructive nativism to the detriment of indigenous peoples and other minorities. Here, Columbus Day is condemned, not celebrated.

Today, "not us" is trotted out so frequently because it defines an entire opposition in one fell swoop. But a question arises: Is "not us" a rhetorical construct or a heartfelt belief? The answer, of course, depends on the individual. There are those cynics who seek to utilize the phrase to their political advantage, but it is the true believers who present a more long-term problem.

For this starry-eyed group, the world needs to be turned around: what is illegal should be legal, what is unconventional should be conventional, what is unconstitutional should be constitutional—whatever is at odds with traditional values must be acknowledged, honored, and accepted—while everything that fits into the "not us" paradigm must be demonized, refused, and extinguished.

This latter point is particularly true with respect to the president, where even disproven charges lodged against Donald Trump are ignored in order for new charges to be posited—and quickly transmitted around the swamp.

In real life, this approach means freedom of speech must be curtailed in order to achieve an offense-less dialogue, respect for religious freedom must be made secondary to the emerging sexual mores of the moment; traditional notions of citizenship and national sovereignty must surrender to borderless nation-states, and self-identified victims (as a function of race, sex, ethnicity, sexual orientation, and identity) must be awarded special status—even reparations in some cases.

Now, this is clearly not the America those of us of a certain age were encouraged to celebrate. Indeed, we've been taught to cherish (even love) our values despite the fact our forbearers were imperfect human beings.

Note that this was never a major obstacle for most of our history. Americans could distinguish between love of country on the one hand and acknowledgment of our sins (slavery, discrimination) on the other, even sins by principals, the Founding Fathers. Still, the new progressive theology rejects acknowledgment of the latter.

Rather, it sees the mistakes of our Founders as rendering the American experience illegitimate—as nothing more than a falsely marketed, delusory failure—with a multitude of victims to boot.

Per this revisionist school of thought, it took the better part of 240 years for our citizens to understand that our America—Ronald Reagan's shining city on a hill—is but a cruel hoax. Accordingly, the glorification of wealth, capitalism, upward mobility, free speech, dissent, privacy, assimilation, national sovereignty, American exceptionalism, and Western civilization itself must be rejected as "not us." Who would have thunk?

Fortunately, this revisionist travesty will not be an easy sell between the coasts. The social contract between our country and its citizens is not so easily torn asunder, the maladies of victimhood and identity politics notwithstanding. Be thankful for small favors.

We Can't Back Down in the Fight for Voter Integrity

Western Journal
August 23, 2019

The State of Maryland has issued new requirements for some Marylanders with older drivers' licenses to supply additional personal identification in order to avoid revocation—former governors not exempted!

The additional requirements are all about submitting the proper paperwork to the DMV in order to comply with the federal "Real ID Act." In the real world, it means that one will be able to access federal buildings and board commercial aircraft.

Little controversy surrounds the new requirement. It's all common sense. Why would a free society **not** have stringent requirements in order to secure a reliable ID card? After all, in today's society, it's nearly impossible to do anything (or go anywhere) without one.

I thought about the new identification requirements while reading about the burgeoning popularity of "ballot harvesting"—the relatively new practice of collecting and submitting absentee or mail-in ballots by volunteers (union workers, campaign workers, etc.).

Yes, you read that right. It is now permissible in 19 states to "harvest" votes in this manner. Those (like me) who have expressed strong views on ballot security over the years are more than mildly perturbed. And it almost goes without saying that those of us who prefer to see only living, legal citizens on the voter rolls, and who readily provide proof of our identity at the polls, are (you guessed it) labeled as "racists" by progressives and their media allies.

The by-now-familiar indictment alleges that requiring valid proof of identity at the ballot box discriminates against minority voters, who allegedly have less access to the ways and means of securing state-issued identity cards. And this during an era wherein even states with stringent federal ID requirements have gone the extra mile to accommodate lesser-served populations in their quest for a photo ID.

Nevertheless, the accusation lives because it fits the popular leftist narrative: Republicans will attempt to suppress the African American vote at every opportunity and at any cost.

GOP initiatives aimed at forcing local election officials to purge dead or otherwise ineligible voters from the voter rolls are likewise labeled unfair, discriminatory, and racist. (Which brings up the old line that Republicans want scrubbed voter rolls because the deceased always vote a straight-line Democratic ticket.) Still, a number of recent court decisions have forced local election officials to clean up their act—and their rolls.

Against this backdrop of distrust and unsupported innuendo comes the harvesting initiative. To be fair, the GOP does not have completely clean hands here: a North Carolina GOP operative was accused of illegal harvesting in the 2016 general election and 2018 Republican congressional primary in District 9. Seems North Carolina–style harvesting is limited to family members or legal guardians.

Still, the questionable practice really took off this past November when California Democrats pulled off seven Orange County, California (traditionally a GOP stronghold) House seats in the 2018 midterms.

You see, California's more liberal harvesting statute (excuse the redundancy) allows anyone to pick up and deliver absentee ballots from the field to the poll. Proponents insist it is an appropriate practice for people who have mobility issues or lack access to post offices; opponents see it more as an invitation to fraud.

And, if you dare oppose this preferred remedy to the problem of poor voter turnout, then you are nothing more than a dirty denier of our most cherished right—and, of course, a racist to boot.

The only way common sense loses this debate is to back down—to let the usual race-conscious suspects capture the moral high ground and stay there.

I, for one, prefer to win on this one. Voting integrity is fundamental to free and fair elections. Just plain ole folks showing up with bundles of votes in tow does not scratch my itch. In fact, it makes me downright suspicious. The bottom line: voters who care about election integrity must not be intimidated, lest a batch of questionable ballots arrives to cloud yet another election day.

By the way, if you think the national Democratic Party does not see this initiative as an absolute priority, think again. The number attached to a congressional bill can mean something. House Bill 1 of the new Congress seeks to federalize election law oversight and require every state to implement a vote by mail system. Each will aid in the adoption of vote harvesting. Informed is forewarned.

Now, get to work spreading the word about this latest affront to our mainstream values...

Don't Forget White-Collar Trump Voters

Western Journal
February 11, 2020

Many of you have watched the tape of CNN anchor Don Lemon's laughing fit while political strategist Rick Wilson assured his audience that "Donald Trump couldn't find Ukraine on a map if you had the letter "U" and a picture of an actual physical crane next to it."

Lemon's chuckling spell continued as commentator Wajahat Ali added with baiting sarcasm, "You elitists with your geography and your maps and your spelling."

The segment produced sharp rebukes from the right, but such is only the latest and most transparent chapter of the mainstream media's relentless demonization of heartland voters.

The reader will recall a number of the most recent egregious putdowns.

There was President Barack Obama's (intended to be off-the-record) indictment of small-town America ("They get bitter, they cling to guns or religion or antipathy toward people who aren't like them").

Then, who could forget FBI Agent Peter Strzok's snarky text to his girlfriend Lisa Page ("I could SMELL the Trump support [in a southern Virginia Walmart]")?

And then, of course, there was candidate Hillary Clinton's now-infamous denunciation of Trump voters ("You could put half of Trump's supporters into what I call the basket of deplorables...they are irredeemable").

That one was a "two-fer": it provided a nascent political movement with a new title and additional energy.

On the upside, these consistently condescending descriptions leave no doubt about how coastal elites view the great unwashed. The dirty secret is out: the progressive Left relentlessly belittles the values, morals, viewing habits, and politics of flyover America because its inhabitants vote "wrong"—and have done so for decades. After all, these are the same people who supported Barry Goldwater, Ronald Reagan, and both Bushes—all to the chagrin of the "really smart" people on each coast. But Donald Trump was the last straw. This guy had once been one of them. He had happily donated to Democratic candidates and causes. Yet there he was espousing conservative views and calling out the establishments of both parties, going so far as to ignore and sometimes belittle career bureaucrats who were (of course) far smarter than he.

But maybe these lefty pundits should not have been so surprised. Was this not the same Mr. Trump who body-slammed, beat, and shaved Vince McMahon at WrestleMania 23 in 2007?

Spoiler alert: this is not yet another piece on why progressives *so* dislike the socially conservative values of blue-collar, WWE-loving America. No, this column concerns the *other* half of Hillary Clinton's infamous critique—those who (according to her) may not be actual racists or nativists or even deplorable, yet somehow remain "lost."

Yes, herein are a few words for those predominately white-collar voters who support border control, free speech on campus, the Second Amendment, charter schools, religious freedom, market capitalism, originalist judges, energy independence, and the electoral college. To boot:

this group really hates identity politics, so many of them beat the odds to achieve (and live) the American dream.

These folks may indeed possess healthy 401(k)s, own their own businesses, maybe even hold a Ph.D.—but they've never been awarded a moniker or even given much attention.

Check it out. In the election of 2016, Mr. Trump famously carried 52 percent (to Clinton's 44 percent) of those without college degrees. Two-thirds (67 percent) of non-college whites supported Trump to just 28 percent for Clinton. Hence the Left's white-hot demonization of those deplorables.

By contrast, those with college degrees supported Mrs. Clinton by nine points, 52 percent to 43 percent, and those with graduate degrees went for the former first lady by a whopping 59 percent to 21 percent margin.

OK, kind of what you expect these days. But what about those college- and advanced-degree-holding folks who supported Mr. Trump? We're talking about millions of Americans here—some of whom attended the same elite colleges and universities that have given rise to modern progressivism and graduate so many of today's progressive activists.

And so let this be a clarion call for at least some analysis of this most inconvenient subset of voters. Let someone take the time to dissect those who tune in to PBS rather than Fox, do not hunt or fish or even own a gun, prefer sushi to Chick-fil-A, or have no trouble finding Ukraine on a map—but still voted for Donald J. Trump.

A timely addendum: I wrote the foregoing prior to the Democratic Party's app/vote-counting meltdown at the Iowa caucuses. Of course, conservative commentators are having a field day, reminding voters of past Democratic technology fiascos, most especially Obamacare's widely panned website debut.

Here, I was reminded of Bill Buckley's famous observation that he "would rather be governed by the first 2,000 people in the telephone directory than by the Harvard University faculty."

Bet there are a whole lot of Iowans who now agree.

In any event, the GOP's preferred takeaway from Iowa—that the smartest, most erudite, most degree-awarded people in the room may not always have the best ideas in the room—could not be a more perfect narrative for the Trump era.

Average Americans May Not Wear MAGA Hats, but It's Clear How They'll Vote

Western Journal
September 4, 2020

On paper, it's not a fair fight.

The Biden-Harris ticket enjoys support from the nation's leading newspapers (the *Washington Post*, the *New York Times*, the *Los Angeles Times*), television networks (ABC, CBS, NBC), cable networks (minus Fox for the most part), big business (Wall Street, big tech, social media, Silicon Valley), Hollywood, the arts, the legal profession (ABA), the academy, professional sports leagues, billionaire socialists, social justice warriors, and the ever-present RINOs and NeverTrumpers.

Together, this may be the most formidable political coalition ever assembled. Within its control is just about every means of communication available to the American voter—with unlimited resources to boot.

And they are not bashful about shameless selective speech shutdowns in order to fulfill their one and only goal: removing President Donald J. Trump from office.

Aligned against this juggernaut are large swaths of flyover America: talk radio fans and Fox viewers, farmers and churchgoers, police and law enforcement, traditional families and homeschoolers.

Alas, much of the heartland feels especially aggrieved. Its people have been forced on the defensive.

One's freedom to wear a MAGA hat in a public place or place a Trump bumper sticker on their vehicle is encroached upon. Indeed, 77 percent of Republicans (according to a recent CATO poll) feel uncomfortable expressing their opinions in the public arena.

They see the angry mobs on the nightly news. They fear for their property and personal safety. They see the lengths to which self-appointed arbiters of conformity are willing to go in order to end the Trump experiment in disruption and American nationalism.

For context, check out Sen. Rand Paul's shockingly life-threatening exit from the White House last Thursday night.

Such chaos is antithetical to all that is good and great and sacred about America.

The proposed revolutionary reimagining of America's most basic values is not a transformation they will support or accept. And so a large contingent of red voters in the heartland are seething.

They hate the rioting and looting and weak-kneed responses from so many politicians. They have tuned out the NBA and will ratchet back their interest in the kneeling NFL. They resent celebrities preaching and dictating to them during 60-second commercials sponsored by suddenly woke big businesses.

Perhaps the ultimate insult has been to watch some commentators preach the importance of social distancing and mask-wearing and school closures for the average family—but bless the lack of these same protections at "mostly peaceful protests" that have destroyed so many of our major Democrat-controlled cities.

It is called hypocrisy—and Joe and Jane Average Citizen have had their fill of it.

Last week I appeared on a Sinclair Broadcasting panel in which a Democratic panelist sought to minimize Sen. Tim Scott's widely acclaimed "cotton to Congress" speech at the Republican National Convention.

She did so by utilizing the term "outlier"—as though there are not millions of successful African Americans in all fields, as though there is not a large black working and middle class in our country, as though there are not growing numbers of African American millionaires from coast to coast.

Of course, such a dismissal is much more than inaccurate; it is insulting to African Americans who refuse to indulge victimhood and dependency, to those who have overcome life's obstacles and now enjoy the American dream.

But it's all the progressives can bring to the table. There are only two ways they treat black people: It's either condescension or you do not exist. Per Joe Biden, "If you have a problem figuring out whether you're for me or Trump, then you ain't black." Come on, man!

This is the stuff that progressives peddle to the young and impressionable.

It is also the kind of thinking that drives conservatives to distraction.

It will assuredly drive millions of Trump voters to the polls. They may not be wearing their red MAGA hats or holding signs, but they will show up to vote. America still has a secret ballot, right?

CHAPTER 6

THE TRUMP DOCTRINE: SPEAK LOUDLY—CARRY A BIG STICK—AND SKIP THE EXPECTED HYPOCRISIES

Per one of his most repeated campaign promises, the president withdrew the U.S. from a deeply flawed Iranian nuclear accord on May 8, 2018. A sanctions regime of "maximum pressure" followed. As Iran's economy tanked and Iranian GDP growth turned negative, the mullahs in Tehran acted out with a series of provocative acts intended to convince Western interests to back off.

A president who had promised no more endless Mideast wars held his powder when the Iranians shot down an unmanned U.S. drone, attacked oil tankers in the Gulf, and sabotaged Saudi oil fields. But a line in the sand was drawn after the U.S. embassy compound in Baghdad was attacked by an Iranian-backed militiaman mob: there would be tangible consequences should an American be killed. When a subsequent militia rocket attack in northern Iraq killed an American contractor, the president acted. To wit: Iranian General Qasem Soleimani, the second most powerful man in Iran and responsible for thousands of American and coalition deaths throughout the years, was killed in a U.S. drone strike outside of Baghdad Airport. Republicans applauded the death of one of the world's most notorious terrorists; Democrats were generally critical of an "undisciplined" president's unilateral action, but a few (including President Obama's Department of Homeland Security Secretary Jeh Johnson) opined that Soleimani was a legitimate military target and that the president possessed the requisite legal authority to take him out. As expected, the regime responded with a (limited) missile attack against two Iraqi military bases housing American troops. The U.S. barracks were not targeted, and no American deaths were sustained. Seems the Ayatollah Khomeini was more interested in a short-term propaganda victory than further escalation against a president who had just sent six nuclear capable B-52s and 3500 paratroopers of the 82nd Airborne to the rogue regime's neighborhood.

But even this short-term Iranian "win" was short-lived as it soon became clear that a commercial plane crash on the night of the Iranian missile attack was caused by an Iranian missile. Eighty-two Iranians and sixty-two Canadians were on the doomed flight.

Tehran initially denied responsibility for the disaster but soon came clean in the face of overwhelming evidence and worldwide condemnation. An Iranian street unhappy over an increasingly dire domestic economy was reignited as angry public protests broke out around the country—a welcome development for a Trump administration intent on regime change in the Middle East *without firing a shot.*

One rather silly take bought into by a number of the Democratic presidential candidates was an alleged Trump-inspired "wag the dog" narrative whereby a suddenly tense engagement with Iran was intended to redirect attention from the president's impeachment. The problem with the theory was that impeachment was *helping* the president per numerous public opinion polls taken over the 2019 Christmas/New Year's break. Indeed, by the end of the Senate's three-week trial, Trump approval numbers had risen 10 points.

Another striking and much under-analyzed aspect of the president's modus operandi is an "unwillingness to indulge expected hypocrisies." Note the phrase is not mine (I first read it in the *Wall Street Journal*) but thought it spot on in differentiating Mr. Trump from other politicians, let alone presidents. Five prominent examples (among many) stand out.

- On October 2, 2018, Jamal Khashoggi, a U.S.-based *Washington Post* journalist often critical of the Saudi government, walked into the Saudi consulate in Istanbul, Turkey. He never walked out. Saudi officials would later blame Khashoggi's murder on a "rogue operation" carried out by agents allegedly sent to return Khashoggi to the Kingdom unharmed. Most of the rest of the world (including Republican and Democrat congressional leaders) saw the Saudi government as compliant in the gruesome murder and accordingly condemned the Saudi leadership, especially Saudi Crown Prince Mohammad bin Salman. Yet, despite intense criticism from both sides of the aisle, Mr. Trump repeatedly refused to call out the crown prince, instead raising questions about the thoroughness of the investigation **and** taking the opportunity to remind the West that the Saudis were essential actors in the American-led coalition (with other friendly Sunni states and Israel) to contain Iran. Here, whether right or wrong, the president blew by the expected hypocrisies in order to get to his bottom line: even when your allies do horrific things—and the world expects you to engage the appropriate condemnations—it is best to keep the long-term strategic interests of your country in mind, even at the price of appearing insensitive.
- Example two concerns the president's reaction to the June 20, 2019, Iranian downing of an unarmed drone operating over international waters. Administration hawks were reportedly happy to use the incident as a starting point for military action against

the terror-friendly ayatollahs in Iran. The president accordingly ordered a retaliatory strike—but backed down minutes prior to launch when informed the action would likely cause up to 150 deaths. Mr. Trump's very public explanation lacked the usual diplomatic niceties, thereby failing to indulge the expected hypocrisies by (again) getting to the very real bottom line: he did not believe the unprovoked loss of a piece of military hardware could justify so many Iranian deaths. Plain and simple language was employed to explain his decision, the usual Washington double-speak be damned.

- A third instance occurred when George Stephanopoulos (in a nationally televised Oval Office interview) asked the president what he would do if a foreign source contacted him with disparaging information on an opponent. In response, despite three years' worth of speculation/investigation over Russia's alleged involvement in just such a scenario…Mr. Trump failed to issue the standard (and politically safe) reply to the effect that he would immediately contact the FBI in such a circumstance. Instead, the man who was daily vilified by the left half of the country said he would "listen" to what the source had to say…. After all, "there isn't anything wrong with listening." Moments later the president did (sort of) assure Americans that if "I thought there was something wrong, I'd go maybe to the FBI." The ensuing media firestorm had little impact on Trump supporters, detractors, or national opinion polls. Still, the blunt response was remarkable for its…bluntness.

- A fourth example presented itself in the wake of critical comments lodged against the president by (the late) Baltimore Congressman Elijah Cummings. The thirteen-term congressman had become a leading Trump critic (and fan of impeachment) from his perch atop the powerful House Committee on Oversight and Reform. In a series of aggressive tweets and interviews the president did not hold back in criticizing the condition of Cummings' inner-city district, decrying Baltimore as rat-infested and crime-ridden while also citing a similar 2015 indictment of the city lodged by Democratic Socialist Senator Bernie Sanders. Of course, the usual suspects (including Al Sharpton) dismissed the tirade as a racist rant against a black man representing a black city—which missed the point entirely. You see, this president lashes out at anyone (regardless of race, creed, or color) when attacked, especially when the "r" word is employed against him. Here again, Mr. Trump did not entertain the expected hypocrisies of holding his tongue and simply taking it (à la George Bushes 41 and 43 and Mitt Romney) when the Left turns to the always reliable, always horrific, and (today) always overutilized moniker of "racist."

- Yet a fifth instance was the way Mr. Trump responded to his election defeat—a loss that will always be clouded in the minds of many due to (alleged) voting irregularities in half a dozen swing states. But even affirmation of a Biden win by the Electoral College did not result in a Trump concession. Just the opposite in fact. There would be no Richard Nixon circa 1960 redux from the man who loathed losing. Donald J. Trump would not go quietly into the night—the way defeated presidential candidates are expected to proceed—even when losses in dozens of court challenges began to pile up in late December 2020.

It was easy for the haters and NeverTrumpers to write off such incidents as a function of an inarticulate, inexperienced president incapable of following the expected diplomatic language—or process. But this easily made charge is mistaken. Any balanced analysis of this president's methodology **must** include his oft-expressed preference for a better (future) deal—even where the final deal follows edgy, often harsh assessments of the opposition. For better or worse, this is the way Mr. Trump interacts with the world. Alas, such a unique second-level approach does not impress those dedicated to hating the man and his methods; those who would never engage the notion that there could be productive thoughts and goals behind the president's idiosyncratic ways.

What Would Jack Kemp Make of Trump?

Washington Examiner
February 1, 2018

I met Jack Kemp when the other three Republicans at Princeton and I visited Capitol Hill during the spring of my junior year. Kemp was a hot ticket among a strong group of young GOP rising stars at the time. Nevertheless, he was quite gracious with his time and advice on behalf of four college kids who did not even live in his district.

Twenty-four years later, former Housing and Urban Development Secretary Jack Kemp was the featured speaker at my inauguration as governor of Maryland. He was, and remains, an inspiration to me and so many others who came to political maturity during the 1980s.

I met Donald Trump and his family on the eve of the Miss USA pageant in Baltimore in 2006. This was the second such time the pageant was presented in Baltimore—a big deal for a city desperately looking to improve its national image. The dinner began a friendship that culminated in my joining his campaign after the old House-Budget-Chairman-turned-Gov. John Kasich of Ohio withdrew from the GOP primary race in May 2016, leaving Trump as the presumptive GOP nominee.

And so I'm left to imagine what the two GOP heavyweights of startlingly different backgrounds and styles would say to one another. Perhaps the conversation would unfold as follows:

> **Trump**: Jack, did you catch my first State of the Union Speech? It presented a strong and inclusive message. I give myself an A+ for that one.

> **Kemp**: You were strong and presidential. Such appearances strengthen your approval with independents and soft Republicans—and does nothing to diminish the enthusiasm of your base. Maintaining this tone will help lower the temperature during what promises to be a hot midterm cycle.

Trump: Nobody could preach the gospel of growth, freedom, and opportunity like you. So…you gotta like my tax bill, right?

Kemp: I do. Your initial deregulatory moves generated credibility and momentum throughout the employer community. The tax bill will spur the economy and markets to historic heights. Lowering the corporate rate, bracket relief for the middle class, immediate expensing for business, and repatriation are all big winners for growth. I could have done without the child tax credits, but understand social conservatives wanted a bite at the apple, too.

Trump: It is a beautiful bill and people are starting to appreciate it!

Kemp: But not because of you. During the tax debate, two-thirds of the country opposed a bill that would put more money in their pockets. You need to continue to talk tax reform every day, just like I did when pushing my popular tax cuts. Ironically, many of the CEOs who so oppose you helped bail you out. Their well-publicized announcements about employee bonuses and business expansion means more jobs and economic growth. And, you got a twofer. Every new announcement makes the progressives look economically incoherent, and small. Armageddon? More like Dow 30,000!

Trump: What about my Reaganesque media strategy? He successfully went around the mainstream media in order to talk with middle America. My Twitter account is simply an updated model of how to communicate with my base in flyover country.

Kemp: Yes…and no. I understand the need to talk to your base, but why all the gratuitous quarrels? A war of words…with Joe Scarborough? Coming out on top of that one is like winning the Hall of Fame Game. Nobody remembers; nobody cares. Churchill reminds us that "progress is difficult when you stop to throw stones at every dog that barks." In other words, choose your battles. Don't get lost in the weeds. Prioritize your goals. I was known as a talker—but everybody knew my central message.

Trump: But it's my nature to fight. My father instilled a competitiveness that burns brightly to this day. It defines me. My base loves it. Why can't I just be myself? It's worked so far, you know.

Kemp: I understand it is your nature to always respond to criticisms large and small with overwhelming force, sort of like Schwarzkopf in Iraq. But the fight is not only about you.

Trump: What do you mean? I'm the most powerful person in the world.

Kemp: You are indeed. But that title carries responsibilities—to your country and to your party. You didn't play team sports (besides a stint as a high school first baseman) so it's a bit more difficult to grasp. You must come to understand how much is riding on your ability to sustain a Republican majority. A new generation of conservative judges only gets appointed if Mitch McConnell is Senate Majority Leader. Additional opportunities at Obamacare reform only exist if Paul Ryan is House Speaker. Your legislative programs go nowhere if the "resistance" controls even one chamber. One more disquieting thought here as you contemplate future unvetted tweets: losing the House means all of your remaining two years will be taken up with defending against weekly impeachment votes. It will not be pretty—for anyone.

Trump: What about race? It was a brilliant campaign move to go to the inner cities and ask how much worse it could all get. And it worked. African Americans did not turn out for Hillary Clinton in Michigan, Pennsylvania, and Wisconsin. Did I tell you that black unemployment is at its lowest point in decades?

Kemp: First of all—don't tell me, tell the country. Tell black churches. Convene a "Save the Cities" forum and tell the attendees. A rising tide does indeed lift all boats. But that's the easy part. For some reason, you tend to make the easy stuff difficult. You know enough about David Duke to condemn his views. You know enough about the white supremacist nut jobs in Charlottesville to eliminate any thoughts of equivocation. Caveats offered in the immediate aftermath of such incidents send the wrong message—and will be exploited by the Left. There are plenty of opportunities to condemn Antifa and lefty nut jobs some other day. Why give your enemies such a gift? Such missed "hanging curveballs" do you far more harm than good.

Trump: You have to be happy with my appointment of Ben Carson for your old job at HUD. He is the embodiment of the self-made man—from the mean streets of Detroit to world-famous brain surgeon. And still the Left hates him. What's the deal?

Kemp: The Left hates him precisely because he is self-made. He has always rejected the victim card. He is also black, a conservative Republican, a man of deep faith, and person of principle unafraid of racial taunts. He is a tangible symbol of hope, and disruptive to the race hustlers of this world. He needs a higher profile in your administration. Use him.

Author's parting observation: a healthy dose of Jack Kemp will go a long way to making politics great again.

Thanks for Taking a Stand for Free Speech on Campus, Mr. President

Western Journal
April 2, 2019

News headline: "President Trump Signs Executive Order to Protect Campus Free Speech."

It is easy to minimize the importance of this recently issued order. I hope you will not indulge the inclination. This long overdue instruction may finally get the academy to recognize that henceforth there will be real costs associated with superficial, politically correct limitations on thought—and speech—on campus.

How did we get to this point? Why would a president lend such gravity to an issue most of us take for granted? A brief retrospective on campus speech provides context.

America's colleges and universities were rather sedate places, albeit places of de facto limited enrollment of African American, Jewish, Catholic, and female students in the aftermath of World War II. Most were experiencing a period of sustained growth as millions of returning GIs resumed their educations.

But the 1960s brought the age of innocence within the classroom to an abrupt halt. The assassinations of JFK, Medgar Evers, Bobby Kennedy, and Martin Luther King (in addition to the Kent State shootings) set the streets—and many campuses—ablaze. These era-defining events provided fuel for the civil rights movement, the anti-war movement, and the women's movement. Suddenly, our institutions of higher learning became ground zero for civil unrest—and sometimes violent demonstrations. Mass protests became the order of the day. A free speech movement arose. The University of California at Berkley became center stage for free speech activism.

America's media praised the newfound social awareness. After all, was not college a microcosm of our society? And what better venue for incubating societal change?

Now fast-forward to the second decade of the new millennium. The free speech movement has become so…1960s. Today, the campus environment is far more about feelings; about some (invented) right-to-be-free from people and/or events and/or ideas that make one uncomfortable. Here, one's right to speak freely—engage in unpopular opinion—advocate minority viewpoints—is circumscribed by a new thought police intent on allowing only "approved speech"—no offense meant or taken!

This new platform comes equipped with brand-new speed bumps: speech codes, trigger warnings, micro-aggressions—and an enthusiastic array of progressive professors and administrators committed to transforming a culture, one micro-aggression at a time. Their body of work—fragile children ill-prepared for the rough and tumble of real-world confrontation—is the predictable result. Many are no doubt experiencing serious anxiety at the realization there are no safe spaces in the private sector.

Not surprising, the advent of thought police on campus has not coincided with a diminishment of enthusiasm for the college degree. In fact, the race for the holy grail has only accelerated as competitive colleges became even more competitive—and expensive. Many parents do not necessarily like the new totalitarianism on campus, but they take it. No parent wishes to put their child at a disadvantage when it comes to admissions.

In retrospect, it is clear how the Left has been able to have its cake and eat it too; how so many of our elite colleges became ever-more competitive at the same time the administrators and faculty who ran them became ever-more hostile to the foundational values that had previously defined the college experience.

Further headshaking is appropriate when college fundraising structures are added to the equation. Talk about chutzpah: the guilt-edged operation known as "annual giving" has morphed into high art, as endowments climb into the (many) billions at our elite universities but always against a familiar chorus of "never enough." At the same time, more and more students are indoctrinated into the downside of free thought and expression, not to mention the particular evils of race privilege, market capitalism, American exceptionalism, and whatever other allegedly racist/nativist constructs the speech code purveyors can think of.

It speaks to the continued aura of the college degree (especially the prestigious degree) that so many parents—the funders who after all pay the tab—choose to ignore the damage being inflicted before their very eyes.

All of which brings us back to the president's explosive executive order. How ironic that a Republican president now borrows a page from the progressive playbook by using economic leverage (loss of federal funds) to attain what is identified as a "conservative" result—but in reality is one only of fairness and balance.

The rats are presently scurrying through their response strategies. Howls of anguish are raised. Some claim with a straight face that language codes are not governors of free speech, while others will look to the courts for relief. The most doctrinaire miscreants are unable to fathom how higher education can survive. It will be interesting to see how it all plays out, but I for one am grateful that the president chose this time to take a stand.

If you think this is not a front-burner issue, that freedom of speech and association on campus are not at a tipping point, recall recent polls that reflect a majority of our young people have a positive view of socialism. Enough said.

Trump Is Making High-Stakes Foreign Policy Plays Like No President Before Him

Western Journal
May 30, 2019

Trump the disruptor. Trump the maverick. Trump the establishment protagonist. All three descriptions fit our 45th president.

No modern president has challenged Washington's bipartisan foreign policy establishment in a more confrontational style. For his efforts, no president has been more ostracized by the foreign policy elite.

Some will argue that the president missed an early opportunity to recruit some members of the elite; that a percentage of the establishment was willing to give the novice politician the benefit of the doubt—and their expertise—country over party, you know.

That observation may indeed be correct; we may never know. But it is of little consequence now. After numerous swings and misses, it appears the president has found a team of senior advisors (Pompeo, Bolton, Lighthizer, Navarro) that reflect his preference for high-stakes threats, high-stakes engagement, and sometimes both. Note that all have adopted the president's "hit and hug" modus operandi on the world stage. Its effectiveness will play out on four extraordinarily important policy fronts over the next 18 months.

China

Recall the president's early move to question "One China" policy but simultaneously engage Chinese President Xi Jinping over North Korea and trade. Principal to principal engagement did follow as an early visit by Xi to Mar-a-Lago met with generally positive reviews. But to what effect remains unclear. Negotiations with Kim Jong Un are presently at a standstill while world markets remained transfixed with more than a dash of pessimism over the status of American-Chinese trade negotiations. The success or failure of the latter will constitute a major part of the president's foreign policy legacy—and the real test of hit and hug.

Talk about breaking the mold. No American president had dared engage the Chinese on ever-widening trade imbalances and the wholesale theft of intellectual property in such an aggressive way. Think about it: what establishment politician would risk the short-term economic health of his political base (midwestern farmers) in an effort to get the Chinese to curb subsidization of their inefficient state industries and stop the blatant theft of Western IP?

The Bottom Line:

Failure here carries a serious downside. Trump needs at least a partial deal that will move the (trade) ball forward in tangible ways.

Iran

Admittedly far more a hit than a hug, the president not only stopped enabling the world's most notorious sponsor of terror (recall the load of cash Barack Obama delivered by plane to the ayatollahs in consideration of his flawed nuclear deal), but he doubled down on a sanctions regime that is wreaking havoc on the Iranian economy.

As usual, our European allies have been less than pleased with the strong-arm tactics. This is not the way the game is supposed to be played—which is the president's point. That game allowed the Chinese to leverage their way into first world economic power status (see above), while the West stood passively by as Iran expanded its Middle Eastern terror empire into Lebanon, Syria, and Yemen. Alas, the Trump administration's crippling sanctions are hitting hard enough to rekindle domestic unrest.

The Bottom Line:

A declining economy that starves the regime of dollars needed to fund its terror activities throughout the Middle East would be a big win. So, too, would a restive Iranian street demanding regime change. There is reason to be optimistic here.

North Korea

Herein is the original field test for hit ("My button is bigger than yours"…"Little Rocket Man") and hug ([Kim Jong-Un] is "very open" and "a very honorable" negotiator). A unique negotiating approach to say the very least. How else to describe an American president praising a ruthless, despotic dictator who has refined the art of systemic starvation? But Trump's response to the resulting bipartisan criticism was (is) on target. To wit: nothing the bipartisan foreign policy establishment has attempted over the past half-century has worked.

Why not try something new?

The Bottom Line:

Early positive movement from Summit #1 was lost when the president prematurely left Summit #2. No opponent has tested Trump's salesmanship skills more than Kim Jong Un. It would be helpful (but probably not a necessity) if the president could point to tangible progress prior to 2020. Otherwise, a North Korean status quo provides little to brag about.

Venezuela

It looks like a Cold War redux. The Russians and Cubans support a corrupt socialist dictator while America and the West cast their lot with the Democratic opposition. But this is different. Venezuela is in the Western hemisphere. The opposition (Juan Guaidó) has been democratically elected but denied office. The Venezuelan economy is in freefall. Neighboring states are increasingly nervous as they receive thousands of starving refugees. And plenty of Florida-based democratic sympathizers are asking for the U.S. to "do the right thing."

To date, the right thing has been harsh sanctions that have further weakened the brutal Nicolás Maduro while placing additional strain on his socialist sponsors in Havana.

The Bottom Line:
A home (hemispheric) game means higher stakes for a Trump administration doing all it can (short of military intervention) for the good guys. A Maduro departure would be a huge win for democracy—and Trump-style diplomacy—over militarism. Again, reason to be optimistic. Enough said.

Six Takeaways from the Trump Presidency after Four Years

Western Journal
April 23, 2020

The start of phase one of our national recovery brings attention back to the presidential campaign.

As we gear up for what will be a brutal contest, now may be the appropriate time to digest the significant ways Donald J. Trump has changed our political and presidential landscape—and why our politics will never be the same.

In other words, how the old rules have changed:

1. *Old Rule: Be Guarded in Your Public Pronouncements*

This may be the most dramatic (and intriguing) aspect of this president and his rhetorical style.

Granted, Mr. Trump has at times shown a willingness to play it conventional—directly off the teleprompter—especially when on foreign soil or addressing the issue of potential military engagements or the scientific components of coronavirus news.

But his daily virus-related media availabilities speak far more to the unvarnished Trump the American people have come to either love, or hate: optimistic (sometimes prematurely so), cheerleading and transparent—especially when angry or frustrated.

For context, recall last week's "LIBERATE VIRGINIA," "LIBERATE MICHIGAN" tweets aimed squarely at Democratic governors exhibiting draconian shutdown orders, or his admission that the U.S. could win in Afghanistan if only he were willing to "kill ten million people," or his harsh criticism of the GOP Senate for an Obamacare replacement bill that could "hurt people," or his rejection of a retaliatory missile attack against the Iranians because it would cause "needless casualties," or his recent criticism of General Motors' alleged change of heart on respirator production or even his early campaign threats to Boeing and Lockheed regarding unreasonable price tags on the new Air Force One and F-35 fighter.

I could go on, but the pattern is clear. The praise, criticism, and opinions are always upfront, always personal, always in the moment. What you see is what you get.

2. *Old Rule: Respect the Media*

Presidential biographies typically speak to the goal of winning over the fourth estate.

If this item were ever on Mr. Trump's agenda, it was jettisoned early on as it became clear that the populist celebrity was striking a dangerous chord in deplorables land.

Some would say the president's relentless campaign to degrade, bypass, or even ignore the press (even friendly media when not so approving) is somewhat Reaganesque. This notion harkens back to the mainstream media's frustration with the Great Communicator's "aw shucks" habit of going around them and directly to the American people.

But upon further review, the analogy fails. Reagan's warm, friendly demeanor with the media is wholly distinguished from Mr. Trump's in-your-face, call-'em-out approach.

Further, the advent of social media has provided this president with something President Reagan never had—a direct means of eliminating the (often hostile) intermediary press: his Twitter account.

3. *Old Rule: Respect Your Opponent*

What was once viewed as comical by Trump supporters and undignified (at best) by Trump detractors is now a familiar Trump campaign tactic.

Not to say that all Trump supporters appreciate the derogatory labels ("Sleepy Joe," "Pocahontas," "Mini Mike"), but one takeaway is impossible to rebut: there has been no GOP or Democratic party challenger who has hit upon an effective response to this favored Trump line of attack.

"Mini Mike" Bloomberg's attempt to slap back—dismissing the president as a "clown" and the object of behind-the-back scorn by fellow New Yorkers—was about as effective as the former New York mayor's presidential campaign.

4. *Old Rule: Engage in Diplomatic Hypocrisy*

I am not the first to make this observation, but I wish that I had been. It concerns the president's propensity to not only be unguarded at times, but also to ignore the expected (and widely accepted) diplomatic hypocrisies that accompany public life at the highest level.

Numerous examples come to mind. The brutal murder of Saudi journalist Jamal Khashoggi? The president's response focused on Saudi Arabia as a valued strategic partner—not the possible complicity of the Saudi government.

George Stephanopoulos asking whether he would listen to a foreign government with "dirt" on a political opponent? The president answered that he would listen—not the safe or expected response for the average politician.

How to respond to the taunts and insults of an unstable North Korean dictator? Mr. Trump answers with taunts and insults of his own—not exactly the expected, kick-the-can-down-the-road diplomatic route followed by every other U.S. president.

5. *Old Rule: Avoid Overexposure*

Another old rule meant to protect a politician from too much public familiarity. A sensible rationale accompanies the admonition that "even popular politicians can wear out their welcome."

Although some may see this guideline as particularly useful in the age of television and social media, it does not appear that anyone associated with the Trump administration is remotely familiar with it.

In other words, like it or not, the original presumption of the first Trump campaign, that Donald J. Trump himself would conduct relentless media messaging on a daily basis, has not changed. In Trump World there is simply no such thing as overexposure.

Reality check for media haters: there will be no change to this approach in the second term, either.

6. *Old Rule: Stay on Message*

What has been gospel for generations of political campaign managers is oxymoronic during the Trump era.

Whether the storyline of the day emanates from early morning tweets or an off-the-cuff response to a reporter's question, there is no doubt that one man has daily set the day's media narrative for the better part of four years.

Still, important messages can get trampled by less important ones, and then there is the occasional inconsistency that opposing media types never ignore.

But such obstacles are temporary, and, after all, tomorrow is another day—and another opportunity to reset the narrative. A nimble press operation, to say the least, is a necessity in this environment.

My last book was about the 2016 Trump campaign. It was entitled *Bet You Didn't See That One Coming*—as true today as it was four years ago.

Polarization a Result of Policies, Not Partisanship

Western Journal
May 19, 2020

One of my great frustrations is to watch how often the media confuse policy differences with partisan differences. And at no time has it been more important to recognize that our deeply polarized nation is a result of the former.

It's not that partisanship is a good thing—it is in fact almost always counterproductive. It states that you are required to oppose the other person because he or she wears a different uniform, that the singular act of identifying with one party requires total opposition to the other.

Partisanship so defined reveals itself as petty, dissatisfying, and unfortunately more dangerous than ever in the age of social media.

Still, our focus today should be on the profound policy differences between the two major parties. Fissures are everywhere—and they are more obvious and pronounced during the current pandemic.

Indeed, naïve Americans who believe that "flattening the curve" through mitigation during this terrifying worldwide health crisis was the hard part have been rudely awakened to the reality of hardball—politics as usual—and a cynical political admonition, "never let a crisis go to waste."

The prescriptions of left versus right have never been more opposed or more obvious.

Gun control? One side believes access to firearms is essential; the other possesses a far more nuanced view of Second Amendment rights.

Lawsuits? One side desires to extend liability protections for manufacturers and suppliers in the midst of a pandemic; the other side always reserves the right to sue, regardless of circumstances.

Immigration? One side wishes to limit extraordinary federal benefits to actual citizens; the other side seeks to provide those same benefits to those who should not be here in the first place.

Censorship? One side rallies on behalf of opening the private economy; the other perpetrates controlled lockdowns in the name of public health.

Church attendance? One side sees services as constitutionally protected medicine for the soul; the other side not so much, going so far as to shut down even outside religious gatherings.

Relief funds? One side wants to focus relief dollars on job creators and small businesses; the other on "ballot harvesting," cannabis "diversity detectives" (in the words of Senator Mitch McConnell), and blue states with a history of high taxes and budget deficits.

Embattled Michigan Gov. Gretchen Whitmer may have said it best for the authoritarian types when she claimed that large protest rallies in opposition to her lockdown orders are "racist" and "misogynistic."

Only a true blue progressive would associate citizens demanding their freedom to conduct commerce with such charges. Alas, it appears many left-leaning governors and officials unsurprisingly agree.

I for one am happy these wide differences on the coronavirus response are playing out in the halls of Congress and on the presidential campaign trail. The unfolding debate is not simply a political play; the differences are real and often emotional. One side identifies with the redemptive value of freedom of commerce and freedom, the other with the authority attendant to government dictates and control.

Back to the realpolitik strategies playing out today.

In light of so many draconian state and local orders, it appears that those with public sector control proclivities do indeed see the coronavirus as an opportunity to accomplish something that competitive elections have failed to deliver: a more socialism-accepting electorate, one that values handouts over self-reliance and one that readily accepts expansive government edicts.

In the words of *Washington Post* columnist Dave Balz, "For the first time, many Americans are looking to government for their very economic survival. In time, that could make them look at government differently."

For further context, recall that Joe Biden has now added Alexandria Ocasio Cortez as his policy consultant on climate change and Beto

O'Rourke as his "go-to" person for personal arms confiscation, and is currently working with Bernie Sanders on an economic manifesto. Talk about a transformed country…

One can only imagine the dent this crowd would make in what was until very recently an ascendant economy and country.

Just a thought as you consider all the depressing news emanating from Joe Biden's basement.

CHAPTER 7

CRISES: MUELLER & UKRAINE

Post-midterms, numerous A-List Democrats announced their campaigns for president—including former Vice President Joe Biden and Senators Elizabeth Warren, Cory Booker, Bernie Sanders, and Kamala Harris. But it was not until Independent Counsel Robert Mueller's long-awaited report on alleged Trump collusion with Russia was published that the real campaign would begin. Democrats needed to know what Mueller had found before they could refine their message. Was it going to be indictment city and a limping Trump administration—as the progressive talking heads and their friendly cable news networks had promised for the previous two and a half years—or more like irrational enthusiasm for a once-promising and long-propagandized theory that would fall on its face, with profound repercussions?

The answer was "B." No collusion and no conspiracy were Mueller's (and Attorney General Barr's) conclusions (albeit a shade of grey was purposely left by Mueller on the issue of obstruction; see below) after 500 witness interviews, 500 search warrants, and $32 million in taxpayer money. As expected, the president claimed victory, Democrats claimed foul, and nary an apology was heard from the media purveyors of a narrative that had begun as an Obama administration counter-intelligence investigation against a political candidate of the other party—fueled by a so-called "dossier" paid for by the Clinton Campaign and the Democratic National Committee. Nevertheless, a dramatic overnight drop in MSNBC and CNN ratings in the immediate aftermath of the Mueller Report reflected the deep disillusionment felt by members of the resistance who had bought the Trump/Russia narrative hook, line, and sinker. To boot, a desperate Democratic attempt to relitigate *any* incriminating tidbit within the Mueller Report went terribly south when a clearly distracted, unfocused Mueller was forced to testify in front of Congress. Many even neutral observers were left to wonder how involved Mueller had been in the writing of the report that bore his name.

For NeverTrumpers and major segments of the media wholly invested in a continuing Trump-Russia narrative, neither the original announcement of Mueller's findings, the publication of the (redacted) 400-page report, or the disquieting testimony of Mueller himself would quell the storm. The new talking points tended to minimize the now discredited case for collusion and the decision of the administration to decline executive privilege, but instead focused on various Trump statements, actions, and near actions to make the case for obstruction of justice. Here, POTUS' well-reported frustration with two-plus years of Mueller's investigation, the firing of former FBI Director Comey, and the allegedly considered but never consummated firing of Mueller provided a predicate for desperate Democrats looking for any colorable claims of obstruction—albeit still a narrative that lacked an underlying crime.

For many long-serving Washington Democrats, Hillary Clinton's email shenanigans and the Trump Russia collusion story became a lot more problematic as newly confident GOP lawmakers began to press the case that the former was (provably) real while the latter was bogus from the jump. Republicans pointed to former Attorney General Loretta Lynch, former FBI Director James Comey, and senior members of the Obama Justice Department to make the case that the fix was always in regarding Hillary Clinton's potential criminal exposure in "Emailgate/Servergate."

Conversely, with regard to then-Candidate Trump, one issue stood out from the rest: How could senior Obama administration officials at the FBI and Department of Justice secure repeated FISA court applications to surveil Trump campaign aide Carter Page on the basis of a salacious dossier wherein even its author (British spy Christopher Steele) could not attest to its authenticity? A related question concerned Mr. Comey's January 6, 2017, Oval Office reassurance to the president that he was **not** under investigation when Comey knew that senior members of the FBI and Department of Justice suspected Page (and possibly Trump) had conspired with the Russians to influence the election. Legitimate questions all—and ones that Attorney General Barr promised to investigate, including the truly scary issue of whether the Trump campaign had fallen victim to a "spying operation" (a phrase strenuously objected to by congressional Democrats) orchestrated by now-disgraced anti-Trump senior officials within the Obama administration. Not one to wear a "Hit Me" button around official Washington, Mr. Barr turned the "investigation of the investigators" over to the widely respected U.S. Attorney from Connecticut, John Durham.

In response, Democrats screamed bloody murder. No surprise there. Few had thought the Obama era's internal campaign to take down Candidate Trump would ever come to light. After all, Hillary Clinton was a slam dunk winner—so why worry? For jubilant Republicans and the Trump administration, it was more like "we told you so"—a refrain that took on added intensity in the strange case of General Michael Flynn.

In May of 2020, newly produced Justice Department memos revealed that Mueller had been given wide latitude to investigate Trump campaign officials—especially the allegations contained in the discredited Steele dossier, a treasure trove of Trump-related lies and misrepresentations paid for, in part, by the Hillary Clinton campaign. With regard to Flynn, Trump's choice for incoming national security director, Mueller was given the authority to examine whether the general had violated the "Logan Act" (a 1799 law that had **never** been successfully used to prosecute an American citizen) per his transition conversations with Soviet Ambassador Sergey Kislyak. Note that the DOJ had previously moved to close its Flynn investigation because no collusion with Russian agents had been found. Nevertheless, the FBI (per the instruction of FBI Agent Peter Strzok) kept the file open—and fed it to Mr. Mueller's team of prosecutors. The Mueller team soon had their scalp when Flynn pled to making false statements to the FBI during a January 24, 2017, White House conversation wherein Flynn was dissuaded from having an attorney present.

But Justice made a return appearance in attorney Sidney Powell, Flynn's second attorney (his first law firm was fired) who not only filed a motion to withdraw the guilty plea, but also successfully persuaded the Justice Department to drop the case. It did so on May 7, 2020. In its filing, the DOJ conceded that it could not make a viable case out against Flynn.[1] Here, yet another piece of the Russian collusion narrative was shown to be illegitimate. Yet still more pieces of the façade were to fall in the succeeding months…

Mere days after the monumental train wreck that was Bob Mueller's congressional testimony, the president had a phone conversation with Ukraine President Volodymyr Zelensky wherein he asked for (among other things) Ukraine's assistance with the investigation of allegations of corruption involving Burisma Holdings (a Ukrainian energy company that had employed Joe Biden's son, Hunter, as a board member) during a time $400 million in previously appropriated foreign aid to Ukraine was pending. Said discussion led to an anonymous "whistleblower" complaint lodged against the president for soliciting interference in the 2020 presidential election…by pressuring a foreign country to investigate one of the president's main political rivals, which shortly thereafter became the basis for a wide-ranging House impeachment inquiry engaging six standing committees.

---

[1]   Only in the Trump era would a motion to dismiss by the government be denied by the trial judge. A series of government motions to force the issue fell on deaf ears until the president issued a blanket pardon to General Flynn on November 27, 2020.

The 24/7 never Trump media immediately switched course from a Russian to a Ukraine narrative. The critics had finally found their smoking gun. It was what they had waited for three long years. And *this time* they had him *on tape*. No way the White House would ever let *that* transcript see the light of day, right?

Wrong. An unapologetic president (it was a "perfect call") doubled down by publishing the transcript for public consumption, to the astonishment of many dissenters. It was here where the impeachment protagonists ran head on into a series of inconvenient facts:

- The "whistleblower" was not a participant in the Trump-Zelensky phone call; he lacked the firsthand knowledge required to possess the requisite standing to file a complaint.
- The recipient of the complaint, Intelligence Community Inspector General (ICIG) Michael Atkinson, nevertheless processed the complaint under a "new" policy that allowed for second-hand information to pass the threshold.
- The whistleblower wished to remain anonymous and remained so throughout the process—which (to Republicans) seemed at odds with even minimal notions of due process. In other words, how does one vet an unidentified person whose allegation sparked a historic impeachment process? Answer: not important when the target is Donald J. Trump.
- The 2020 campaign was never discussed. Rather, the focus of the president's request was the *2016 campaign* since the president believed the genesis of the Trump—Manafort—Russian narrative emanated from Ukrainian government officials. Hence, Mr. Trump's request: "I would like you to do *us* a favor though because our country has been through a lot" (referencing three years of relentless Russian collusion coverage).
- The Justice Department had an active investigation into the origins of alleged Ukrainian electoral involvement prior to the Trump-Zelensky phone call.

- The whistleblower himself violated the predicate statute by communicating with House Democrats (Adam Schiff's staff) prior to filing his complaint. He also reportedly had professional ties to a prominent Democrat.
- Zelensky repeatedly stated that he did not know the aid package was held up at the time of his phone call with the president.
- The Ukrainian government never did commence the suggested investigation, despite the fact the aid was distributed.
- Former Vice President Biden had famously bragged about pressuring the Ukrainian government to fire a prosecutor who was investigating Burisma Holdings.

Undaunted, House Democrats forged ahead with their investigation, structuring a "formal" inquiry (i.e., setting ground rules) in preparing the case for impeachment. Of note, only two of the 31 Democrats (in Trump districts) broke party ranks and voted against the resolution. Hearings would occur first in Chairman Adam Schiff's House Permanent Select Committee on Intelligence, wherein State Department witnesses would testify to Mr. Trump's alleged inappropriate "quid pro quo" discussion with the Ukrainian leader, in addition to numerous other occasions wherein the often-undiplomatic president would ruffle feathers within the foreign policy establishment. Here, Democrats and their media allies applauded as establishment bureaucrats repeatedly questioned Mr. Trump's unique modus operandi (and disregard for contrary opinions) while Fox-watching deplorables had their worst "deep state" fears confirmed.

Chairman Schiff's extended hearings were followed by a Judiciary Committee hearing wherein three liberal law professors assured the assembled that Mr. Trump had without doubt committed impeachable offenses. Notably, a fourth left-leaning professor (Jonathan Turley of George Washington University Law School) testified in convincing fashion to the contrary.

But the public vetting missed its (political) mark, as public opinion polls reflected diminishing support for impeachment, especially among independents. Despite the best efforts of the usual media suspects, the

Democrats were accordingly forced to ditch the difficult-to-understand "quid pro quo" standard to the more easily digestible "bribery" as the basis for the entire exercise. But even this recalculation fell short, as television ratings **and** public support continued to soften. In the end, no bribery Article would emerge from the House.

Still, Speaker Pelosi and her merry band of progressives marched into the fire, all the while bemoaning how "solemn" the process had become. But their alleged empathy was of no help to the aforementioned House Democrats who had captured Trump districts in the 2018 mid-terms. Their world was suddenly turned upside down in a well-publicized series of unpleasant town halls. Alas, after weeks of intense media coverage but general indifference around the country, only two Articles were reported and passed on the House Floor: "Abuse of Power" and "Obstruction of Congress." Neither of the Articles alleged a criminal act.

The House had acted swiftly. The entire process had lasted two months, one week, and two days. House leaders defended the accelerated schedule with a now-familiar narrative: they **had** to speed up the process due to the clear and present danger that *is* the Trump presidency. Yet, Speaker Pelosi slow-walked the newly passed Articles out of the House, waiting a full month before transmitting them over to the Senate. Pundits generally panned the strategy, a conclusion shared by growing numbers of Americans as the president's approval numbers continued to tick up. Historic economic growth and record low unemployment were proving to be fierce countervailing political forces against the Democrats' impeachment gamble.

As expected, the Senate proved to be a new ballgame. The 35-year veteran Mitch McConnell quickly took charge through party line votes that forbade new documents and witnesses from being introduced in a Senate trial. The majority leader also limited each side to 24 hours of oral argument. There was no chance the GOP-controlled Senate was going to indulge Democratic requests for additional discovery. After all, had not the House leadership declared their case for impeachment as "overwhelming," "a slam dunk"?

Still, television viewership continued to dwindle as Representative Schiff and his fellow managers argued ad nauseum that the president's interest in Ukraine corruption was in reality a thinly veiled attempt to damage Joe Biden—and that any attempt to impede foreign aid to Ukraine met the standard for a high crime or misdemeanor. To nobody's surprise, the Senate trial ended in acquittal—on a near party line vote. Only Utah Senator Mitt Romney would support a single Article—"Abuse of Power." In the end, impeachment never did register on the list of issues most important to the American people. The entire charade changed precious few minds.

More Excuses for Democrats to Impeach Trump

Western Journal
December 3, 2019

A condensed history of the Democrats' longstanding promise to impeach President Trump runs through numerous storylines.

A fair review includes pre- and post-inaugural promises to impeach on both general grounds (Hillary Clinton's supporters being really mad she lost), and the initial, slightly more specific grounds (Trump's failure to divest from his business empire). Then there were the associated charges of illegitimacy because…Mrs. Clinton won the popular vote…and… the electoral college is an archaic process invented by a bunch of racist white men. This was followed by the persistent allegation that "Trump is a Russian asset," a charge that gave birth to the 35-month, $32-million Mueller-Russia investigation. The embarrassing conclusion to that lame affair was of course followed by the Trump-Ukraine pre-impeachment process, which may now indeed lead to a House vote in the near future.

Alas, it is crystal clear that even if the House finally pulls the impeachment trigger, a GOP Senate will not convict. In fact, the president will no doubt declare victory and go about his re-election efforts. But what then? Well, I'll tell you: more impeachment shenanigans. You can take it to the bank.

At this point, you may ask, "On what grounds?" Haven't we had enough impeachment vitriol over the past three years? One might think so, but that conclusion would define you as a Trump sycophant, unable to appreciate the pure evil that is Donald J. Trump. Indeed, a fertile mind can imagine unlimited grounds to hold Mr. Trump responsible—and impeachable:

The NFL's New Pass Interference Video Challenge Rule

You may not realize it, but this rarely enforced call was voted upon and passed…during the Trump administration. Maybe, just maybe, Roger Goodell discussed this incomprehensible remedy with the former owner of the New Jersey Generals? Further investigation required.

Eleven Years Left

Earthlings are now reliably informed the world as we know it has 12 years (and counting) left, per the renowned climate scientist Alexandria Ocasio-Cortez. This is big news, as previously, few climatologists have hazarded a precise prediction as to when we are all toast (literally). And who do you think has been president as the timetable for Armageddon has accelerated? You guessed it. Further investigation required.

Iran

Just over three years ago, President Obama sent $1.7 billion in cash to the mullahs in Tehran, money allegedly owed as part of an arms settlement from the 1970s. It took three flights to Switzerland by unmarked chartered aircraft to get the job done. Mr. Obama also negotiated a nuclear deal with the Iranians, a negotiation that was supposed to be the signature foreign policy accomplishment of the Obama era. Both actions were intended to placate a murderous regional power that 1.) has promised to wipe Israel off the face of the earth and 2.) remains the world's most notorious state sponsor of terror.

Then along comes Mr. Trump and his decision to hit Iran with draconian sanctions that are sucking the lifeblood out of the Iranian economy and give support to Iranian street protesters intent on regime change. More investigation required.

Modern Country Music

Have you noticed how popular this genre has become? It is no secret that many country stars lean right (note: lefty T. Swift crossed over to pop a few years ago) and their music is enjoyed by millions of flyover state deplorables who simply do not know better. This displacement of rock 'n' roll lefties from our national consciousness is an unfolding tragedy. Where is Bon Jovi when we need him? Further investigation required.

Hollywood

A series of big-money, woke blockbuster movies have proven busts at the box office, resulting in angry reactions from the directors and producers of these supposedly transformative works. To make matters worse, Clint Eastwood (yep, Dirty Harry himself) keeps churning out hit after hit, many with a decidedly anti-progressive bent. And who do you think Mr. Eastwood supported in 2016? Only another arduous $32-million inquisition will get to the bottom of it. Further investigation required.

Jeffrey Epstein Is Still Dead

The former financier and convicted sex offender was found unresponsive in a Manhattan jail cell. Donald Trump used to live in New York. Epstein allegedly used a bed sheet to commit suicide. Donald Trump owns hotels that use bed sheets. Coincidence? Further investigation required.

Feel free to invent your own case in support of further impeachment inquiries. Washington's new favorite parlor game may be suffering from low television ratings and increasingly poor polling, but there appears to be no end in sight.

Opposition to Trump Is Rooted in Anger

Western Journal
December 16, 2019

There is a unique angle to all the political anger going around these days, but few pundits bother to focus on it.

To wit: 99 percent of the angst you see on your television screens and read about on social media platforms proceeds from one direction—far left field.

And I'm not simply talking about the unbridled vitriol unleashed from the losers' side beginning the very moment Donald J. Trump declared victory on Nov. 8, 2016. The angry chorus includes ongoing progressive tantrums that have become part of the political landscape in the second decade of the new millennium—especially during the Trump era.

You know them when you see them, as the perpetrators are the "usual suspects": lefty "intellectuals," Hollywood celebrities, and snowflake students regularly lighting up about the latest insult or injury to their progressive sensibilities.

Think of a De Niro full of sound and fury, signifying nothing, in one of his patented late-night television tirades or just about any stump speech from Elizabeth Warren or Bernie Sanders.

In this world, Berkeley burns again—but this time in angry protest *against* free speech; Republican officeholders and administration appointees are accosted in public places, sometimes for simply sitting down to eat dinner; lefty comedians and actors take to stage and screen to lodge often vulgar attacks against any and all things Trump.

Safe to say the melodrama that began with Madonna famously dreaming of blowing up the White House at the inaugural women's anti-Trump march has never slowed down.

I have been thinking about this one-way street while forcing myself to watch (OK, not every minute—there *are* limits to self-punishment) the witnesses called by Reps. Adam Schiff and Jerry Nadler in the Trump impeachment inquiry.

With regard to the former, the Democratic majority produced numerous career diplomats displeased with the president. Each of them let us know how downright frustrated (angry) they were with the bare-knuckled treatment they received at the hands of the cantankerous Mr. Trump.

Similar disgust emanated from the Democratic (law professor) witnesses called by Mr. Nadler—especially Stanford Law School's uber-progressive professor Pamela Karlan.

Yep, this was the good professor's long-anticipated opportunity to strike back at Mr. Trump and all the Trump-loving deplorables (presumably those not admitted to elite colleges and universities) she so despises. She did not miss her mark. Her appearance may, in fact, be the most instructive of the lot: serious, unmitigated anger from start to finish. The parting gratuitous insult directed toward Mr. Trump's 13-year-old son, Barron, (although she later apologized), only served as the icing on top of her progressive cake.

Bet she was a big hit at the faculty lounge back at Stanford.

Now juxtapose for a second the most commented upon GOP "angry moment" over the last three years: Brett Kavanaugh's emotional self-defense in the face of allegations of sexual misconduct from over 30 years ago. Recall how the previously vetted and Senate-approved jurist defended his reputation in a demonstrably angry tone—for which he was torched by the establishment media for his alleged lack of self-control.

Talk about having it both ways.

The good news for Republicans is that unmitigated anger and overt hostility seldom carry the day in competitive elections—especially the no-holds-barred, over-the-top, and often unhinged kind recently peddled to the American public.

As the impeachment process winds down toward a House vote, I am reminded of a May 15, 2018, column I wrote for *National Review* titled "Don't Throw Stones at Barking Dogs."

The opinion piece analyzed Winston Churchill's famous maxim to the effect that persistent (and angry) overreactions to things large *and* small are typically self-destructive; that sooner or later the voters will stop paying attention or turn on those who insist on throwing stones at *every* barking dog. For non-Churchill fans, the story of "the little boy who cried wolf" will suffice. A bottom line appears: choosing to whine at every perceived slight or opponent's success tends to wear out an audience.

Still, it is difficult to find a time in recent political history where so many angry comments—and so many stones—are being slung at a single politician. Indeed, entire media operations have given themselves over to an unrelenting 24/7 search for barking dogs wherever they may lie.

But the angry opposition's smarmy, snarky, and snarly ways now appear to have limits. Public opinion polls published since the start of Adam Schiff's inquisition are trending in favor of the embattled president.

No doubt Mr. Churchill is looking down on this circus with a wry smile.

CHAPTER 8

APOLOGIES & ACTING OUT: DEMOCRATS TURN HARD LEFT

Race was one but certainly not the only focus for the endless apologies pouring forth from the leading Democratic contenders. Each sought to make amends for past (real and imagined) indiscretions that were now interpreted as violating the planks of a newly instilled progressive platform—one that was undergoing rapid construction on the campaign trail. It was accordingly here where Joe Biden sought forgiveness for a multitude of past sins, especially his criticism of '70s-style busing, alleged poor treatment of Anita Hill in the Clarence Thomas hearings, and dozens of Senate votes deemed contrary to the Democrats' now uber pro-choice position. Biden's sudden policy turnabout did not stand alone, however, as Senator Kristin Gillibrand would renounce her own record as a freshman upstate New York moderate, and Senator Cory Booker (lately of Spartacus fame from the Kavanaugh hearings) would forever shed his once differentiating moniker of a pro-business, big city mayor.

A related tactic (perfected by President Barack Obama) was to create and then take down strawmen on the stump. Perhaps the best example here was the way openly gay South Bend, Indiana, Mayor Pete Buttigieg indicted Vice President Mike Pence's alleged bigotry against gays in an early campaign speech. The mayor's strong defense of his Christian faith and lifestyle was guaranteed to engender strong reaction among Democratic base voters, which it did. The only problem with the charge was when Fox News began to run old video reflecting friendly comments Pence (then Indiana's governor) had directed Buttigieg's way over the years. Indeed, there was no evidence of *any* previous ill will between the two men—until "Mayor Pete" felt the need to break out the homophobe strawman at an opportune time. After all, it *was* a crowded field of 25 candidates. The charge was lodged in short order and on the accuser's terms. Our 44th president must have been smiling while watching from the sidelines.

But it was wins in the Iowa and Nevada caucuses and New Hampshire primary that gave self-described "Democratic Socialist" Senator Bernie Sanders momentum entering the Super Tuesday primaries. Still, all was not well with America's labor/progressive party.

The Democratic establishment was feeling the burn—not the "Bern"—as the party's so-called moderates (until quite recently re-ferred to as "liberals") began a very public vetting of their concerns about Sanders' electability—and his potentially devastating impact on down-ballot Democrats. This fear of a political wipeout helped propel for-mer New York City Mayor Michael Bloomberg into double digits nation-ally. But the rapid rise of the charisma-challenged technocrat billionaire (and former Republican) set off alarm bells in progressive land, and for good reason. It was only four years ago wherein "Bernie Bros" had stood by helplessly as the Democratic Party establishment manipulated party nominating rules to ensure that Hillary Clinton prevailed over Sanders. And now the media was full of reports that party elders were set to do it all over again. Suddenly, more critical reporting of Sanders appeared on the likes of CNN and MSNBC—further antagonizing Sanders' bur-geoning army of true believers.

All the while, the president sat back and tweeted often critical re-views about the Democratic Party's identity problem—and its competing candidates. Underlying many of Mr. Trump's comments (and tracking the thoughts of millions of conservatives) was a query: Could the septuagenarian Sanders, a mere afterthought for the majority of his political career, actually secure the Democratic nomination?

The 24 hours leading up to Super Tuesday provided a hint, as supposed "moderate" alternatives Pete Buttigieg and Amy Klobuchar bowed out in favor of Biden. These last-minute endorsements and continued strong support from African American supporters boosted Biden to big wins in nine states (to Sanders' four). A week later, Super Tuesday produced similar results, as Biden won in Mississippi, Washington, Missouri, Michigan, and Idaho. The swift turnaround in Biden's fortunes could not be overestimated: the pundits had declared the early frontrunner all but dead just a week prior. Bloomberg's exit the next day guaranteed Biden sole possession of the supposed middle road all the way to the Milwaukee convention.

More good news for Biden arrived two days later as Senator Elizabeth Warren exited the race after placing in third in her home state of Massachusetts on Super Tuesday. The progressive lane was now clear for Sanders. The respective wings of the Democratic Party had now chosen their leaders to carry forward into the spring and summer primaries—or so the pundits believed. On April 13 Sanders announced the suspension of his campaign. Not enough Democratic primary voters had felt the Bern this go-round. The establishment had struck back at the Democratic Socialist yet again. Biden was now the presumptive nominee.

But Bernie's hard left constituency needed reassurance. And so on July 8, 2020, a once-unthinkable headline led in all the major newspapers: "Biden and Sanders Allies Unite on Policies." Phrased another way, the establishment liberal who had beaten the anti-establishment progressive-socialist was now...supportive of the latter's platform. The party's hard-left move was now official, all that 2016 talk about "recapturing" white, working-class, blue-collar workers notwithstanding. In no particular order, free college tuition, Obamacare expansion, liability limits for police, and dramatic cuts to fossil fuel production would be included in the Democratic Party platform. Even more progressive planks on immigration, education, and free speech would be ironed out at the convention. Long-time observers were left to ponder whether this easily confused version of Mr. Biden comprehended precisely what his party was selling to the voters in 2020. Had not the former VP lived through the George McGovern fiasco of 1972?

The public will of course never know if Mr. Biden truly understood how far left his party had come. He often appeared confused in campaign appearances, easily losing his train of thought and temper. Yet, in one sense it did not matter all that much. Mr. Biden's job was simply to remind voters that he was still good ole Joe—the Amtrak guy—and not Darth Vader, a.k.a. Donald J. Trump. This central fact and a few platitudes regarding America's better nature comprised Mr. Biden's acceptance speech at the Democrats' virtual convention. The Biden campaign strategy soon came into focus. Keep the voters so transfixed on removing Mr. Trump that they would pay no real heed to what the party now stood for—and against.

Where Have All the Liberals Gone?

National Review
March 29, 2018

"Where have all the liberals gone?" I find myself asking this question a lot these days, and, truth be known, I miss them. Sure, I've had my share of very public battles with them. A number of our uglier encounters were splattered over the pages of the *Washington Post* and the *Baltimore Sun*. Still, our underlying *values* were not so far apart; we simply differed on how to get there—how to make Maryland (and America) better. Today, however, those former colleagues with whom I served in two legislatures are a vanishing breed: gone from the national political scene; gone from the ranks of Democratic leadership; gone from our daily political debates.

Now, I'm not talking about Truman–JFK–(Scoop) Jackson Democrats here. But for the recent anomaly of a Congressman Conor Lamb (who ran as a squeaky-clean version of the president), those good folks have unfortunately gone missing for quite some time now. I witnessed their demise as a member of the Maryland legislature in the late 1980s and early 1990s. Each election cycle saw their long-held outer-suburban and rural seats turn a deeper shade of red. Seems the local folks simply decided to go with the "real thing"—to replace a conservative Democrat with a conservative Republican when given the opportunity. It was new blood versus dinosaurs—and even the right-thinking dinosaurs never stood a chance.

For the GOP, this realignment brought a significant increase in seats, especially in the South and West. I rode the wave of this historic bump (in 1994) to Congress along with 73 other Republican freshmen. The dozen and a half remaining "Blue Dogs" soon went the way of the horse and buggy. But the loss of this important third-party voting bloc did more than bolster House Republicans. By shrinking the Democratic base to (primarily) urban and coastal districts, it also signaled the decline of many old-fashioned liberals, as ascendant progressives challenged "safe" blue seats.

These liberals were further pressured by the demise of private-sector labor as a vote-generating machine. Here, the old New Deal "base" of socially conservative blue-collar ethnics has been replaced by young and minority voters attracted to the progressives' big-tax, slow-growth, and very green agenda. Indeed, "Joe 6-Pack" quickly figured out that his local progressive Democrat had little interest in preserving industrial-era manufacturing and mining jobs (recall Hillary Clinton's tone-deaf promise to West Virginians that she would put their mining livelihoods out of business—forever).

But traditional liberals have felt the heavy hand of progressive ideology on two issues more than any other: immigration and (free) speech.

Generations of grade-school kids learned how waves of turn-of-the-century immigrants from Poland, Italy, Greece, Germany, and Ireland launched FDR's coalition. These new arrivals would soon populate America's inner cities, assimilate into American culture, and join one political party—the party of the "workingman." For decades thereafter, Democrats from right and left took great pride in this melting-pot immigrant identity, including an abiding respect for the rule of law and their (Ellis Island) legal entry into this promised land. Such a worldview lasted until and during the presidency of Bill Clinton, who famously declared in his January 1995 State of the Union address:

> All Americans, not only in the States most heavily af-
> fected but in every place in this country, are rightly
> disturbed by the large numbers of illegal aliens entering
> our country. The jobs they hold might otherwise be held
> by citizens or legal immigrants. The public service[s]
> they use impose burdens on our taxpayers.… We are a
> nation of immigrants. But we are also a nation of laws.
> It is wrong and ultimately self-defeating for a nation of
> immigrants to permit the kind of abuse of our immigra-
> tion laws we have seen in recent years, and we must do
> more to stop it.

You may also recall Hillary Clinton's opposition to driver's licenses for illegal aliens during her presidential campaign of 2007. To wit: "As president, I will not support driver's licenses for undocumented people and will press for comprehensive immigration reform that deals with all of the issues around illegal immigration, including border security and fixing our broken system."

Now fast-forward a decade and the world is upside down. Democratic mayors and their enablers in Congress champion "rights" for illegal aliens and sanctuary cities. And there appears to be no end to their "no-borders" platform. Every night, the cable news shows are full of Democratic leaders promising to resist…federal agents in charge of locating and deporting *illegal felons*. (Note: President Clinton uttered the above-cited words to *bipartisan* applause.) Can anyone in this audience imagine Hubert Humphrey championing the rights of alien felons over American citizens?

Free speech is another obvious victim of the progressive tide. Seemingly overnight, American campuses have been transformed from bastions of liberal protest to bastions of *illiberal* opposition to speech.

Not so long ago, college activists marched for civil rights and women's rights and in opposition to the Vietnam War. Liberals were in the vanguard; free speech and dissent would be utilized to bring about social change. A couple of generations later, millennials and their faculty enablers march, protest, shout down, and destroy property...in order to deny those with alternative opinions their free-speech rights. Again, what would Hubert Humphrey say? He wouldn't recognize his party. Neither do most Americans.

Elitist Left Won't Be Satisfied Until Trump Is Out of the Oval Office

LifeZette
October 19, 2018

Conservative media are having a field day reporting on the daily, targeted, and very public confrontations perpetrated by the progressive Left. Seems a right-winger can't buy a hamburger and soda these days without some angst-ridden protester wrecking the occasion.

Things have gotten so out of hand that none other than New York Mayor Bill de Blasio is now calling for some restraint—recognition that social bullying may not be the correct foundation for a Democratic comeback in three weeks. Alas, de Blasio's call for a modicum of civility is far more the exception than the rule these days.

Of course, such protests began the very moment Donald Trump was declared president-elect. Progressives immediately took to the streets in order to register their disgust at losing a third Obama term, let alone the chance to elect our first female president.

Underlying it all was profound resentment at what flyover America had dared pull off, a result of "misinformation" possessed by "low information voters" (translation: stupid), according to left-wing pundits and politicians.

The central villain was (is) Trump. And why not? The political novice encompasses all that progressives truly resent: he is a wealthy businessman hellbent on rebooting the military, protecting the border, cutting taxes and regulation. And he is decidedly anti-PC to boot.

Worse, this president would refocus his office on American interests. Maintaining high poll numbers in other countries was never going to be part of Trump's DNA.

So a domestic opposition quickly morphed into a resistance: a radically different movement intent on immediate reflexive, utter, and complete opposition to everything proffered by the new Republican administration. It is this widely held attitude that should concern all who worry about our deepening cultural divide.

A few reminders:

We have seen this movie before. The modern Left acts out whenever threatened—whenever their access to governmental power is at risk. Think Bush/Gore, Bork/Thomas, and any number of "Million Man/ Woman" marches on behalf of progressive causes.

I would add the now largely forgotten but instructive progressive takeover of Minnesota Democrat Sen. Paul Wellstone's wake—the one wherein Republicans were called out and demonized during a memorial service. The emotional opposition to Judge Kavanaugh applies here, too, because a long-term originalist Supreme Court majority is simply too much for progressives to countenance.

Compare my eight-year despair over the Obama presidency wherein I (and many millions of other Americans) would mutter to like-minded deplorables about the latest progressive assault on our values—but never once thought to riot, knit funny hats, or shout down a leftist speaker at a college campus.

The contrast is clear. When the Right loses, we tend to cry in our beer, retreat to our conservative think tanks—watch more Fox News— and get to work on winning the next election.

The new Left looks to act out—now mulling nullification (recall December 2016 and more recent collateral attacks on the Electoral College) and even more recent calls for "court packing" in their never-ending attempt to retain power.

The other half of the equation is more dangerous because it concerns a virulent dogmatism more than legitimate disagreement over issues. It's called "elitism," a sense of intellectual superiority that compels wholesale rejection of opposing viewpoints.

Webster defines "elitism" as leadership or rule by an elite; the selectivity of the elite especially; snobbery elitism in choosing new members; consciousness of being or belonging to an elite.

In the real world, we know it when we see it. Flyover America saw it front and center in President Barack Obama's infamous (intended to be off-the-record) condemnation of the great unwashed between the coasts:

> They get bitter, they cling to guns or religion or antipathy to people who aren't like them, or anti-immigrant sentiment or anti-trade sentiment as a way to explain their frustrations.

Here, "professor" Obama covers all of the hot-button issues in one easy indictment: guns, religion, immigration, trade. Such a concise condemnation was no doubt enthusiastically received in faculty lounges and newspaper editorial boards throughout the land. The deplorables likewise received the message. Their distrust of the Washington elites only grew stronger.

Diagnosis, of course, leads to treatment. In this case, the hoped-for removal of Trump from office. Impeachment? Yep. Invoke the 25th Amendment? Why not! But leave it to our old friend California Gov. Jerry Brown to capsulize the charge: "Something's got to happen to this guy."

The none-too-subtle point is impossible to miss: POTUS needs to go. He challenges our assumptions—he disrupts our values and conventions—he feeds the worst inclinations of those who are too simpleminded to understand what is best for them. He gets in our way.

Brown and his progressive sycophants simply know better—just ask 'em. Elitism, indeed.

"It's Always Something" with the Campaign to Delegitimize Donald Trump

Western Journal
February 11, 2019

"It's always something."

Those of us of a certain age recall Gilda Radner's beloved *SNL* character Roseanne Roseannadanna. She was the chatty, dim-witted reporter who always got pronunciations wrong—always to hilarious effect—before being educated by the straight man/anchor. Invariably, once corrected, Miss Roseannadanna would minimize her mistaken verbiage with a dismissive, "It's always something." In other words, we'll just go on to the next story.

I think back to that famous punch line every time a frustrated media seeks to delegitimize the outcome of election 2016. The continued viability of the underlying storyline speaks to the establishment's (read: "swamp's") inability to wrap its head around what went down over two years ago. For those of us keeping score at home, "It's always something" looks and sounds more like this:

"But Hillary won the popular vote."

A crowd favorite, and oft-repeated on the lefty networks, as though the national popular vote counts, which of course it does not. This "break glass and use in case of emergency" line was heard anew in the aftermath of the 2018 midterms wherein Senate Democrats protested they had won the national popular vote but were still in the minority. Imagine...

"But the electoral college is antiquated."

An increasingly popular narrative now that heavily voting New York and California have emerged as two of our most reliably progressive states. This one is, of course, related to number one above, and focuses on how unfair it is that those short-sighted framers of ours saw fit to give smaller, rural states equal say in how our democracy operates. Look for the uber-left to continue its attacks on our Constitutional framework every time an election cycle does not go their way.

"But the Russians did it."

This one sure looked promising in those early, heady days of 2017. But of course, it was that KGB-trained Putin and his army of social bots and media influencers that swung American social media over to "The Donald." And why not? Vlad and DJT are two peas in a pod—both autocrats bent on consolidating their power and making a private fortune in the process. Seems no amount of FISA Court abuses or FBI missteps can dissuade purveyors of this conspiracy theory. Note that the expiration date on this one will be reached once Robert Mueller completes his investigation—and the president remains unindicted.

"But voter suppression is widespread."

I get the staying power of this one. Anyone who has studied slavery, Reconstruction, Jim Crow, and the long violent road to civil rights has to get the context. But advocates of this theory lose me in the here-and-now. Particularly galling is the persistent use of the race card to attack commonsensical security measures such as mandatory photo ID (or its equivalent) or the purging of voter rolls after prolonged periods of (voting) inactivity. How did our country get so far off base that minimal requirements imposed to protect the integrity of our sacred franchise now give rise to allegations of racism?

"But dark money was the culprit."

This one sounds so good when you say it real fast. After all, who is willing to defend dirty contributions? Aggrieved Clinton supporters know: it was those evil corporate polluters who pumped tens of millions of dollars into Trump's coffers—that's who! That Democratic candidates also benefit from progressive super PACS and tech America's nouveau wealth never quite bubbles up in the popular narrative. It's always easier to indict corporate America and its GOP allies on K-Street, facts on the ground notwithstanding.

"But Citizens United did the trick."

Herein is a first cousin to the dark money narrative. Recall Hillary Clinton's repeated stump demonizations of this Supreme Court decision. Recall also her promise to appoint Supreme Court justices who would overturn the case. No surprise here. It was an anti-Hillary film, (*Hillary's America: The Secret History of the Democratic Party*) that brought the issue of corporate First Amendment protections to the head of the class. Call me cynical, but I would bet my house that a clear majority of those Hillary-Elizabeth-Bernie fans screaming bloody murder at the mere mention of Citizens United during campus campaign rallies couldn't tell you the first thing about campaign finance.

For the last two years, the progressive-leaning cable networks have devoted a majority of their programming to one or more of the foregoing narratives. You can check it out any night—and twice on weekends. But the prudent reader might be on the lookout for new and novel narratives leading up to 2020—including the extraordinary remedies of impeachment and the 25th Amendment. Here, "It's always something" means a constant stream of rationalization—innuendo—denials about the rise (and sustained appeal) of Trump.

The bottom line: the campaign to delegitimize everything and anything Donald J. Trump will continue apace…right up until 8 p.m. on Nov. 3, 2020.

There's Still Hope for Race Relations in America

Western Journal
May 1, 2019

Remember when President Obama called for a long-overdue national dialogue on race? Most of us recall the well-publicized call to arms. That a gauntlet had been thrown down by our first black president was without doubt, but few on either side of the aisle were willing to pick up the kryptonite and run with it.

The feeble response was not surprising. Discussions on race are so… awkward. Everyone is on edge, on guard. Too many of us are scared about how what we say will be interpreted that we just shy away from the really tough stuff—the thought-provoking opinions that challenge individual safety zones. As a result, we talk past one another far too often.

Our 44th president's challenge is never far removed from my mind these days, as race-based appeals carry us further away from Dr. King's vision of "character first" judgment.

It is indeed a disappointment, as many Americans (myself included) have long believed that race relations in America would improve over time. I was able to maintain this conviction throughout my public career, and not only because I wanted to believe it.

My rationale was solid: I thought the first black president would prove to be a moderating presence regarding race relations—that a growing African American middle class would generate more philosophical buy-in from self-appointed black leaders—that, in the end, green (as in dollars) would ultimately trump (excuse the pun) the black and white divide.

Today, I'm no longer so sure.

My pessimism centers on the emergence of two inter-connected but equally dangerous cultural movements—victimhood and identity politics. Each is destructive in its own right, but together they represent serious and perhaps permanent problems for the future of race relations in America.

Victimhood (and its consequences) is the new bright shiny thing on the left. It has the benefit of covering a lot of ground. For example, it's convenient as it explains/rationalizes negative life results through a racial lens. The narrative has especially metastasized on the extreme left where the country and culture are seen as bastions of unyielding racism, where life's uneven playing fields are offered as excuses, not explanations. Per this narrative, racism and racial insensitivity explain instances of failure, poor result, or lack of upward mobility.

Another iteration is equally available but so weak. Here, purveyors of the political trade who have enjoyed America's advantages—strong families, elite educations, high-paying jobs, and professional success—unapologetically cling to their victimhood. Apparently, these children of privilege recognize no other rhetorical option—such is their shallowness.

Alas, while the specter of Ivy League graduates playing this card may be embarrassing to us, it will continue to be used until it doesn't work anymore.

A first cousin is identity politics—the theory that pre-supposes the color of one's skin or ethnicity or sexual orientation or religion must dictate one's political views. This affliction is the other rage among progressives because such a narrow perspective is easy to teach and too often politically rewarding (and expedient) as those whose political identities fail to conform are easily cast aside, marginalized as inauthentic.

For context, check out the treatment of black conservative intellectuals and politicians by the establishment Left and their media allies. Here, defining down is so much easier than having to...think. It is accordingly easy to discern why the Thomas Sowells, Condoleezza Rices, and Ben Carsons of this world are not appropriately celebrated. They are counterfeit. Their politics does not fit their assigned race or sex. Their high profiles are also mightily inconvenient for the narrative makers and sustainers on the left.

At the end of the day, their careers, life stories, and professional successes are sacrificed on the altar of identity politics. The message to young people is accordingly clear: no role models to be found here—keep turning left…

Some friends of mine believe my rose-colored glasses are blocking out the stark reality of racial politics circa 2019. Still, I have not given up my belief that demonstrable economic progress may indeed reduce racial tension in America.

A good barometer may be the 2020 election. If the Trump economy holds up—and in the process the historic economic progress of minority communities, especially African Americans—it may at the very least help turn our racial dialogue in a more positive direction.

Such would be a timely development in a nation that remains far too divided by skin color.

Acting Out

Western Journal
July 15, 2019

The Donald Trump era has witnessed many unique displays of opposition over the past three years. These very public, well-reported incidents are guaranteed fodder for the anti-Trump media, as they typically include well-known celebrities acting out their dissatisfaction with any and all things Trump.

Check it out:

> **Madonna**: The well-attended Women's March on Washington to protest the 2016 election included a speech by the aging pop star wherein she first told the event's detractors "F— you!" She then continued to express her outrage by saying she had "thought an awful lot about blowing up the White House."

The Cast of 'Hamilton': In November 2016, the cast of the Broadway hit had unscripted words for Vice President Mike Pence (sitting in the audience) at the end of its performance—words that spoke to how "anxious" the cast was about the new administration's views on "our planet, our children, our parents, [and] our inalienable rights."

Gillette: The razor company that has long-championed "manly men" ran a two-minute, pre-Super Bowl commercial aimed at today's often-discussed and allegedly out-of-control "toxic masculinity." The preachy commercial met with a decidedly mixed reaction, with plenty of Gillette's long-time customers pledging to boycott the company for its "anti-male" ad.

Robert DeNiro: The Oscar-winning actor has repeatedly used vulgar language in his public appearances to describe President Trump, punctuating his desires with a public wish to "punch Trump in the face."

Lindsey Vonn: The U.S. skier assured the world that she attended the 2018 Pyeongchang Winter Olympics to represent "the people of the United States, not the president." She added she would decline a White House invitation if she were to win gold (she did not).

Megan Rapinoe: The soccer star promised to boycott the "F—ing White House" if the U.S. Women's National Team won the World Cup (they did). She has said her teammates would follow suit, and they plan to come to Congress (at Sen. Chuck Schumer's invitation) to emphasize their opposition to President Trump.

House Democrats: Eighty-five House Democrats are signed up to begin impeachment proceedings against President Trump despite special counsel Robert Mueller's finding of no collusion with Russia.

Dining Out: Senate Majority Leader Mitch McConnell of Kentucky and Sen. Ted Cruz of Texas were confronted at different restaurants in the aftermath of Brett Kavanagh's Supreme Court confirmation hearings. Both incidents had the intended effect: an uncomfortable meal and a negative national news story.

Colin Kaepernick: The pig-socks-wearing one-time NFL quarterback has repeatedly degraded the president, law enforcement and America while leading the kneeling protest movement during the playing of "The Star-Spangled Banner." His latest outburst was to induce Nike to remove its Betsy Ross flag shoes from store shelves (it did).

I could make this list five pages long, but the point is clear: Numerous of America's high-profile elite have been acting out during the Trump presidency.

Some may wonder why the incidents have not decreased in frequency or intensity given that the president has been in office nearly three years. I am not in that group. Indeed, there are a number of reasons the angry resistance is as emotional today as it was on Nov. 9, 2016:

The Economy: Where to begin? Try as they might (and they will), it will be a tough sell for detractors to minimize the Trump era's sustained wage growth, record low unemployment, quiet inflation, expansive energy sector and record-setting stock market.

Teflon: The ultimate test will, of course, occur in November 2020, but President Trump's public ratings have steadied in the mid-40s despite a predisposition toward Twitter wars, senior staff turnover, belittling of political opponents and super-aggressive salesmanship.

Mueller Report: That dull thud heard round the world a few weeks back represented two years' worth of dashed progressive hopes for a truncated Trump administration. But what was a major disappointment got worse as a new attorney general set his guns on how and why so many Barack Obama-era officials at the Justice Department and the FBI could have signed off on a transparently phony dossier while simultaneously going out of their way to protect former Democratic presidential candidate Hillary Clinton in the investigation of her email debacle.

The Democratic Field: The Democrats have attracted a large and diverse field of competitors, many of whom have won state-wide races in the past. Yet it does not take a political genius to figure out that the policy positions advocated by the leading contenders are far outside the political mainstream, even angering the difficult-to-anger House Speaker Nancy Pelosi. It's a stretch to run to the center after you have spent a year in the far recesses of the left field bleachers.

In 2018, I wrote a column wherein I alluded to Winston Churchill's widely quoted admonition to refrain from "throwing stones at every dog that barks."

Churchill knew that too many thrown stones would simply overwhelm public attention—the shock value and shelf life of a political attack would be lost in the process.

Nevertheless, it is unlikely the angry mob will back off President Trump anytime soon. They just can't help throwing those stones...

A Guide to Understanding the Language of the Left

Western Journal
September 11, 2019

In politics, as in life, words count. It is therefore important to keep abreast of how our cultural value makers manipulate the English language to their political benefit.

Accordingly, I offer the following definitions/contextual examples for those of you attempting to understand the tone, tenor, and vocabulary of the progressive Left.

Enjoy, if you can.

"Normalize": Typically used in the pejorative sense ("Trump's actions are normalizing anti-social behavior," etc.), the word became trendy shortly after the resistance began its counterattack in the aftermath of Nov. 8, 2016.

The verb is an especially effective weapon as the new Left attempts to curtail conservative—traditional—un-PC speech. For example, any and all attempts to protect religious liberty are now lumped together as "normalizing" prejudice and bigotry.

But two can play this game. The Right has also begun to employ the term in its efforts to marginalize progressive policies advocated by the leading Democratic presidential contenders. Hence, the Left's relentless efforts to nullify the legal requirements of immigration enforcement (eliminate ICE, tear down borders walls) serve to "normalize" progressive immigration policy to America's detriment.

You can bet this increasingly popular verb will continue to be employed by both sides in light of our highly polarized election cycle.

"That's not us": A second cousin to "normalize," this brief phrase was first perfected by candidate and then-President Barack Obama during the GITMO/torture debates post-9/11. The words are of course intended to convey a sense of moral superiority on the one hand; moral depravity on the other.

In the tenor of that era, this meant that American values would never countenance torture or even non-torturous tough treatment, no matter the circumstances or intelligence to be gained.

Per the president, we were too civilized to indulge, which by definition meant that those who continued to defend the practice were…uncivilized.

Today, "that's not us" has expanded to include just about every political position rejected by progressives: free markets, abortion restrictions, gun rights, border enforcement, mandatory sentences, due process on campus, and religious liberty just to name a few.

Conservatives beware: "that's not us" remains a most effective rhetorical phrase, always intended to place conservatives on the defensive.

"Woke": The progressive group "Black Lives Matter" is credited with the popularity of the phrase in today's politics. The adjective is reportedly a term of African origin intended to convey deeper awareness of social and racial justice. Of course, progressives use "justice" as a one-way street: the term refers to a progressive awakening as to inequalities within American society, especially on issues relating to criminal justice reform and the disparities inherent in market capitalism.

Those of us who subscribe to another type of awakening—along the lines of appreciation for law enforcement, free speech rights, and the incredible wealth produced by capitalism are decidedly "un-woke." Wonder if I just made up a word?

"Aspirational": Most of us will recognize the use of this always positive adjective by those for whom reality has reared its ugly head. And sooner or later it always rears its ugly head.

The most recent (and illustrative) example concerns the almost comical overuse of the word in the aftermath of "Green New Deal" media events. It is best to think about GND media events as two-part occurrences. First, the highbrow lofty goals (peace on earth, equality, socialism, Fox News goes off the air) are announced with an air of breathless anticipation and widely covered by CNN, MSNBC, the *New York Times* and the *Washington Post*.

Then, comes the much less aspirational follow-up presser. Here, the advocates (sometimes) are able to indulge reality for a fleeting minute or two. They accordingly recognize that the immediate elimination of fossil fuels, airplanes, cows, and Sean Hannity may indeed be lofty, but must remain merely aspirational for now due to all those burger-eating closed-minded deplorables running to and from the pistol range in their gas-guzzling SUVs.

"Social Justice": This may be the most commonly employed phrase in today's progressive universe. What began as a catch-all phrase to encourage criminal sentencing and re-entry reform now means…anything progressives want it to mean. Lately, the likes of Kirsten Gillibrand have used it to "educate" working-class, blue-collar whites about their "enhanced" social/race status.

Unsurprisingly, this one did not fly very high. But this useful phrase will remain wildly popular because it seeks to guilt-trip anyone viewed as privileged into supporting just about any social remedy that degrades the privilege.

Can you say reparations?

Democrats' Lurch to the Left Is Unprecedented

Western Journal
December 30, 2019

For most of the 20th century (and the first decade of the 21st) both major political parties engaged in battles "between the 20s."

You know the phrase—where most plays from scrimmage are run in a typical football game. Candidates who possessed more extreme ideological positions typically picked up and went their own way (think Henry Wallace and Strom Thurmond in 1948, George Wallace in 1968, Ralph Nader in 2000).

The primary reason why both established parties could avoid "red zone" (closer to the end zone) candidates is clear: most of their respective bases would not stand for it.

Think about that last statement for a second. Even the most ideological candidates of the post-war era never dared question the basic assumptions (values) undergirding the American experience. To boot, when the voting public came to believe—rightly or wrongly—a particular candidate was too extreme, that candidate lost big (see Barry Goldwater in 1964 and George McGovern in 1972).

Today this history lesson is butting up against the reality of an ascendant (some would say dominant) progressive influence within the Democratic Party. You want to talk red-zone offense, well…take a quick glance at a typical Democratic party presidential debate. There you will find regular offerings of positions—foreign and domestic—that only a few precious years ago would have been anathema to major-party presidential candidates.

A good starting point is religious belief. For two centuries, a far less secular culture believed that religious practice constituted highly protected speech, despite occasional outlier lawsuits from the likes of the ACLU.

Not so much today, when just about every religious tradition and practice that contravenes progressive positions is labeled a "hate crime"; when the laws of the organized church are simply dismissed as a cover for discrimination against the no-judgment "values" of the new Left.

"American nationalism," a newly minted pejorative on the left, is another good example. Until very recently, blatant pro-Americanism was seen as a political asset. (Personally, I plead guilty—I root for America to win every Olympic medal, to lead the space race, to triumph over every despotic regime.)

Indeed, celebrations of all that is good and exceptional about America used to be blessed by both political parties. As I've written in previous columns, these celebrations of American successes were never intended to erase or excuse America's sins (slavery, Jim Crow, discrimination)—far from it. Most people believe America's shortcomings can and should be illuminated, the better that future stains can be avoided. But most adult Americans are also able to calibrate the shortcomings and the glories of America—an art that seems lost on those who work backward from the conclusion that America is evil and today seek to destroy parts of our history that are inappropriately un-woke.

Ironically, these are the same folks who so easily label patriotic, Trump-friendly deplorables as "fascists."

Perhaps the most perplexing narrative from the new progressivism is the simultaneous call for open borders and the denigration of the American blue-collar worker. Economics 101 teaches that an influx of cheap, illegal labor into local labor markets disproportionally hurts low- and semi-skilled American workers. In fact, it freezes their progression from working class to middle class dead in its tracks. Yet, progressives insist on inviting ever more unskilled workers to our shores—and our voting booths.

Moreover, the newfound animosity for even clean-burning fossil fuels (natural gas) has the likes of plain ole "Amtrak Joe" repeating Hillary Clinton's infamous dismissal of high-paying energy jobs in favor of a quixotic "Green New Deal." No wonder Western Pennsylvania and other energy-rich, rebounding regions in the midwest are running to Trump's call for "American energy independence." As for the opposition, is this really the same group that promised to listen and learn more about working-class voters after getting hammered in deplorable strongholds in 2016?

The intellectual arrogance of the campus left (so well documented by Democratic witnesses during the recent impeachment circus) may be the most subtle of the recent progressive drives into the red zone.

In retrospect, Hillary Clinton did everybody a big favor four years ago. Her "basket of deplorables" line both accurately captured the Left's contempt for middle America and provided those same voters with a handy reminder of how so many lefty intellectuals view those who still work with their hands.

One surmises that such condescension, often not so clearly stated, has always been the dominant view from within the ivory tower—it was just covered up when previous generations of deplorables constituted the core of the Democrats' New Deal coalition.

How interesting that the alleged elitist empathy that kept FDR's coalition together for decades has now morphed into an unhinged resentment of those same voters during the Trump era. A further question arises: What genius told the elitists that the best way to save or rehabilitate the great unwashed between the coasts was to repeatedly insult them and take their jobs? Talk about a game-changing fumble!

There Are No "Moderate" Democratic Presidential Candidates

Western Journal
February 26, 2020

I have a serious problem with the media, and it is not confined to the left-wing press.

My issue concerns the repeated identification of the major Democratic candidates for president (other than Sens. Sanders and Warren) as occupiers of the "middle lane" of our politics.

This prized middle ground is where Messrs. Biden, Buttigieg, and Bloomberg and Mrs. Klobuchar are alleged to live.

None of this "democratic socialist" nonsense for this crew; at times, one or more of them can even be heard speaking a few ritualistic words in defense of market capitalism or keeping one's private health insurance. For the Democratic establishment, this lane constitutes a nominally anti-socialist haven that may house the kryptonite required to defeat the irrepressible Mr. Trump in November.

Unfortunately, this con-job of a narrative is not limited to the usual suspects. Reliably conservative outlets such as Fox News and the *Wall Street Journal* also employ the moderate label for this group. I have no reasonable explanation for this indulgence.

A wake-up call is therefore in order: lifelong liberals are not miraculously transformed into middle-of-the-roaders simply because two uber-progressives have captured a significant portion of the Democratic Party's base.

In other words, despite the fact that most of humankind is to the right of Sanders and Warren, there still exists those who until very recently were known as "liberals."

Not so long ago, this proud group defined the Democratic Party. Their members occupied such a large lane within the party that every one of the Democratic candidates for president going back to 1968 happily owned the moniker. It was where The Honorable Hubert Humphreys, Walter Mondales, Mike Dukakises, John Kerrys, and yes, even Joe Bidens (circa 1980) lived.

On the policy front, these liberal leaders could be heard advocating for free speech on campus, due process, secure borders, assimilation, religious freedom, and working-class tax cuts. Some went as far as supporting (some) abortion restrictions. Others were "pro-gun" for a time (see the early Howard Dean and Bernie Sanders).

Still, this group always supported an aggressive federal role in our daily lives. Class-warfare rhetoric (the "evil" rich) was standard fare. Activist judges were their cup of tea. And there was always a call for a downsized military in exchange for increased domestic spending. (In the old vernacular, "Fewer guns, more butter.") As a result, conservatives always had plenty to fight them about.

Now fast-forward to the progressive crisis that is 2020's Democratic nominating process.

In this new world, *all* of the so-called moderates have raised their hands in support of free health care for illegal aliens, *all* of the moderates have called for gun registration and/or confiscation measures, *all* of the moderates have dismissed the concept of "religious freedom" as a mere dog whistle for homophobia and racism, and *all* of the moderates have called for the maintenance of sanctuary cities and the elimination or reconstituting of ICE.

You might add to this list a growing number of incongruous apologies issued by the likes of Biden and Bloomberg for past policy errors. The voting public has seen this movie before. Recall Hillary Clinton's latter-day apologies for past positions that are now deemed unacceptable to the progressive intelligentsia. Alas, that late-term conversion proved unconvincing.

Often forgotten in this race to identify heretofore liberals as moderates is the long-ignored, long-suffering conservative wing of the Democratic Party. This forlorn group, last seen on the back of milk cartons, is simply beaten down these days. Their social conservatism is no longer allowed in a party controlled by the PC police.

That many of them may have voted for President Trump (and other Republican presidential candidates before him) appears to be of no interest to the powers that be. To be sure, those who "feel the Bern" have no interest in conducting deplorable-focused listening tours throughout the heartland!

One thing you can take to the bank, however: if the Trump campaign does its job, millions of conservative Democrats will not be confused by the supposedly heavy traffic in the middle lane.

Those vehicles will simply be AOC and her "squad" cutting them off in the slow lane in order to swerve back to the far left—where most of this crowd truly belongs.

Dems Were Sliding toward Socialism Long Before Bernie

Western Journal
March 9, 2020

That the present campaign to stop Sen. Bernie Sanders is an all-hands-on-deck enterprise is without doubt. You may accordingly expect the

Democratic establishment to continue to use any and all tools at their disposal. Such is a natural response by a political party interested in self-preservation.

A portion of the forthcoming media coverage will focus on the internal machinations of party bosses to manipulate the rules in favor of former Vice President Joe Biden. It will be interesting to watch how the army of "Bernie Bros" reacts to these maneuvers.

Will it be a redux of 2016, when the candidate and his base proved acquiescent to the other big fish in the pond, a former first lady and U.S. senator, or will 2020 witness a backlash from the young, newly aggressive progressives that constitute Sanders' base? Any reaction short of full acceptance of their (and their candidate's) plight will assuredly damage Mr. Biden in November.

But the political maneuvering is but a sideshow compared to the realpolitik "come to Jesus" movement that the Bernie candidacy represents. To wit, "the Bern" and his acolytes are the logical (if unwelcome) culmination of the creeping social welfarism/quasi-socialism that has gained a substantial following within the Democratic Party over the last four decades.

This, of course, is a bitter pill for traditional liberals to swallow. After all, New Deal–style liberalism had been around for 80 years without devolving into a more sinister mutation. Accordingly, it is logical to ask, why now?

The answer lies in an important lesson I learned as a young legislator.

A conservative Democratic leader and mentor of mine (in the Maryland legislature) was always fond of asking bill sponsors about "next year's bill." In other words, if the bill at issue would expand the reach and means of government under this year's bill, was not the legislature just as likely to justify further expansion next year—and the next?

Invariably, the sponsor would deny the allegation—and then seek to do precisely what had been predicted the following year.

For a young legislator, it was a classic lesson in the way government grows, and typically to the detriment of liberty.

All of which brings us back to what has caused the Democratic establishment's head-on collision with the likes of Sanders-style "socialism." My conclusion: next year's bill has arrived—all at once. Take a look:

- What began as an "America needs a raise" movement to hike the minimum wage evolved into demands for a "living wage" and then into the "fight for $15." That this proposal is guaranteed to cost millions of marginal, low-skilled workers their jobs seems lost on the activists. Spoiler alert: Comrade Bernie is talking $20 to $25 an hour on the stump, but that's next year's bill…

- What began as lax enforcement at our southern border has now metastasized into calls for free health care for illegal aliens and the elimination of Immigration and Customs Enforcement. Note that these proposals have caught on despite consistent reports of illegal aliens committing violent acts against U.S. citizens. Now, numerous progressive jurisdictions are experimenting with allowing illegals to vote in municipal elections, a notion that was not so long ago—you guessed it—next year's bill.

- What began as standard class warfare rhetoric ("tax cuts for the rich") has evolved into calls for a return to Carter-era tax rates—and even demands for income caps in the private sector—as the Left advances the principle that government knows best how much money you should make. But, not to worry, that will be next year's bill.

- What began as calls to close the gun show "loophole" or limit the commercial purchase of firearms (and ammunition) has morphed into calls for a national gun registry and, in some quarters, mandatory "turn-ins" of certain types of semi-automatic weapons. You may have read that Joe Biden has tasked the always reliable Beto O'Rourke with this job—and, presumably, with leading the charge on behalf of next year's (confiscation) bill.

- What began as the pro-abortion movement's attempt to protect the *Roe v. Wade* status quo led to Obamacare's requirement for nuns to secure birth control and, more recently, support for expanding late-term abortion—even what appears to be infanti-cide—amid a new enthusiasm for an unfettered right to abortion on demand at any point in a pregnancy. Sounds like next year's bill to me…

I could go on, but you get the point. Modern progressivism has *accelerated* traditional liberal positions to their logical (illogical) conclusions. In the process, it has inflicted real damage on the Democratic brand. Will Joe Biden attempt to reign in these excesses or will voters be left to wonder about next year's progressive insult to our sensibilities?

Timely questions for a party coming to grips with its newly energized wild side.

Trump, Like Grant, Faces a Multi-Front Challenge

Western Journal
June 5, 2020

The excellent mini-series *Grant* (a must-see for any student of American history) analyzed General Ulysses S. Grant's ability to wage and win simultaneous military campaigns in different theaters of the Civil War.

The point is made—and history reflects—that Grant alone above all other Union generals possessed the right values and unique vision to get it done, all of which got me to thinking of how the politician and two-term President Grant would fare against the multi-front challenges facing President Trump.

True, Grant faced plenty of political challenges in his second public life, but maybe not as many as those confronting our 45th president. Talk about a daunting landscape…

A Divided Country

What was a polarized electorate prior to George Floyd's death is now further divided.

What began as appropriate outrage over a brutal death has disintegrated into nightly lawlessness. What could have been a national reminder of how negligent policing degrades the cause of justice became an excuse to rob and loot businesses and even kill police officers.

Ludicrous defenses of the chaos offered by so-called intellectuals and the familiar 24/7 narrative-driven coverage of the cable news networks, however, have also made things worse. Now, a president vehemently opposed by 45 percent of the voters is tasked with leading, healing, and governing this divided country.

The Democrats

Congressional Democrats took their role as the loyal opposition to heart from the very beginning of the Trump presidency.

In short order, the defeated Mrs. Clinton and the Democratic National Committee cried "voter suppression" with no supporting evidence.

This initial barrage was followed by challenges to the Electoral College itself and then a failed attempt at encouraging so-called faithless electors.

Next came questions regarding the president's mental health and then lawsuits alleging violations of the Constitution's Emoluments Clause. Still, all of this was a mere prologue to the three-year-long opera known as Russiagate, including a narrative that featured the targeting and persecution of an incoming national security advisor (General Mike Flynn) and Special Counsel Mueller's embarrassingly overhyped report.

Once that hoax was exhausted, a new investigation ("Ukrainegate") came about that led to only the third impeachment trial in U.S. history. Currently, the House is gathering materials from the early days of the administration's coronavirus response, presumably to again revisit a baseless narrative and maybe get yet another bite at the impeachment apple.

The Media

Suffice it to say the antagonism that began during the 2016 campaign now reaches new depths every day.

The Left's leading platforms (the *New York Times*, the *Washington Post*, MSNBC, CNN) have happily and aggressively assumed the leadership mantle despite having to retract or apologize for a variety of egregious reporting "mistakes."

For his part, the president has hit back in ways large and small. "Fake news" is now a part of our political vernacular. Without a doubt, the left-leaning media have been plenty put out by the president's belligerent approach. They had become acclimated to far more acquiescent behavior from GOP standard-bearers. Not so much Mr. Trump.

Federal Judges

To borrow a phrase from Ronald Reagan, the scariest words in the English language remain, "A federal judge today…"

Indeed, Obama-appointed activist judges have been the bane of numerous Trump-era executive orders. Judge-shopping is more in vogue than ever as it only takes one liberal judge to place a nationwide halt on executive actions.

But help is on the way. A new generation of originalist appointees (197 at last count) is now getting the federal judiciary back to the business of interpreting, rather than legislating, federal law. Accordingly, judicial selection may again be a front-burner issue come November.

The Billionaires

Progressive rich guys are the latest rage on the left.

And I'm not talking about George Soros. Why, even "lock-em-up" Michael Bloomberg had a liberal epiphany once he decided to run for the Democratic nomination.

But the political track record of the uber-wealthy is not so good. Starbucks' Howard Schultz, Farallon Capital's Tom Steyer, and the aforementioned Mr. Bloomberg enjoyed only brief and unsuccessful runs for president (Schultz never even made it to the starting block).

It's just tough to run against success, wealth, and entrepreneurship when you are successful, wealthy, and entrepreneurial.

But the rich guys all agree on one thing: that other rich guy Trump is a ne'er-do-well. Their progressive political action committees are spending millions of dollars to drive home the point.

Social Media Platforms

The pre-riots news was all about the back and forth between the president and his very own social media platform, Twitter.

The issue is not terribly complicated. To wit: How much censorship can a social media platform exercise without placing its liability shield in legal jeopardy?

That Silicon Valley has been vehemently anti-Trump from the beginning (and is a breeding ground for all shapes and sizes of political correctness) promises to make this yet another election-year fight.

The Campuses

Polls reflect the enormous success that progressive administrators and professors have enjoyed in their campaign to degrade free speech, and in the words of one pundit in the Daily Caller, "crush" conservatism and conservatives in academia.

As a result, the First Amendment is out of favor at our nation's institutions of higher learning.

If you doubt me, try wearing a MAGA hat on just about any college campus. Then, prepare for the worst. You may rest assured that the considerable powers of America's campus-based elites will be brought to bear against Mr. Trump when classes reconvene in September.

Joe Biden's sudden pivot to the hard-left will only further energize these folks.

General Grant passed his multi-front test with flying colors. The president must now do the same.

The Left Has Completely Abandoned Free Speech

Western Journal
June 17, 2020

What theory of governance encourages the banning and burning of books, coerces agreement with its central tenets, practices revisionist history, perfects virtue-signaling, disparages dissenting opinion, invents social constructs to minimize speech, indoctrinates gullible students, revels in civil disobedience, holds idealistic appeal for young people, specializes in utopian platitudes, and never, to be charitable, quite works?

If you guessed socialism—or its cousin, fascism—go to the head of the class. If you guessed anything else, you are likely a victim of progressive instruction at a tender age. But can you spot the missing element in these descriptions?

The answer, of course, is freedom—a response that is unfortunately not so automatic for so many of our educated elites.

Indeed, there is a reason that so many of the really smart people are so often the ground troops for the latest iteration of authoritarianism. These folks tend to dismiss the uniquely American principles of limited government and individual liberty, values that have been far out of fashion with a tremendously high percentage of those who have been administering and instructing on our college campuses for decades now.

But the dangers associated with taking our way of life for granted is nothing new.

A number of our more important leaders have cautioned about this attitude for years. Why, ol' Ben Franklin famously admonished us that we indeed had a republic "if you can keep it."

Two centuries later, President Ronald Reagan reminded us that the loss of liberty is "never more than one generation away from extinction."

Perhaps the most prescient lesson came from the revered Australian economist Friedrich Hayek, who opined in *The Intellectuals and Socialism* (1949):

It may be that a free society as we have known it carries in itself the forces of its own destruction, that once freedom has been achieved it is taken for granted and ceases to be valued, and that the free growth of ideas which is the essence of a free society will bring about the destruction of the foundations on which it depends.

Not so long ago, Right and Left wholeheartedly agreed with these thoughts. Free speech was sacrosanct, especially after it provided the intellectual fuel for the transformative movements of the 1960s: civil rights, women's rights, the anti-war movement. You can bet that few of today's "safe zone"–friendly college students know that Berkeley, California, was the epicenter for free speech circa 1968.

But a dangerous turn occurred approximately twenty years later, about the time most Americans naively hoped that the fall of the Berlin Wall and the Soviet Union would end Western intellectuals' fascination with socialism.

On the contrary: a renewed appreciation for authoritarianism and its offspring, speech control, began to take root. Even as new autocratic regimes popped up in Central and South America and a reconstituted Russia once again returned to its despotic ways, it became increasingly acceptable to degrade diverse opinions in America—especially within the academy.

Free speech advocates of different political philosophies began to worry and write about the problem (think Bill Buckley on the right, Christopher Hitchens on the left).

But then another important corner was turned: liberals began to disengage from the fight. Their silence created a vacuum and further energized progressives who were as willing to indict Democratic liberals as they were conservative Republicans. Here, dogmatism recognized no party labels.

As time wore on, more of these progressives challenged traditional Democrats in their "safe" seats. A few won. More importantly, liberals got the message. Most stayed quiet as the campaign to denigrate and even eviscerate free speech gained momentum.

All of which brings us to our present conundrum, and a personal note.

Being born and raised in Maryland meant early and relentless exposure to left-leaning blue-state politics. Nevertheless, I repeatedly challenged the status quo during my public life, winning and losing campaigns in the process.

But rare was the circumstance in which an opponent would attempt to silence me, to make it politically and socially unacceptable to espouse my positions. Most would never have thought to degrade an opponent in such a manner. That would have been the demagogue's way out. They would rather have won the argument on its merits.

Today, times are a-changin'—and not for the better.

The Real Joe

Western Journal
July 14, 2020

Maybe this time the traditional old rule applies: "It's all about the incumbent." Or, more precisely, "It's only about the incumbent."

Such an arrangement seems suitable to all. Per former Virginia Gov. Terry McAuliffe, the Democrats and their media enablers: the less coming from Joe's basement, the better.

It follows that little else about presumptive Democratic presidential nominee Joe Biden is deemed particularly newsworthy—not his procrastination in making his VP pick, not his platform, not his son's questionable ethics, not his neurological instead of mental health, not his barely visible campaign structure.

NeverTrumpers of both parties are also on board. They are determined to keep the focus on all (negative) things Trump. And so far, so good. A man who has serious difficulties stringing two sentences together or finishing thoughts is up 9 points over President Donald Trump in the latest Real Clear Politics average. Who would have thunk?

Still, it is difficult to believe this status quo will hold for another 115 days. A couple of percentage points worth of undecideds are always available in the up-for-grabs purple states. At some point, these voter-kingmakers will look to the current status of Joe's "big ideas"—the prominent policies that have defined his public career. Here is a sampling of what will they find:

Busing

1970s-era school integration was met with a decided lack of enthusiasm in many Northern precincts. Biden reflected this selective taste for civil rights in his public pronouncements. But perhaps unsurprisingly, the young senator's otherwise solid liberal credentials made the memory of this stance disappear over time.

Even now, the mainstream media is remarkably uninterested in this unsavory chapter of the Biden saga.

Parenthetical thought: imagine the consternation among the media if a young Senator Trump had the same stain on his early public record...

China

Robert Gates, who was defense secretary under President Barack Obama, put it most succinctly when he observed that Biden "has been wrong on nearly every major foreign policy and national security issue over the past four decades." This indictment is especially accurate with respect to China.

Besides acquiescing to Beijing's coronavirus narrative, Biden has regularly dismissed the notion that we should be concerned about China's economic sabotage: "They are not competition for us.... China is going to eat our lunch? Come on, man." Come on man, indeed.

1994 Crime Bill

It may be easy to forget today, but Rep. Newt Gingrich and an energized Republican base were just waiting to pounce on a weakened Bill Clinton and congressional Democrats as the 1994 midterms approached.

The suddenly defensive Democrats were accordingly intent on strengthening their tough on crime bona fides—which they did in the form of the 1994 crime bill. Notably, the legislation did nothing to fix the disparate weight ratio between crack (then an allegedly black drug) and powder (then an allegedly white drug) cocaine required to trigger enhanced criminal penalties. Hence was born a rallying cry for the Congressional Black Caucus that lasted until the Fair Sentencing Act was passed in 2010.

In the end, Biden helped create the problem; he had no part in its resolution.

Green New Deal

Biden's handlers have been smart enough to distance him from a full-scale endorsement. Yet the campaign has been strong in its condemnation of the fossil fuels economy.

It is fair to conclude that "Scranton Joe" opposes Western Pennsylvania's natural gas revolution and the thousands of union jobs that have been produced by new drilling technology.

America's newfound energy independence under President Trump is real. All those Pittsburgh-based union Democrats have a right to know if Joe intends to close them down—as do all voters.

Obamacare

Live mics captured the VP's inappropriate quip ("This is a big f—in' deal") to President Obama at the news conference to celebrate passage of the Affordable Care Act ("Obamacare"). Biden's enthusiasm was not replicated by an American public who actually had to participate.

A faulty website and accompanying negative media coverage may have been the high watermark as millions of Americans soon learned that they could not, contrary to promise after promise after consistently undiluted promise, "keep their doctor...or their insurance."

In the end, Obamacare was utilized to expand Medicaid coverage far beyond poor people and into the lower working class. It also became a symbol of government mismanagement—and GOP pick-ups—over four election cycles.

Notably, Biden has not made health care a cornerstone of his 2020 campaign.

Education

The union-dependent senator from Delaware has been in lockstep with national teachers unions for his entire career. Just last week, Biden bragged that his White House would have at least one dues-paying NEA member—his wife, Jill Biden.

It is accordingly clear that the important—and wildly successful for the less well-to-do—charter school and school choice movement under the Trump administration would be brought to an abrupt end with the Bidens in power. As usual, predominately poor African American and Hispanic children would be the unfortunate losers.

Second Amendment

Consistent support for just about any gun control measure that comes down the pike is a required entry on every liberal Democrat's resume. That the measures typically only impact law-abiding citizens—not the criminal element—is rarely made part of the discussion.

But Biden's recent gun rhetoric is three degrees deeper. How else to characterize his decision to place the embarrassing former Texas Rep. Beto O'Rourke in charge of his future administration's gun confiscation program?

I have purposely not included the long (and getting longer by the day) list of Biden's faux pas here. Even in his heyday, "Amtrak Joe" was a bit goofy, prone to the inappropriate remark. Today, his recurrent inability to speak coherently is both unfunny and uncomfortable and genuinely worrisome should he become president.

But that's the small stuff. Here's hoping those late undecideds will step back and take a long look at the big stuff—the kind of stuff that makes or breaks campaigns in the Heartland.

What the Left Is Doing Right Now Will Never End, Even if You Give In

Western Journal
July 30, 2020

Maybe it's time to reacquaint ourselves with Ronald Reagan's "A Time for Choosing" speech.

The 40th president's words sought to ensure that we would never have to teach our children what America was like "when men were free." Mr. Reagan knew true liberty was an anomaly in human history, that despotism tends to survive despite its history of suffering and brutality.

Maybe it's also time for Republicans to suck it up, to remind ourselves that politics is not a game of perfect (to borrow a phrase) and that even the most popular political leaders are flawed.

This thought should be kept in mind when weighing the binary decision that looms on Nov. 3.

And then maybe it's time for millions of relatively silent Democrats who are appalled by the direction of their party to take it back, to reject the underreported devastating violence of the looters, the insanity of the "defund the police" movement, and the unbridled antagonism toward America and American history.

Maybe the foregoing is simply too much to expect. I hope not. Americans are typically optimistic, especially in challenging times.

I cling to hope despite a historic pandemic and a racial divide that threatens the very underpinnings of our culture.

Think about that last observation for a second. A country that has triumphed over slavery, reconstruction, segregation, and Jim Crow now faces a progressive movement that has moved far beyond the noble demands of equal rights for its citizens.

Indeed, one hears little about police training and retraining and appropriate response in minority communities these days (and nothing relating to those matters in the mainstream media).

Instead, we are subjected to anarchy and violence, brought to your town primarily by angry, young, white progressives and tolerated by Democratic mayors. These children of the well-to-do, having been well-indoctrinated on revolutionary theory on campus, now strike at the very fabric of American values.

By now, all of us should have learned to take this campaign seriously.

The stated goal of these revolutionaries is transformation, which is to be achieved through speech and thought control. Remember, these young people have been indoctrinated into the world of speech codes, trigger warnings, and safe spaces—all in the interest of protecting them from opposing views.

These constructs empower the notion that contrary or unpopular opinions could be fairly outlawed, simply forbidden from public discourse because such viewpoints constitute "hate speech."

Underpinning it all is a new "right": the right not to be upset or inconvenienced by disagreeable speech, people, or history. And so the brilliance of the Founding Fathers, the uniqueness of the Constitution, the foundational values of our Judeo-Christian heritage, the centrality of religious belief and practice, the benefits of capitalism, and the beauty of liberty need to be "canceled" because human beings are flawed and so is their history.

For the riotous malcontents, the present drama does not end with the removal of statues or the adoption of revisionist history. It will never end.

Theirs is an endless list of demands, a lesson lately learned by their heretofore big-city mayor benefactors who now face a hard truth: revolutionaries are never mollified.

Accordingly, the demands multiply, from open borders to the elimination of ICE to voting rights for illegal immigrants to a war on fossil fuels to a downsized military ("defund the Pentagon") to confiscatory tax rates.

A compliant press, energized academy, and newly woke professional sports leagues and business communities are all in. The Right is seething, but currently quiet, as are centrist Democrats. Yet, at the end of the day, all this energy and activism is represented by the basement-dwelling Joe Biden.

Openly aligned against the former vice president and his enablers are Fox News, talk radio, right-leaning websites (including this one), and Donald J. Trump. And the people who watch Fox, listen to talk radio, and read these websites tend to live between the coasts, work hard, attend religious services, wish their children better lives than theirs, and strongly reject the out-of-control chaos infecting many of our largest cities.

Still, the election presents a perplexing problem for those who demand a return to normalcy but have decidedly mixed feelings about this president.

This is the relatively small, all-important cadre of Republicans, Democrats, and independents who generally like what the president has accomplished but do not like or appreciate how he goes about his daily business. I hear from many of them. They desire an "option C," but none is available. Hence, the aforementioned binary decision.

I, for one, choose order over chaos, law over criminality, sovereignty over open borders, capitalism over socialism, speech over silence, raw honesty over political correctness, and hope over fear. Here's hoping that 270 electoral votes will emerge with a similar calculus.

Biden Has Broken a Longstanding American Tradition & It May Cost Him the Election

Western Journal
August 13, 2020

"If I'm elected and this [plan for racial economic equality] passes, I'm going to go down as one of the most progressive presidents in American history."—Joe Biden

The 2016 campaign saw President Trump break with alacrity all of the traditional rules of presidential politics.

He ran as the anti-politician, more on a cult of personality, as an outsider with a small staff and little organization, using social media to challenge the establishments of both political parties.

He promised he would be the bull in the swamp's china shop. By any measure, he has accomplished that goal: swamp creatures of all ilks simply hate him. The accompanying vitriol directed his way daily is one measure of his success.

A different type of tradition is being broken this year.

It concerns the time-honored rule that candidates run to their base in the primaries, but turn to the middle come the general.

But "Biden 2020" is proving the exception. His advisers evidently see little gold to be gained in those moderate hills.

As a result, this latest iteration of Joe Biden has veered left from the jump—and kept on going. In the process, he has convinced the Democratic Party's progressive stars to enthusiastically join his parade.

Check it out. Beto O'Rourke eagerly leads on gun confiscation. Alexandria Ocasio Cortez happily on the environment. Bernie Sanders with ominous self-assurance he can affect Biden on health care—and just about every other important plank as well.

Reliably progressive VP selection Kamala Harris fits in perfectly with this crowd.

This progressive juggernaut then asks you to engage in a new game: "Imagine."

But this is no John Lennon song. It's more like ordering à la carte off a menu of "defund options," where you can choose to defund the local police department, a federal police agency such as ICE, the Pentagon, or your local charter school.

Biden even defends the feckless Democratic mayors who have with cringeworthy diffidence allowed their cities to burn rather than cooperate with Trump-led federal police agencies.

As recently as four years ago, this path would have been seen as McGovern 2.0—and a surefire way to re-elect a Republican president.

American voters have traditionally operated "between the 20s." For what purpose would a major-party candidate recklessly enter the socialist red zone?

But this is 2020. Nothing is traditional.

Big business is officially woke. Political correctness is now mandatory.

And so Joe Biden feels free to race down the progressive highway, ignoring the speed limit and the police. Indeed, law enforcement and the corrections system have but a very small space in his new world order.

The primary reason for this strategy is the opponent.

Biden's handlers know that Mr. Trump is polarizing; no one would argue to the contrary. They also know that the pandemic and resulting shutdowns have inflicted real damage on the president and put the American people in a sour mood.

And so why not make the election a referendum on the incumbent?

Why not hide out in your basement and only emerge for the occasional controlled, lollypop interview? Why not run as if "Trump" is the only name on the ballot?

Of course, this strategy only works in conjunction with a compliant media, one that would allow a presidential candidate to avoid difficult questions, one that would never ask why the candidate's current positions are so at odds with his 35-year voting record in the Senate, one that would acquiesce to a presidential campaign without debates (as Biden has now been repeatedly asked to do by Democratic principals.)

There is one other reason for the hide-(and seldom)-seek strategy. It has to do with Mr. Biden's apparent difficulty in spontaneous speaking.

The media repeatedly refuses to acknowledge the 800-pound elephant in the room. But even the Biden campaign's de minimis strategy has produced its share of gaffes—unforced errors and contradictions, e.g., on police defunding, that will be magnified should Mr. Biden ever find himself (sans teleprompter) required to fend off personal attacks from one Donald J. Trump.

(How would you like to be the Biden staffer who has to trot out Mr. Biden's "clarifications" after each interview goes off the rails?)

You now better understand why so many prominent Democratic strategists have opined, even publicly, against Mr. Biden's participation in direct debate.

Biden's no-show strategy has worked relatively well to this point in time. Still, whether a presidential candidate in 2020 can win while running an invisible and hard-left campaign remains an open question.

If the combined power of the swamp can pull this one off, God help us.

Here's a Great Option for Sticking It to the Left without Giving In to Cancel Culture

Western Journal
August 6, 2020

You are a conservative, God-fearing, law-abiding citizen. You pay your bills, love your family, give to charity and root for the U.S. to win every medal at the Olympics. You still tear up while watching "Miracle" for the tenth time.

But your world has been turned upside down.

A pandemic has upended the economy, chilling the hottest market in decades. Major cities burn, but their Democratic mayors seem more interested in scoring political points than quieting the streets. Bizarrely, the destructive rioting is no more than touched on in major media.

Daily, you watch 20-something young women spout F-bombs at African American police officers whom the women wish to "defund."

A husband and wife "caught" defending their home with firearms in the face of an encroaching large mob are themselves arrested and charged. You cannot turn on a sporting event or watch a movie or comedy show without receiving a political message smack in your face. College professors are disciplined or even fired for spouting politically incorrect (conservative) opinions.

Your kids are not going back to school. Your neighborhood associa- tion sent you a warning for failing to wear a face mask—while walking your dog. You can no longer have a civil political discussion with your neighbor. Your normal excitement at the prospect of another NFL season has soured; you will take a knee instead of watching on Sundays.

Then, you learn of a recent CATO Institute poll that reflects 62 percent of the American public is intimidated about expressing political opinion. Yep, a revealing 52 percent of liberals and an astonishing 77 percent of conservatives say that they are afraid to exercise their First Amendment right to freedom of speech.

You are next asked to swallow that Joe Biden is now ahead by 5–10 points—as if those last two numbers are unrelated.

All of this puts you in a bad mood. Your sense of humor suffers as well. You mutter to yourself constantly. It seems there is no escape from the daily pounding. All of which leads to two possible options.

Option One is to further a nascent right-wing cancel culture.

Here, you have unlimited options. Boycotts of lefty actors are easy as 98 percent of Hollywood tilts hard left. But bypassing periodic viewing of *The Office* (Steve Carell has gone off the rails) might prove more difficult.

You now have a menu of professional woke sports leagues to tune out. Bypassing the usual media suspects (MSNBC, CNN, the *New York Times*, the *Washington Post*) is another easy task. After all, how much spinning narrative (as opposed to hard news) can one person bear?

Still, your general optimism about life—and America—does not easily lend itself to *negative* action. You are an optimist by nature; boycotts, protests, riots, and civil unrest are counterculture activities, not your cup of tea.

Just ask yourself: When was the last time the College Republicans took over a university president's office? If any such incident did go down, it was to redecorate the place, not burn it down.

And so I have been thinking about an Option Two—a positive, boycott-less path to protest the attempted dismantling of our culture.

Just within the last week, I have daily purchased Goya cookies at our local Wawa. (I never thought the mere purchase of cookies would be so liberating.)

Also at Wawa (yes, guilty, I am there every day) I bought lunch for a guy dressed in a Capitol Police uniform. He appreciated but objected to my gesture until I reminded him that he had protected me for eight years on Capitol Hill.

I also asked my police friends what police-supporting organization they would recommend. A check was soon in the mail.

Speaking of contributions, there are many effective organizations dedicated to the restoration of free speech on campus. The Leadership Institute and Young America's Foundation are two that come to mind. Support them.

My wife will shortly make another purchase from "MyPillow"—the company that stepped up when the Twitter mob attempted to take down Fox's leading political shows. It and other Fox advertisers should be supported.

And then there is "Black Rifle Coffee Company." What a great idea: a group of veterans banding together to sell coffee to "people who love America." Count me in.

The foregoing is a brief sampling of steps you might choose when considering your options in opposition to progressive chaos and the undemocratic strategies of taking away constitutional guarantees of freedom of speech and freedom of assembly for conservative citizens.

There is no perfect response, but I bet you'll feel better after doing something.

Oh, and one more thing: cast your ballot for the Republican ticket on Nov. 3.

Make it known you want your life back—and that you are not going to put up with the mob and its cancel culture campaign. After all, another four years for you-know-who is the ultimate payback.

Trump Is Robbing Democrats of Their Base Across the Country

Western Journal
September 21, 2020

Voters are being called to "reimagine" an awful lot these days, but one major development is profound and occurring in real time.

I refer to the ongoing realignments within both of our major political parties.

Think about it. Big business has been a stalwart GOP ally for decades. Indeed, many congressional Democrats correctly viewed the U.S. Chamber of Commerce as nothing more than a wing of the Republican party.

Even moderate Democrats had difficulty securing the Chamber's attention—and fundraising prowess. The focus was always on the speakership—which party would control the House—and few Democrats were willing to cast *that* vote against their own leadership.

Today, we operate in a vastly different dimension. A social issue–driven Wall Street is fertile territory for Democratic fundraising. Check out Joe Biden's Wall Street contributions for context. But the most remarkable (and rapid) change has been a large segment of the business culture ready, willing, and able to spend billions in order to virtue-signal their newfound wokeness.

Look no further than a happily progressive NFL for evidence.

The average person may find this confusing, but there is context.

Think of your college-aged children. Many parents go into debt in order for their son or daughter to attend an expensive university. The institution uses your tuition dollars to pay professors, many of whom then make it their business to indict your traditional values—the ones you have spent seventeen years instilling in your kids.

You are nevertheless supposed to feel good about the indoctrination, err, education, even if your once-polite child now deems it socially acceptable to riot, loot, and scream F-bombs at police officers. Biting the hand that feeds you it surely is—a lesson big business will learn too late should Mr. Biden be elected.

Another Trump-generated dilemma concerns trade policy.

In the modern era, at least, the GOP has been the party of free trade. For their part, Democrats have proudly heralded their union-driven protectionist positions. But here again, the tables have turned.

Trump's GOP has developed a taste for bilateral trade and punishing tariffs, especially in regard to a predatory and perpetually cheating China, while Democrats have taken to singing the praises of mega, multi-lateral trade agreements.

As cited above, a more Democrat-friendly business community is one tangible result, but so is a blue-collar, working-class voter far more open to Trump's Republican party and conservatism.

This tradeoff really counts. There are outsized numbers of these Democrats (once called "deplorables" by you-know-who) in the vital blue-leaning states of Pennsylvania, Michigan, and Wisconsin.

A third realignment pertains to law enforcement, but the significant change here is limited to the Democrats.

A police-friendly GOP has long been the norm, despite resistance from some union leadership types more preoccupied with union rather than public safety issues. But recent events have diminished even this remnant of FDR's New Deal coalition. Almost daily, the media reports yet another Trump police union endorsement, including some who have bravely retracted their Democratic support to do so.

What other choice do they have? The Democratic Party's remaining moderates are reticent to show support for the blue, given the possibility of retribution from the "defund" wing of the party. Recent well-publicized resignations of high-profile female African American police chiefs reflect the frustration and angst of police leaders—and the depth of anti-police sentiment among progressives within the party.

This may be one explanation for Mr. Trump's recent relatively high approval numbers with African Americans. Poll after poll has shown that a large majority of black Americans oppose efforts to defund police in their communities, one as high at 84 percent. No surprise here. Law enforcement is most needed in our most vulnerable communities.

And then there is perhaps the most startling realignment of all. A suddenly dovish GOP, recently forsaken by numerous high-profile neo-cons, now opposes an internationalist Democratic Party invested in military adventures around the world.

There are caveats: Trump's defense acolytes will spend heavily on hardware (especially where military sales to allies are concerned) and personnel, while ascendant progressives continue to control the anti-war wing of the Democratic Party. Still, the attitudinal changes are surprising, given where the respective parties were a mere four years ago.

The bottom line: the profound differences between the parties are real, and anything but static. Blame or praise the "Great Disruptor" for all the commotion. He would have it no other way.

CHAPTER 9

CHINA, COVID-19 & TRADE

The economy's impressive three-year "Trump Bump" ran head on into an insurmountable obstacle—the coronavirus. Seemingly overnight, state shutdown orders quieted America's consumer-driven economy. The Dow plunged from historic highs to a bear market (down 10,000 points). The NBA cancelled the remainder of its regular season, and the NCAA shut down March Madness—and spring athletic schedules. Hundreds of thousands of American college students were told to leave campus, while federal and state political leaders instructed Americans to begin practicing "social distancing." "Stay at Home" orders were issued by most of America's governors. By mid-March, millions of America's "non-essential businesses" were forced to shutter.

A primetime presidential address from the Oval Office failed to calm the markets and a jittery public. One thing that remained status quo however was the partisan divide. Here, it was business as usual—and a sorry reflection of the state of American politics. How else to characterize a Democratic response to the president's early travel restrictions ("nativist," "racist") that morphed into "not enough" a mere three weeks later?

In the short term at least, COVID-19 accomplished what Russiagate, Ukrainegate, and all of the other resistance-inspired "gates" had failed to do—place the indefatigable president on defense.

Indeed, Mr. Trump's early words of optimism concerning the depth and duration of the pandemic were repeatedly criticized by media and political opponents as daily media briefings produced ever more dire predictions regarding the length and severity of the outbreak. Soon thereafter, the usually optimistic salesman Trump began to adopt a decidedly more stern demeanor at press briefings.

The federal government's considerable arsenal of fiscal tools was brought to bear as the Fed cut its benchmark rate by 1 percent (close to zero after an emergency cut 14 days prior). The central bank further announced a program of unlimited asset purchases and set up three loan facilities to support employees, businesses, and consumers. For its part, Congress passed four packages of bipartisan relief. Phase One targeted $8 billion for tests and treatment. Phase Two included $104 billion for paid emergency leave and nutritional assistance to families. But these initial steps failed to stem a tidal wave of business closings and new unemployment claims. Some economists predicted a severe recession—an unthinkable notion a mere month prior.

In further response, Congress passed a $2 trillion Phase Three relief package—the largest fiscal rescue package in U.S. history. The bill was initially blocked by House Democrats agitating for a long list of progressive policy initiatives. The proposed add-ons added up to nothing more than a left-wing wish list, including limits on ICE and the border patrol, same-day voter registration, carbon offsets directed to the airlines, grants to the Kennedy Center and the National Foundation for the Arts and Humanities, solar and wind energy credits, a postal service bailout, and a $15 minimum wage.

In the end, this third relief tranche (entitled the "Cares Act") funded $260 billion in unemployment insurance benefits; allocated $349 billion in loans for the "Paycheck Protection Program" (PPP, targeted to businesses with less than 500 employees to cover payroll expenses—loans to be forgiven where used to cover payroll); $250 billion in direct payments to individuals and children (including $1,200 to most adults and $500 to most children); $150 billion to states and localities; and $150 billion to hospitals for equipment and infrastructure.

When the PPP depleted its $349 billion in less than two weeks, Congress passed an additional round of funding to the tune of $310 billion, as well as $50 billion in Small Business Administration economic disaster loans and $10 billion in direct grants.

Once government-mandated shutdowns of those businesses deemed non-essential were accomplished, it did not take long for the American economy to crater. An historically low unemployment rate of 3.5 percent in February soared to 14.7 percent by the end of March. Even the infusion of trillions of dollars into the economy by Congress and the Fed could not keep tens of thousands of small businesses out of harm's way: bankruptcies and layoffs began to skyrocket. As spring began to bloom, two developments offered promise: (1.) the infection curve in most states began to flatten; and (2.) epidemiologists and medical professionals began to downgrade their virus-generating morbidity rates. The virus was proving to be highly transmissible but not nearly as life-threatening to otherwise healthy people. Indeed, it soon became clear that young people and healthy adults were at minimal risk for severe illness, while the elderly and those suffering from medical pre-conditions were far more susceptible to complications from the virus. Accordingly, states and localities with low infection rates began to (incrementally) reopen, albeit with appropriate personal protection and social distancing guidelines in place.

Unsurprising, red state governors took up the reopening mantel with greater frequency and enthusiasm than their blue state counterparts. These decisions in turn sparked increasingly hostile "reopening" protests in blue state capitals—and along the (closed) beach communities of ultra-blue California.

The reopening/shutdown policies of the respective chief executives reflected the ongoing philosophical differences between the two major parties. To wit: one group instinctively looked to market capitalism to revive their suddenly hurting state economies, while the other instinctively preferred continued government control—extended lockdowns and additional government sponsored bailouts as recovery efforts began.

The contrast played out in similar fashion at the national level with the president and GOP congressional leaders applauding the administration's early travel ban on China and its suggested three-tier process for state reopenings, while candidate Biden and Democratic leaders fretted about how America had been ill-prepared for a pandemic that was rapidly becoming the central narrative in the race for the White House.

Predictably, House Democrats offered a $3 trillion additional funding round (the "Heroes Act") with $875 billion targeted to state and local governments—a reprise of the earlier $1200 direct payment to qualifying individuals—and an extension (until the end of 2020) of the $600 per week federal unemployment benefit contained in the "Cares Act"—in addition to still more progressive priorities (so-called "vote harvesting," prohibitions on voter identification, cannabis "diversity directors"). Fiscal conservatives noted the first three tranches of coronavirus relief totaled $3.6 trillion compared to a total federal budget of $4 trillion in 2019. The coronavirus pandemic got even more expensive for Uncle Sam when an additional $900 billion aid package was signed into law on December 27, 2020, thereby providing a second round of stimulus checks ($600 per child and adult) after prolonged negotiations between the president and House Democrats…

Another of the many high stakes China-involved issues was highly anticipated trade negotiations with China. The backdrop fit Mr. Trump's now-familiar indictment: an indulgent West had allowed a third world economy to grow into a first world competitor. Here, as elsewhere, the charge was lodged against *both* party establishments. Indeed, no feelings were spared as the administration asked why trade representatives of both parties had stood by as the Chinese unfairly subsidized their state-owned industries, all the while engaging in large-scale economic espionage through relentless theft of American intellectual property.

The on again/off again meetings between U.S. Trade representative Robert Lighthizer, Treasury Secretary Mnuchin, and China's lead negotiator, Vice Premier Liu He, were closely watched as either positive or negative reports were reflected in real time by stock markets around the globe. A Republican president's ready preference for tariffs added to the intensity and uniqueness of the negotiations. Here was a president at once striking at the heart of the GOP's free trade establishment (a.k.a. the U.S. Chamber of Commerce) while placing a key political constituency (midwestern farmers) at risk of retaliatory moves by the Chinese. A plainly nervous GOP caucus cautiously stood by their unconventional leader. But for how long?

Lessons Learned from Coronavirus

Western Journal
March 24, 2020

Three questions to contemplate while you are taking a break from your daily telecommute:

1. Where have all the open border zealots gone now that our country is in virtual lockdown due to a worldwide contagion?
2. Why a sudden case of media amnesia regarding Joe Biden's claim that the president's early travel restrictions on China constituted "hysterical xenophobia"?
3. I wonder what Golden State Warriors Coach Steve Kerr ("Mr. Moral Equivalence" on China) and superstar LeBron James ("Mr. Misinformed" about human rights in Hong Kong) now think of the Chinese government's lies and distortions regarding the depth, size, and origin of the COVID-19 virus?

Rhetorical questions, yes, but nevertheless timely queries—and lessons—for an America that just may graduate from this pandemic with important, realpolitik lessons learned in dealing with challenges presented by America's most formidable foe.

First, a background reminder for those who have been transfixed by the media's relentless focus on Russia (and Ukraine) for the past three years: Donald Trump won the presidency in large part due to deep heartland angst over questionable trade deals and the demise of America's industrial base.

An important but generally ignored subtext was Mr. Trump's telling inquiry as to why the most powerful nation on earth insisted on treating its fastest-growing competitor (China) as a third world power? In the process, Chamber of Commerce Republicans and indulgent one-world progressives were exposed—to their great frustration.

You may take that last sentence as an understatement.

On the right, free-trade establishment types saw Mr. Trump's unabashed nationalism and (feelings-be-damned) tariff threats as proof of an uncomprehending mind, more interested in scoring cheap political points than understanding the complexities of free trade.

On the left, the celebrity casino owner was similarly dismissed as an intellectual lightweight and further condemned as a xenophobe and nativist to boot. Both sides remained rather unimpressed, even dismissive of the pleas of flyover country laborers who still work with their hands.

Further to the point, the mainstream media and Russia-obsessed lefties never understood that Mr. Trump was primarily focused on our most serious opponent/economic competitor/situational ally—China—from the jump.

Recall the new president's first major policy pronouncement: he would reappraise America's "One China Policy."

Both party establishments blanched, and the Left immediately assumed "Trump Derangement Syndrome." A familiar refrain began: we told you he was crazy—he is going to start a war with the Chinese. But buried beneath the short-lived, shot-across-the-bow initiative was a new president's desire to secure China's immediate attention. The president needed Chinese President Xi Jinping to intervene with North Korea's saber-rattling Kim Jong Un.

Shortly thereafter came a sustained Trump administration attack on America's ever-spiraling, out-of-control trade deficit with China—a fact of life even conservative economists had minimized for years.

Not so Mr. Trump.

China's willingness to engage in currency manipulation and the wholesale theft of American intellectual property became battering rams in a protracted trade negotiation that achieved phase-one success in January but reserved more difficult issues for a forthcoming phase-two negotiation later this year.

All of which brings us back to a dangerous virus strain that has its genesis in the Chinese city of Wuhan—a virus outbreak that was negligently covered up and foisted on the world by an autocratic government that simply could not get ahead of its own lies. A worldwide health crisis and many thousands of deaths are the unfortunate results.

At some point, of course, this too shall pass. Once it is mostly over, here's hoping the president will take the opportunity to again utilize his bully pulpit—similar to the way he postured China into engaging with North Korea and entering into a trade summit.

Specifically, there are two important takeaways from this brutal go-around with the Chinese politburo:

1. A timely reminder for a suddenly socialism-accepting America that no socialist or communist state can replicate the cleansing transparency of Western democracies—real looks behind the dictator's curtain will always reveal the negligence, heavy-handedness, and brutality (how many critics of the Chinese government's response have recently vanished?) of autocratic rule.

2. Perhaps it's not so xenophobic or nationalistic to question why America's essential medical supply chains remain captive to a hostile power that in recent days has openly threatened to leverage its pharmacological manufacturing advantage against the U.S.

That the wannabe diplomats from the NBA may also learn a lesson here is without doubt. I wonder if Messrs. Kerr and James now know there are over one million ethnic Turkic Muslims (primarily Uyghurs) imprisoned against their will in the Chinese gulag?

On second thought, I think I know the answer to that one.

Coronavirus Offering Students a New Opportunity to Learn

Western Journal
March 31, 2020

Millions of America's best and brightest students have returned home only midway through their spring semester.

Their coursework will continue, of course, as online education assumes center stage for the foreseeable future. Only those of us of a certain age recall how "distance learning" was once such a curiosity.

The considerable downside of this course of events is obvious, especially for the talented athletes and artistic types forced to miss their spring performances or games. A special sadness is reserved for the seniors, most of whom will choose to forgo their final opportunity to compete again next year even if given the option.

The upside of this new normal for America's undergraduates is an opportunity to step back and re-examine newly acquired opinions, to think anew—maybe even begin to question some of the progressive indoctrination they have been force-fed by overwhelmingly leftist professors in the social sciences and humanities and their administrative enablers.

Here, a First Amendment redux is long overdue. Why not a reminder of how the '60s-era free speech movement changed our culture—and how the political correctness–inspired campaign to curtail speech through made-up constructs such as "trigger warnings" and "safe zones" represent serious challenges to our First Amendment freedoms.

You might also remind the kids there is no Constitutional right to proceed through life unbothered by those with opposing viewpoints—and that the simple dismissal of contrary opinions as "racist" or "nativist" or "homophobic" is intellectually dishonest, anti-intellectual, and empty.

In lieu of a protracted remedial course in American history (an academic experience denied many high schoolers these days), a concerned parent might suggest Dr. Martin Luther King's *Letter from Birmingham*

Jail and Nat Hentoff's *Free Speech for Me—But Not for Thee* as instructive, thought-provoking reads.

Another timely exercise would be to revisit the history of socialism, beginning with the impressive body counts compiled by a political philosophy that values government over the individual, egalitarianism over merit, autocracy over freedom.

There is an abundance to read here, of course, but a few "have-to's" stand out: George Orwell's *Animal Farm*, Aleksandr Solzhenitsyn's *The Gulag Archipelago*, and Christopher Hudson's *The Killing Fields*.

Much of the material covered herein is disturbing—snowflakes might even label it triggering—but that is the point. In-the-flesh socialism invariably kills; its history is full of bloodshed and terror. You can bet your son or daughter will be far less inclined to attend a Bernie rally after *these* reading assignments.

A third area ripe for re-visitation is basic economics—you know, the science of how market capitalism creates competition and wealth. True, market economies have their shortcomings. Not everyone is able to compete (and win) in a free economy. But despite some well-analyzed warts, free market capitalism remains the reason our country is so rich, and why so many people from around the world continue to want to come here.

Again, there is a long list of texts worthy of a young person's time, but must-reads here include Milton Friedman's *Capitalism and Freedom* and anything written by the brilliant economist Thomas Sowell.

The silliness (and danger) of political correctness is another timely exercise. Indeed, examples abound in the time of the coronavirus. Recall how quickly Joe Biden associated the president's early travel restrictions on Chinese nationals with "xenophobia," "fear-mongering," and "hysteria."

A senior Biden campaign aide went so far as to say that labeling COVID-19 a "Chinese virus" was a racial slur, thereby ignoring the usual practice of associating a new disease with its point of origin ("German Measles," "West Nile Virus," "West African Ebola"). A compliant media of course piled on until the appropriateness of the executive order became apparent to all.

Finally, these challenging times remind us of how fragile life—and liberty—can be.

Such is a difficult lesson for the young and healthy, but our present circumstance serves to remind us of the importance of self-sacrifice and selflessness in times of danger and uncertainty. Such times also help us appreciate the importance of leaders, as opposed to mere politicians.

There are no better reads in this space than all three installments of William Manchester's *The Last Lion: Winston Spencer Churchill* and David Herbert Donald's *Lincoln*.

Those who have raised children (and paid the considerable freight for their education) have the absolute right to instill their values into their sons and daughters. Too often, those values are lost by attrition or indoctrination by the progressive elites that control American public secondary and higher education.

With the collective timeout recently imposed on our coronavirus-ridden society, now may be the right time to revisit the social and moral mores you instilled in them in the first place. It may indeed be your last opportunity.

COVID Proves China—Not Russia—Is World's Most Formidable Authoritarian State

Western Journal
April 7, 2020

> "The capitalists will sell us the rope with which we will hang them."

This familiar quote, widely attributed to Vladimir Lenin (though likely spurious), remains a central tenet of Marxist/Leninist thought. And nowhere is the assurance contained therein more engrained than in the rhetoric and policies of the People's Republic of China.

President Xi Jinping has in fact been the purveyor-in-chief of China's long march of influence and infiltration into South America, Asia, and the Middle East. Accompanying the money and military might brought to bear is fear—a necessary commodity of domination well understood by the Chinese politburo.

By any measure, Mr. Xi has been effective. The West has proven quite acquiescent in the face of soft—and hard—Chinese aggression.

Here, the demands of Hong Kong's dissidents for Chinese adherence to the 1997 "handover agreement" is met with rubber (and real) bullets.

More foreboding, the protesters surely understand that tanks—lots of tanks—are always an available option for a repressive government. Those of a certain age will recall those same tanks massacred many thousands of democracy protestors in Tiananmen Square over 30 years ago—a historical fact the Chinese government continues to officially deny.

Here, the Islamic world looks past the ongoing imprisonment of a million ethnic Uyghur Muslims in the Xinjiang gulag, strong-armed into silence by Beijing's economic investments and military might.

There is, after all, real gold in that "Belt and Road" initiative, as well as so many other economic development projects fueled by Beijing's cash. In the developing world, it's just so much easier (and safer) to offer up yet another condemnation of Israel's "occupation" of the West Bank. That one never misses its mark.

Here, the World Health Organization slow-walks its declaration of a coronavirus pandemic in deference to the Chinese government's "commitment to transparency," while the famously dysfunctional United Nations Human Rights Council adds a Chinese representative to a prestigious panel—where he will help pick monitors on freedom of speech, forced disappearance, and arbitrary detention.

Here, those profit-loving NBA types who envision millions of jersey and shoe sales in a basketball-loving nation of 1.4 billion people are likewise mute as the body counts continue to pile up on the streets of Wuhan, a count that includes the brave Chinese physicians who early on had the courage at the manifest risk of their lives to question their government's failure to act.

Here, the Chinese government's aggressive saber-rattling and relentless artificial island-building in the South China Sea—aimed at establishing Chinese control of the area's commercial sea lanes—provokes only occasional protests from China apologists around the world (albeit plenty of sleepless nights in Tokyo and Seoul).

Here, the practice of some American politicians (almost exclusively Republicans) to associate the coronavirus with its true city of origin leads the Chinese government to threaten America's generic medical supply chains with a shutdown in the middle of a pandemic.

These Chinese endeavors illustrate how misguided the mainstream media's "Russia, Russia, Russia" narrative has been over the last three years.

Mr. Putin may indeed remain the consummate KGB bad guy, fully capable of creating chaos in his immediate neighborhood (just ask Georgia and Ukraine).

But the bottom line is difficult to escape. Modern Russia is economically backward, overly reliant on its energy sector, and laden with corruption. Putin's cash-strapped regime generates a lower GDP than the state of Texas.

Of course, the foregoing does not constitute a call for a shutdown of bilateral relations with China. The Chinese remain our largest trading partner and may (hopefully) become a more accommodating trading partner during the forthcoming phase-two trade negotiations.

They can also play a vital intermediary role should negotiations with Kim Jong Un ever become serious. President Xi no doubt sees upside for his country as well: stability on his eastern border.

Still, the present crisis reminds us of the lethality so often associated with authoritarian governments. For these nation-states, self-perpetuation always trumps transparency and individualism and freedom. We might accordingly think anew about the wisdom of giving—and selling—so much rope to a regime chock-full of harmful intent.

COVID & China Have Exposed How Globalism's Virtues Were Exaggerated All Along

Western Journal
May 22, 2020

During my twenty years in public office, I would regularly take batting practice on the hypocrisy of the business community.

Why, I would ask, do business interests regularly write checks to politicians who oppose job creators, while liberal special interests reject such game playing?

In private, a weak response was typically offered: we give because it gains us "access." Phrased another way, business interests gave to anti-business politicians because they had become acclimated to the crumbs that fell *if* they fell from big labor's table. I nevertheless screamed bloody murder on behalf of the entrepreneurs who refused to indulge such games—to little avail.

One unforgettable aspect of my crusade was the furious reaction of anti-business legislators to being exposed.

They hated being found out; having your cake and eating it too had been such the perfect shakedown. Who needed some troublemaker shining a flashlight in the corner?

I think back to this "Patty Hearst Syndrome" (identifying with your captors), as the mainstream media continues to report on how dues-paying progressives are viewing the coronavirus pandemic as a rare opportunity to forcibly change American culture and capitalism itself.

To their credit, those who wish to do so are front and center and plenty transparent about their rare opportunity to effect transformative change.

Take "Mr. Progressive"—George Soros—for example. His take is crystal clear: "This is the crisis of my lifetime. Even before the pandemic hit, I realized that we were in a revolutionary moment where what would be impossible or even inconceivable in normal times had become not only possible, but probably absolutely necessary."

Similarly, democratic socialist Bernie Sanders now doubles down on his demand for single-payer "Medicare for All" health care, while the senator formerly known as "Liberal Joe Biden" (now "Progressive Joe Biden") sees the shutdown of the American economy as "an incredible opportunity…to fundamentally transform the country."

How ironic would it be if the very captains of capitalism who have lined the pockets of progressive politicians all these years end up getting beaten up by those same ascendant socialists should Joe Biden win in November!

Further irony reveals itself in the business community's long-running, successful marketing campaign on behalf of globalization as beneficial to the larger culture.

This talking point of both party establishments seeks to depict the rapid integration of "third world economies" (such as China's) into world markets as a significant net positive for the American consumer and America generally. Recall the common refrain of how much the typical consumer benefits from all those cheap Walmart goods manufactured in China.

Another aspect of this argument stresses how the inter-connectedness of supply chains leads to more efficiencies and a more peaceful world. After all, what country would want to threaten its acquiescent trading partners?

The weakness of this narrative, of course, is the presence of a subsidy-driven, not-so-law-abiding trading partner in the form of the People's Republic of China. Indeed, the coronavirus catastrophe has re-educated the world about the downside of dealing with a saber-rattling regime that appears more than willing to intimidate, manipulate, and utilize supply line leverage against its largest trading partner, the good ole U.S.A.

Thoughtful people should not call for a shutdown of bilateral relations with Beijing.

The world's sole superpower *must* deal with its number one economic and military competitor. But America must take note of the coronavirus' principal lessons:

1. Leftist politicians see opportunity whenever capitalism takes a hit.
2. Henceforth, those who promote the advantages of interdependency must be far more realistic when signaling the virtues of globalization with cunning and duplicitous countries that do not share our fundamental values—especially the rule of law.

Biden's "Back to the Future" Plan Is Going to Destroy American Workers

Western Journal
December 10, 2020

For conservatives, many important issues may have "lost" on Election Day: religious liberty, charter schools, gun rights, energy independence, and freedom of speech on campus, to name just a few.

But the most important prospective loss will be sustained by America's working class through a Joe Biden–sponsored "back to the future" relationship with China.

To be fair, Mr. Biden has never attempted to hide his disdain for the tough-on-China, America-first approach of President Trump. Biden has in fact long maintained dovish views toward America's primary economic and military competitor. Recall the famous assurances, "They are not bad folks…they are not competition for us" from the campaign trail.

Indeed, China engagement and economic assistance were in vogue during Biden's long Senate tenure, and especially during his vice presidency. All along, Biden and leaders of both party establishments minimized China's competitive edge—and rapidly swelling and dangerous military might. Nine years ago, Biden went so far as to endorse Beijing's "one-child policy"—before being forced to walk it back in the face of intense criticism.

Former Obama Defense Secretary Bob Gates once quipped and later reiterated that Biden "has been wrong on nearly every major foreign policy and national security issue over the past four decades."

With respect to China, the denominator for bad decisions is the prospect of over a billion Chinese consumers. For Wall Street, that's an awful lot of automobiles, athletic jerseys, and pancake mix. Of course, the price of admission is high: sustained acquiescence to the Chinese government's authoritarian control. And so no anti-China rhetoric from you, NBA!

It is an indulgent behavior that Washington had grown quite accustomed to pre-Trump. Both party establishments provided lip service to

China's notorious campaign of intellectual property theft for decades. (The federal government estimates such theft cost the U.S. as much as $600 billion a year—not to mention gigantic ill-gotten profits going forward.)

A lesser-known element of China's theft and indoctrination network has been the establishment of so-called "Confucius Institutes" on our college campuses, a network of partnerships funded in part by the Chinese ministry of education.

These stand-alone institutes were supposed to advance understanding of Chinese language and culture, but have more recently been viewed as Trojan-horse propaganda organs of the Chinese government.

Such concerns were tangibly addressed in the 2019 Defense Authorization Act that forced colleges to choose between maintaining their institutes or receiving program dollars from the Defense Department. More and more schools are choosing "B."

Today, China's aggression extends to the four corners of the globe.

Military provocations in the Formosa Strait aimed at Taiwan are regular occurrences. Relentless artificial island-building in the South China Sea leaves Southwest Asia unsettled and intimidated. Increased suppression of speech and assembly is crushing Hong Kong's pro-democracy movement. And offensive cyber campaigns directed against U.S. political and defense targets grow exponentially.

None of this is surprising to long-time observers of the regime. Its brutality is matched by a relentless censorship machine. History reminds us that all of the killer "-isms" (Marxism, communism, fascism, socialism) deconstruct history rather than teach it. It's the only way they can survive—and thrive. (Quick question: How many American college students even know about the Tiananmen Square massacre of 1989?)

And so today the cover-up and accompanying propaganda regarding the origins of COVID-19 continues apace, enabled by the World Health Organization—a once-respected entity now almost completely compromised by Chinese money and influence.

Chinese President Xi Jinping well understands the ways and means of projecting power and influence around the globe. His influence campaigns are supported by an economy that is now the second-largest in the world and a military (2.8 million soldiers) that is twice as large as Uncle Sam's.

Back to the present. A Trump-inspired momentum has the American working class leaning GOP these days. Biden and a new internationalist Democratic Party understand the trend—and appear willing to pay the political price (their candidate presumably won the presidency, after all).

And so a more important question arises: Is Joe Biden so blinded by Silicon Valley and Wall Street commercial interests that he will follow a laissez-faire attitude toward Beijing's unrelenting aggression? His China-friendly staff selections to this point in time ominously lean in that direction. Further bad news: if he wakes up from his misconceptions, the danger of Chinese miscalculation looms large.

Americans are not accustomed to "also-ran" status. But China engagement from a position of weakness will ensure just that. So, will 74 million deplorables—and other out-of-fashion America-firsters—come to accept second place? Don't bet on it.

CHAPTER 10

GEORGE FLOYD & THE 2020 CAMPAIGN

On May 25, 2020, a white Minneapolis police officer kneeled on the neck of a 46-year old African American suspect named George Floyd. The maneuver appeared to cause Mr. Floyd to lose consciousness and die. The entire incident (eight minutes and forty-six seconds worth) was caught on video wherein Floyd is heard complaining, "I can't breathe." The video immediately went viral, and Minneapolis—in addition to numerous other major American cities—was soon engulfed in flames. Thirty-one states mobilized National Guard units. Predictably, the violence trumped (no pun intended) the many peaceful protests that had followed the killing. (The Floyd family itself pleaded for nonviolent protests, to no avail.) A heretofore fringe social justice group, "Black Lives Matter" (BLM), quickly assumed a leadership role with regard to the public protests. Of the more violent demonstrations, a number of anarchist groups—especially Antifa—claimed credit. In city after city, their violent escapades often went unpunished, as big city mayors allowed widespread looting and property damage while ordering their police to stand down. A reported 17 deaths and billions of dollars of property damage ($400–500 million in the Twin Cities alone) was the result.

As the inner cities remained tense, a unique plea was suddenly added to protestors' list of demands: "Defund the Police." Remarkably, a number of local and even national Democrats picked up on the emotional appeal—so much so that Joe Biden was forced to announce his opposition to wholesale defunding (in favor of incremental reforms) such as "demilitarization." That the ludicrous demand had legs reflected the depth of emotion surrounding the Floyd case and the incredible reach of progressivism into mainstream Democratic Party thought. That there was no clear answer to what or who was supposed to replace the police (a few rather looney commentators suggested that social workers could pick up much of the workload) spoke to the unseriousness of the advocates. A back-on-its-heels GOP was thereby given a temporary lifeline: polls showed few members of either party supported such a draconian move.

Still, detached from reality agendas did not stop rioters from literally taking over a six-block-wide section of downtown Seattle, Washington. Their so-called breakaway republic ("CHAZ" and later "CHOP") included a police station that was overrun in the initial Floyd-related riots.

Remarkably, Seattle Mayor Jenny Durkan instructed her police to indulge the occupation—famously stating that the protests could turn into another "Summer of Love" (circa San Francisco, 1968). The "left coast" had struck again. Alas, Durkan's appreciation for the Love Fest ended when several thousand uncivil and uninvited protestors showed up at *her* residence.

Yet additional unrest followed the arrest and subsequent death of Rayshard Brooks, an intoxicated African American driver who had fallen asleep in a drive-thru lane at a Wendy's in downtown Atlanta. Once placed under arrest, Brooks fought with the arresting officers, in the process stealing one of their tasers. When the taser was pointed at Officer Garrett Rolfe, he fired, killing Brooks. A week later, *before* the Georgia State Police could conclude its investigation, Fulton County District Attorney Paul Howard (already under investigation for corruption) brought a felony murder charge against Rolfe. This time, however, public opinion was far more mixed. Police unions around the country protested the blatant over-charging, while public opinion polls continued to reflect little public enthusiasm for the "defund" experiment.

Notably, both incidents energized a BLM movement that was immediately propelled into the national conversation on race and police brutality. Corporate America quickly fell in line, as BLM garnered tens of millions of dollars from a business community in perpetual fear of racially driven boycotts. A sidebar but still instructive vignette on the march to political correctness was the removal of The Quaker Oats Company's "Aunt Jemima" brand—an image that was quickly deleted due to its allegedly negative racial connotation. But, as usual, there was the "rest of the story." The original Aunt Jemima was Nancy Green, a former slave, storyteller, cook, and missionary worker who had been signed by General Mills in 1890 (two other African American women, Anna Short Harrington and Lillian Richard, portrayed Aunt Jemima in subsequent years). Relatives of both Green and Harrington opposed the change, citing the injustice of eliminating an important chapter in black history, let alone a successful African American woman who had played a key role in the development of such a universally recognized brand product. Alas, the objection fell on deaf ears. Seemingly overnight, Aunt Jemima disappeared from America's grocery shelves, likely never to return.

Politically correct orthodoxy continued to infiltrate the culture as Hollywood, the arts community, the academy, and professional and college sports quickly advocated newly energized progressive takes on social justice. Here, the NBA had "Black Lives Matter" painted on its floors, while the Boston Red Sox sponsored a huge BLM billboard for opening day at Fenway Park. But it was the NFL that made the most notorious statement: helmet decals reflecting the names of alleged victims of police brutality were prominently displayed. Per Commissioner Roger Goodell, a suddenly woke, BLM-friendly league should have "listened earlier" to Colin Kaepernick. That all this support was bestowed on a group with a mission statement reflecting avowed Marxist positions and a stated desire to eliminate the nuclear family was remarkable. To be sure, many left-leaning influencers saw this as their chance to transform a "racist" culture.

A subchapter of the domestic unrest narrative concerned what to do about persistent rioting and looting in Seattle, Chicago, New York, and especially Portland. In each venue, feckless Democratic mayors ordered their police departments to stand down, thereby indulging continued property destruction and personal injuries. Crime rates in those cities accordingly skyrocketed as news coverage depicted nightly chaos—including the attempted destruction of federal properties. In response, the president sent federal agents to both protect federal property and work with local law enforcement to capture and prosecute the wrong doers. A number of the mayors ordered their police departments to rebuff the federal assistance, even going to court to force the issue. Democrats in Congress joined the chorus, bemoaning the federal government's "jack-booted" tactics while alleging that unidentified federal police agents were kidnapping "peaceful" protestors from the street. The Left's sudden regard for federalism, although ironic, was transparent. For progressives, it was all hands-on deck—anything and everything to defeat Donald J. Trump.

Progressive leaders had no interest in discouraging the protestors or in giving the president an opportunity to claim a law and order victory in the midst of a bitter campaign—the protection of their own citizenry and economic interests notwithstanding. Observers wondered how much more the situations could deteriorate—and how much impact the continued disorder would have on the election. In other words, how much longer could Joe Biden and other leading Democrats soft-peddle and/or literally withhold their criticism of nightly chaos in America's most progressive cities?

And yet at the same time, and in startling fashion—reports began to circulate in early summer that the GOP was targeting African American voters—particularly males—in its campaign advertising. The offensive would continue throughout the Republican Party's virtual convention, led by a dynamic speech ("From Cotton to Congress") by South Carolina Senator Tim Scott and featuring testimonials by African American athletes, small business owners, and celebrities. In the short term at least, the offensive appeared to achieve a bit of progress: post-convention polls reflected African American support for the president exceeding 20 percent.

Democrats fired back with both barrels, employing the always reliable "but he's a racist" charge against the president. A full-court press on race was essential. Party strategists knew that a bleed of 5–10 points among this base voting block would spell doom for Mr. Biden. Starkly contrasting narratives were soon in play. Democratic rhetoric doubled down on a "systemic racism" theme begun in the aftermath of the Floyd incident. On the other side of the aisle, a Trump-led GOP rejected the victim route, instead utilizing a familiar "up by the bootstraps, only in America" narrative. For four days at least, the American dream was again alive and well. But would an appeal to traditional American values (and a widely touted criminal justice reform law pushed through by Mr. Trump) be enough to detach African Americans from generational voting habits?

This "Murderers Row" Lineup Is Set on Destroying Donald Trump in 2020

Western Journal
June 7, 2019

The 1927 Yankees, widely proclaimed baseball's greatest team, sported Hall of Famers throughout the lineup. The heart of the order (Combs, Koenig, Ruth, Gehrig, Meusel, Lazzeri) was famously dubbed "Murderers Row," a moniker that reverberates to this day.

There is another incarnation of murderers row in 2019. But this hit-happy lineup plays on the political stage, not Yankee Stadium. Their goal is not to slam home runs or to beat the hated Red Sox.

Rather, they live to inflict enough damage over the next 18 months to beat one man, Donald J. Trump. Make no mistake, this lineup carries enough power to inflict serious damage on the president and his administration.

As the battle for 2020 is now fully engaged, it's time to better understand the ways, means, and ends of this anti-Trump juggernaut.

The Media

The so-called mainstream media has been at DEFCON 5 ever since the evening of Nov. 8, 2016. As the blue wall came crashing down and the tears began to flow at the Javits Center that fateful night, this group would be the first to take up arms against the incoming administration.

They have not disappointed. The usual suspects (*New York Times, Washington Post, L.A. Times*, MSNBC, CNN, PBS) have worked overtime, ignoring presidential accomplishments and focusing almost exclusively on alleged, often irrelevant, weaknesses to degrade anything and everything connected with Trump.

That this unrelentingly critical coverage of the president and his supporters is one of the primary reasons he won in the first place seems lost on this segment of the fourth estate.

Nevertheless, Special Counsel Mueller's gratuitous parting shot (a not-too-subtle call for impeachment) has further stoked the fires of those who buy ink by the barrel. Suffice to say it's gonna be really ugly going forward.

Barack Obama and the Obama Administration

The Obama administration appears to have inflicted serious damage on their way out the door. The list of suspicious activities includes slow walking the Hillary Clinton email investigation to aggressive "unmasking" of American citizens in the course of a counter-intelligence investigation to reliance on a bought and paid for Russian dossier repeatedly submitted to a FISA court in the course of said investigation.

Alas, the failure of these (and other) operations has prompted Attorney General William Barr to appoint the so-called "bulldog" U.S. Attorney for Connecticut (John Durham) to investigate the investigators. The resulting howls of protest and manifest nervousness from aggrieved Democrats speak to the potential seriousness of this additional investigation.

Progressive Tech/Investor Billionaires

How ironic that some who have gained the most from American capitalism are now in the vanguard of a movement intent on doing harm to American capitalism. Nevertheless, well-known entrepreneurs such as

Tom Steyer, Chris Sacca, Donald Sussman, Reid Hoffman, and numerous others are serious, deep-pocket progressives willing to spend a whole bunch of dollars in order to make Trump a one-term president. (Steyer has also funded numerous state-based initiatives intended to convert red states into blue states.)

These folks saw their midterm investment in the Democrats pay off in a big way. Now, they are turning their attention (and wallets) to the big prize.

Progressive State Attorneys General

Little understood by the average voter, a number of the nation's most hard-left attorneys general have brought lawsuits against the president on a number of front-burner issues, including the rescission of DACA, numerous travel bans, the FCC's repeal of net neutrality, a new border wall, a citizenship question on the census, and Trump's alleged violations of the Constitution's Emoluments Clause (a rarely pursued prohibition on a president's ability to accept money or benefits from foreign governments).

The aggressiveness of progressive state AGs is a rather new phenomenon but one that must be taken seriously by Republicans who now have yet another front to defend in the lead up to 2020.

Academia

I am not breaking new ground here, but things are getting worse on campus. Never has the American academy been more hostile to free (i.e., conservative) speech; never has religious freedom, border control, gun rights, market capitalism, or American exceptionalism been under such unrelenting and unapologetic attack by those charged to "teach" our children.

Precious few of our so-called institutions of higher learning are exempt from the progressive onslaught. What to do? Readers of my columns over the years will recall my repeated pleas to withhold annual giving dollars to these laboratories of indoctrination. It seems to me that hitting weak college presidents and their lefty administrators where they live provides the best opportunity to make our dissatisfaction known.

Hollywood

Where to begin? Robert De Niro? Johnny Depp? Jim Carrey? Alec Baldwin? Still, the specter of Hollywood actors using their celebrity to make political pitches is not new. (Recall Frank Sinatra was quite helpful to JFK, while John Wayne helped a succession of GOP presidents.)

What is new is corporate America's threat of boycotts to protest conservative state laws. Witness Disney CEO Bob Iger's recent lament to the effect that his employees would likely object to working in the state of Georgia should that state maintain its new anti-abortion statute. Look for additional action on the boycott front, as Hollywood explores the outer limits of its reach within flyover America.

Biden, Defunding Cops, and a Few Other Thoughts on America's Summer of Discontent

Western Journal
July 23, 2020

- Today's chameleon-like Joe Biden would not recognize his 35-year voting record in the Senate, and not just because Joe has a difficult time remembering anything these days.

  That Biden was the reflexively left-leaning "Amtrak Joe"—a Northeastern liberal operating squarely within the Teddy Kennedy wing of the party. Today's knockoff takes his cues from the likes of Alexandria Ocasio-Cortez, Bernie, and Beto—placing him squarely within the neo-socialist wing of his party.

  Biden's sudden left turn recalls the similar journey of Hillary Clinton at this point in her campaign. It may be difficult to believe now, but for most of her political life Hillary also operated on the Democrats' traditional labor-left island—that is until she decided to drink the progressive Kool-Aid during her fall campaign.

  The next sound we heard was that supposedly impregnable midwestern blue wall tumbling down on the evening of Nov. 8, 2016.

- Is anyone really surprised the mob has now made its destructive way to our places of worship and religious statues?

  The rioters are not your run-of-the mill protesters (one wonders if they even know the George Floyd story). Rather, these are the relatively small in number but truly committed anarchist- and Marxist-influenced young people seeking the elimination of our Judeo-Christian heritage.

  Their criminality is real, open, and unapologetic.

- The statistics from the "defund the police" era are startling: at least one police officer death, property damage into the billions ($400–$500 million in the Twin Cities alone), and well over 10,000 (and counting) arrests.

  One has to believe that the remaining moderates within the Democratic Party will soon begin walking back some of the more insane "defund" advocacy. Waiting to do so until after the election is a catch-22: if Biden wins, defunding police agencies will have become normalized; if he loses, the rational middle will have again rejected a more ludicrous inclination of the far left.

  The two best lines I have heard in opposition to the defund madness: (1.) "Wonder how many social workers would have run up those Tower stairwells on 9/11?"; and (2.) "Why not have all defund proponents register on a 'No-911' app so the police will know where their presence is not welcome?"

- Not so long ago, the most dramatic split within the Democratic Party pitted traditional New Deal Democrats against more liberal environmentalists. With the rapid ascendancy of the party's progressive wing, that war has now been won.

  Today, the most obvious intramural fight is the one-sided affair between national teachers unions and those (predominately minority) advocates of school choice. How ironic that a wildly successful, grassroots movement of African American women begun in Wisconsin would evolve into a rallying cry for conservatives attempting to break the union stranglehold on public education.

- Speaking of which, the next big (post-Trump election) showdown in our nation's Capitol will be over control of federal dollars on campus.

  The academy's recent campaign to limit speech while promoting newly popular socialist and Marxist thought will collide head-on with a re-elected administration aiming to even the First Amendment playing field.

  The nation's colleges and universities have had it their way for a long time—until Mr. Trump came along with his Title IX (due process) reforms and now a free speech fight for which the American right has been itching for years.

- A bright spot on an otherwise nondescript weekday afternoon occurred recently when *New York Times* writer and editor Bari Weiss resigned because she just couldn't take progressive persecution anymore.

  The angle is that Ms. Weiss was hired (after the Trump election) to be the diverse voice the *Times* has lacked. But the newsroom mob would not countenance such diversity, all that high-sounding free exchange of ideas stuff from our "paper of record" notwithstanding. The only real surprise here is that it took so long for all those supposedly woke defenders of diversity to eliminate diversity within their workplace. What a farce.

- Remember the old days when national Democrats ran campaign ads castigating GOP control of big business and Wall Street and when right-wing CEOs were seen as nothing more than cheerleaders for the Republican agenda? Neither do I.

- Truth be told, many of our nation's distressingly progressive, anti-police mayors and prosecutors are safe bets to win re-election. (This despite their fecklessness in the face of organized rebellion.)

  Their cities are overwhelmingly left; there is no fear of a silent majority response come next election day. Moreover, many of these failed executives are beneficiaries of uber-wealthy sponsors, including the ever-present George Soros. Of course, there may be some movement from those who simply can't take city life anymore—similar to the thousands of businesses that have exited California over the last 10 years.

But overall, our deteriorating big cities are in for many more years of dysfunction and malfeasance. It's the unsurprising result of ultra-left one-party rule.

- As New York City continues to descend into anarchy reminiscent of the David Dinkins era, I keep wondering how Rudy Giuliani got it done, how a legitimate right-of-center, law-and-order former prosecutor made so many decisions that turned the city around—and got himself re-elected in the process.

  Students of history will recall that Giuliani cut taxes, drastically reduced crime, cleaned up corruption (and Times Square), and took on New York's most powerful unions in balancing his budget. The cops loved him. As Joe Biden might conclude after examining Bill de Blasio's rapidly deteriorating city: "C'mon, man!"

- Rays of light: Goya Food's pro-Trump CEO Bob Unanue's courageously standing strong in the face of the Twitter mob's attacks—and sales exploding as a result; a coalition of large and important police unions (the National Association of Police Organizations) that had endorsed Obama/Biden twice overwhelmingly endorsing Trump for re-election; the shocked look on the face of MSNBC host Craig Melvin when all five physicians interviewed for his back-to-school story said they would happily send their own kids back to school this fall; and the RNC's national grassroots operation announcement that it has registered more voters to date than it did during the entirety of the 2016 campaign.

If Gun Sales Are Any Indicator, Race Rioters Are Creating New Trump Voters as We Speak

Western Journal
August 20, 2020

A couple of recent news reports have caught my eye.

Each speculated (with some anecdotal supporting evidence) that a sampling of voters in deep-blue cities hard-hit by riots, looting and property damage are showing signs of "enough," that the combination of anarchy in the streets and cuts to law enforcement is reframing opinions shared by those who have never seen a MAGA hat in person—let alone thought of voting for a Republican.

A related but not coincidental storyline is of an enormous uptick in gun purchases in our most liberal cities.

A pause is appropriate here.

These news items do not mean that thousands of latte-loving, anti-plastic straw drinking, Prius-driving urbanites have suddenly become card-carrying Republicans. It does not mean they have a newfound appreciation for President Donald J. Trump.

Indeed, their devotion to windmills, health care for illegal aliens, and "woke" learning in the public schools is likely not much altered.

What is novel may be a renewed appreciation for the difference between the sacred American right to protest and the illegal, dangerous and terrorizing acts of a mob.

So many of these good folks have now experienced the difference: from the legitimate protests in the wake of George's Floyd's death to the unreconstructed violence of street thugs who have brought widespread destruction to the most beautiful of our urban business districts and neighborhoods.

In a word, they didn't sign up for this.

There is of course nothing surprising here.

The old line about a "conservative is nothing more than a liberal who has been mugged" applies. Who in their right mind could support "protesters" who attempt to destroy a Ronald McDonald House occupied by terribly sick children and terrified parents?

Who does that sort of thing? Certainly not those who wish to participate in a national conversation about law enforcement practices in the inner city.

But there is another aspect to some of the media reports, and it has to do with these impacted liberals taking a second look at how their chosen party has responded to all the civil unrest.

Recall these burning cities have been led by Democrats for half a century or more. Most have all Democratic councils. Republicans often fail to offer even token opposition.

It's one-party rule. Straight blue. No questions asked.

Nevertheless, the mayors and elected prosecutors in these cities have demonstrated a stunning level of indulgence vis-à-vis the criminal element.

Without a doubt, the "most pitiful" award goes to Seattle Mayor Jenny Durkan, who famously speculated that a six-block breakaway "republic" in the middle of Seattle could experience another "summer of love." A couple of murders (and mounting nationwide scorn) ended that imbecilic experiment.

A close second in perfidy is Portland Mayor Ted Wheeler, who was most perturbed by the presence of federal police agents assigned to protect federal property in his city—but not so upset at the nightly rioting and property damage inflicted by "mostly peaceful" protesters who have brought chaos to his city for nearly 90 straight nights.

In Chicago, Mayor Lori Lightfoot's patience finally wore thin when a large mob showed up at her home. Still, the out-of-control gun violence and murderous mayhem continues unabated on the streets of America's "Second City."

Imagine being the president of the chamber of commerce in that godforsaken town today!

But what of condemnation from national Democratic leaders? What indictments about the riots have issued out of Joe Biden's presidential basement bunker?

The answer, of course, is (primarily) … crickets.

Speaker Pelosi and numerous other Democratic leaders have voiced strong opposition to federal agents using tear gas to protect … federal property in Portland.

The presence of federal agents in riot-torn cities is peddled as a Trump administration tactic to generate public support for a "law & order" campaign.

The Biden campaign has adopted a similar line. Pronouncements in support of law enforcement have been few and far between from this crowd.

Only by 2020 standards is this normal politics.

It's as though national Democrats perceive little risk in hanging law enforcement out to dry.

It's as though they either fail or do not wish to understand that even CNN viewers desire a return to normalcy, to safe streets, to peaceful protests that respect the rule of law.

That some of these reliably left Democratic voters are asking whether that is expecting too much in this summer of discontent is not a positive development for the Biden-Harris ticket.

Let's Rename "The Lincoln Project" to "The Benedict Arnold Project"—That Makes More Sense

Western Journal
August 31, 2020

Media attention always follows those who disrupt.

In 2016, President Trump parlayed this law of politics all the way to the presidency. Four years later, a number of once-prominent Republicans also seek to disrupt a re-election campaign.

The rallying point is the so-called Lincoln Project.

Its founders were smart to co-opt a revered name. The American people (with the notable exception of a few rioters and woke college children who never learned about the "Great Emancipator") are attracted to anything that carries the 16th president's name.

No surprise here. Lincoln's life story defines not only the American dream but also incredible courage in the face of a truly existential threat to the country. He remains arguably our most beloved president.

Today, the Lincoln Project goes about the business of using the Lincoln moniker to convince enough undecided voters that a clearly limited Joe Biden is an acceptable alternative—a mainstream Democrat who is in no way a threat to the Constitution.

They will tell you plain ol' "Amtrak Joe" has never suffered from wokeness (you can look it up).

Parenthetical note: many of the organization's supporters are former middle-to-left-leaning congressmen from marginal districts who have grown increasingly uncomfortable with a socially conservative, America-first GOP.

But the group's central focus is not Joe Biden. Its dominant mission is to remind one and all that Donald J. Trump is evil.

Its list of grievances grows by the day. In no particular order, complaints include the president's use of Twitter to communicate outside the mainstream press, his disdain for both party establishments, his unrelenting salesmanship, his decision to give family members jobs in the West Wing, his use of simple (and at times coarse) language, his habit of ignoring career bureaucrats, his love of golf (at his own properties), and his support for a "big beautiful wall" at the southern border.

And then come the media's favorite hits: he praised racists at Charlottesville (well, not really—read the transcript), he is anti-Semitic (well, not really—his son-in-law and grandchildren are Jewish), and he struck a deal with Vladimir Putin to win the election (well, not really—four years of relentless investigation and still not one shred of supporting evidence in sight).

Regardless of facts on the ground, however, members of the Lincoln Project want you to know that Trump is *really* evil.

Listen any hour of any day to CNN or MSNBC or NPR and you too can add to this never-ending list of Trump shortcomings.

What to do?

My first thought is to take the high ground by acknowledging the Lincoln Project's right to dissent. It shows that conservatives can withstand what at least NeverTrumpers believe is speaking truth to power.

All of this should be rather easy as the First Amendment lives on the right. We are not afraid of opposing views. We do not cancel. We defend the right to engage. It is what separates us from Joe Biden's campaign—those who wish to limit our most precious rights as American citizens.

After these preliminaries, we can proceed to the bottom line, to what really counts on election day: school choice, private health care, legal immigration, enforceable borders, originalist judges, fair trade deals, opportunity zones, an isolated Iran, energy independence, standing up to China, religious liberty, Israel (and its Sunni-Arab allies), hunting down and killing terrorists, the Second Amendment, criminal justice reform, re-funding the police, growing your 401(k), honoring our flag on our feet, getting your kids back to school, and playing high school football.

Come Nov. 3, the foregoing agenda should prevail over professional victimhood, riots, identity politics, defund campaigns, the *New York Times*, George Soros, and socialism.

Accordingly, the Lincoln Project's benefactors do not want you to think about how four or eight years of a Biden-Harris administration would damage our culture and make our country unrecognizable.

That the Biden-Harris agenda makes the Obama administration look downright mainstream by comparison should scare you to death.

Alas, not everyone has read their platform. I seriously doubt our beloved restorer of order, Mr. Lincoln, would approve.

The Trick to Trump Winning the Next Debate Is to Make Biden Debate Biden

Western Journal
October 2, 2020

Former Vice President Joe Biden's ability to meet the low bar of mental fitness and stamina, which he demonstrated during Tuesday's debate, does not extinguish the issue.

Indeed, in more normal times, the intellectual capacity and stamina of a major-party nominee would be an all-important, front-burner issue. But not so much during the historically weird election year of 2020.

For my taste, too many conservative pundits on TV engage in gratuitously mean-spirited reviews, employing selective videos of the former vice president's more infamous memory lapses.

Note these are not the type of faux pas everyone—including elected officials—typically commit. Rather, the scenes are uncomfortable, making me hearken back to the clearly limited Ronald Reagan at the end of his second term.

Still, outside the base, these videos probably do little to advance the Trump cause. And they in fact may add to "mean-spiritedness" as a reason to reject the president.

On the flip side, too many Democrats (and their media enablers) pretend they do not see what is obvious to everyone. One byproduct is loss of credibility—what used to be the kiss of death for media types who wish to be taken seriously.

The few who have bothered to acknowledge the issue tend to dismiss it quickly, as though questioning a nominee's mental capacities is an exempt line of criticism. To wit: the media's uncritical acceptance of Dr. Jill Biden's refusal to "go there"—an effective response in the face of an acquiescent media.

All of which gets us back to the issue of how we arrived here in the first place.

Hard to believe now, but not so long ago Joe Biden was dead in the water.

An uninspiring campaign, unenthusiastic supporters, and lack of funds made for many premature political obituaries until the African American vote in South Carolina's primary saved him. It was the first state primary he had ever won in three national campaigns, and it could not have come at a more opportune time.

But it was not only the African American vote to the rescue. It was also a Democratic establishment correctly scared to death about what a Bernie Sanders or Elizabeth Warren nomination would do to their party's chances in November, not to mention their party in general.

And so all those who had passed on drinking the progressive Kool-Aid boarded the Biden train. Everybody knew this was a long way from Obama-era enthusiasm, but at least a possible Biden loss would not likely take the House down with him.

Back to the present. Biden's staff has gone to great pains to limit their presidential nominee's campaign. They fully understand their candidate's limitations and have (so far, at least) been successful at their low-key strategy.

Of course, a virtual campaign is more plausible in the time of the coronavirus. But even so, Mr. Biden engages in few public appearances and seldom does he leave the confines of his Wilmington, Delaware, basement. Even when he does so, his "crowds" are socially distanced and almost creepily limited to single digits.

As for real unscripted press availabilities, forget it. The few questions Mr. Biden takes are carefully chosen and apparently embarrassingly scripted down to the answers on his teleprompter.

Still, the campaign (and how he would govern if elected) is but a sideshow for the Biden staff. Their wish is to make the election all about the evil occupant at 1600 Pennsylvania Avenue.

Republicans are confronted with a far different challenge, one that played out during the first presidential debate. Their candidate is hyper-aggressive: he loves to mix it up, to counterpunch against one and all who dare attack him. He prides himself on hitting hard, a modus operandi that has largely worked in both his business and political careers.

But how to deal with Joe Biden in his present state of platitudinal diffidence? That is a tough one, and a problem that the president's staff must remedy prior to the next presidential debate.

I hope the president will tap the brakes. After all, he possesses a stalwart record of accomplishment, foreign and domestic, that should be front and center in a re-election campaign. And, if required, he can still be the counter-puncher in response to Biden's more ludicrous attacks (e.g., every life lost to coronavirus is Trump's fault).

Independent and moderate voters do not appreciate over-the-top aggressiveness. The president should accordingly toe a delicate line, perhaps exploring the increasingly uncomfortable relationship between the Democrats' traditional liberal establishment and its suddenly ascendant progressive wing.

In other words, make Biden debate Biden. Now that's a winning strategy.

My Favorite Pollster Has Boosted Trump's Chances by 10 Percent

Western Journal
October 12, 2020

The vast majority of my professional friends are lawyers, lobbyists, public officials, or those otherwise engaged in some aspect of politics or public policy.

Taken together, these groups are known as the "chattering class." It is not a sympathetic moniker. Moreover, we (I include myself), of course, inhabit "the swamp."

The latter may be my favorite pejorative of all time because everybody says they hate the place, yet it never gets eradicated.

The inconvenient reason being that although everyone loves to castigate the political class, most folks (be they mail carriers, plumbers, doctors, real estate agents, secretaries, stevedores, nurses, steelworkers, gravediggers, stockbrokers, wind turbine salesmen, police, business owners, journalists, carpenters, or you fill in the blank) want their views reflected on Capitol Hill. But I digress.

Currently, with precious few exceptions, the aforementioned occupants of the swamp fervently believe Joe Biden will easily carry the day on Nov. 3. We know this because the swamp's official media organs—the *Washington Post*, the *New York Times*, the *Los Angeles Times*, CNN, MSNBC, and NPR—daily tell us so with alacrity.

Of course, these charter members of the cultural elite tend to rely on the very same class of operatives and pollsters who told us with complete assurance that Hillary Clinton would be elected in a landslide on Nov. 8, 2016. Some of you may even recall the now-infamous *Washington Post* headline of Oct. 24, 2016: "Donald Trump's chances of becoming President are approaching zero."

Most of the D.C. establishment (both parties) choose to believe Mr. Trump will be defeated as it has been their most ardent goal for close to four years now, and we all know how wishing for a certain result can provide a distorted view of reality ("Trump Derangement Syndrome" being the diagnosis herein).

For further context, check out the daily headlines from the aforementioned official organs. More times than not you will read bits of hard news intertwined with a softer narrative—more a story of how the media wants you to interpret what occurred than what actually occurred.

Throw in the irrational exuberant emotion of finally getting rid of the devil incarnate and you have the hot mess that passes for news on CNN and MSNBC most days.

But enough of the left. What are conservatives to think?

They are daily pounded with anti-Trump media narratives—and more dire poll numbers. Numerous GOP establishment types have fled the island, believing four years of Biden/Harris is preferable to an additional four years of daily disruption.

Then the president gets wracked for his performance in the first debate—after which the polls get even worse. Then he comes down with COVID. Is there no end to the bad news?

The truth of it is that nobody really knows how all this will play out. Joe Biden is the least exciting front-runner in memory, running a mostly subterranean campaign that is difficult to gage.

On the other side, the president and his movement have been difficult to judge from the jump. Mr. Trump has never consistently polled above 50 percent—even when he won.

Then there is the "silent majority," sometimes known as the "I'm scared to talk to pollsters because I don't want my car door keyed tonight" crowd.

This is likely a large group: the Cato Institute has reported that up to 77 percent of conservatives are uncomfortable sharing their political beliefs. Note that these GOPers are not simply paranoid.

The media has regularly reported stories in which Trump supporters are confronted or attacked in public or at school—and not just college campuses. In this environment, MAGA hats are considered provocative. What has happened to free speech in this country?

My favorite pollster (name withheld to protect the guilty) gives the president a 40 percent chance of winning on Nov. 3. Before you get too depressed, I should tell you that he gave candidate Trump a 30 percent chance last time.

Now, don't you feel better?

The Mainstream Media Is Now Employing Boulders in Order to Tip the Election for Biden

Western Journal
October 26, 2020

No one truly knows how the election will play out. We do, however, know how the media want it to go.

The continuing mainstream media blackout regarding emails reflecting Hunter Biden's nefarious activities in Ukraine as well as sordid implications of father Joe's complicity and possible financial gains would have been blowout news in a normal year—but not so much when Donald Trump is on the ballot.

Just think of the media circus if the roles were reversed and Don Jr. or Eric Trump were the ethics-challenged child at issue.

Indeed, we have been forced to watch from the sidelines as Big Tech exerts its enormous clout in shutting the story down. Adding insult to injury, Mr. Biden has cited the shutdown as cover for his continuing failure to respond. Orwell must be spinning in his grave.

Recall the old metaphor about inappropriately placing one's hand on the scale of justice. A typically left-leaning media is now employing boulders in order to tip the election to their favored candidate.

Should the president prevail—and with him a Republican Senate— look for a serious effort to combat the ever-growing abuses of Silicon Valley regarding how, when, and even whether the public receives political news.

Yes, many conservatives have finally had their fill of this dangerous game. A contingent of First Amendment–friendly GOP members will lead in what promises to be bruising fights over liability and antitrust protections currently enjoyed by the social media giants.

Speaking of those for whom this election is a very big deal, that ever-growing, loose confederation of POTUS-hating NeverTrumpers have serious skin in the game.

For these shut-out GOPers, the continued employment of Mr. Trump as the leader of the free world presents an existential threat. They are the establishment, and they want their status quo back. But theirs is an interesting quandary. Think about it.

A Trump win raises real questions about their continued relevance on the national political stage. After all, a one-off win over a polarizing and unlikeable Hillary Clinton can be rationalized away, but a second win over good ole Amtrak Joe after four years of brutal resistance and in the midst of a worldwide pandemic would show the world a new main street, America first–oriented GOP is here to stay.

Another four years outside the tent for these Lincoln Project types would indeed be hard to swallow as their temporary Democratic allies will surely jettison them in a heartbeat. Who needs temporary allies with no push inside their party? In any event, two losses to the great devil Trump will have the Democrats preoccupied with their own intra-party problems.

A Trump loss presents a different set of issues. A few jubilant NeverTrumpers may get rewarded for their efforts with goodies such as appointments, but ascendant progressives would have little tolerance for newly arrived, right-of-center Republicans in their neighborhood.

For just one example, John Kasich's fiscal conservatism (let alone pro-life record) would never sit well with the Bernie bros and AOC types who will be directing policy in the new administration.

If you doubt my opinion, take a good look at last week's threatening letter to Mr. Biden, issued by uber-left progressives demanding that he eschew corporate America from his new administration…or else. Trust me, this time the uber-lefties mean business.

But how Trump-supporting Republicans would view the turncoats is even more interesting.

Most would view their former brethren with jaundiced eyes. Those who fought—and lost—the re-election effort would require the NeverTrumpers to own the Biden-Harris legacy, especially if it proves to be the next installment of "Progressives Gone Wild." Some of the anti-Trumpers may not care about being identified with the pseudo-socialist, open-borders crowd, but others surely would.

For the latter group, it will be a long, uncomfortable road ahead.

The Deplorables, Clingers & Chumps Are About to Shout "We. Count. Too."

Western Journal
November 2, 2020

OK, George Washington defeated the Brits; Truman beat Dewey; Trump beat Clinton; Appalachian State beat Michigan; the Jets beat the (Baltimore) Colts; Douglas beat Tyson; Chaminade beat Virginia; and the U.S. (miracle) beat the Soviets.

Monumental upsets all. Heavy favorites lost; the smart money had it wrong.

I know, Trump vs. Biden is not quite the same. An incumbent president has serious resources at his disposal—just check out the recent miles logged on Air Force One. Still, the width, depth, and reach of the interests in opposition to the 45th president is quite impressive.

How impressive?

Well, start with the power, influence, and money of a united Democratic Party, big-city newspapers, the big four broadcast networks, two out of three of the major cable news networks (except Fox), public broadcasting, Hollywood, Broadway, professional sports leagues, the foreign policy establishment, Big Tech, Wall Street, Silicon Valley, teachers unions, the reliably progressive public college and university professorate, most other public employee unions, the billionaire class, and NeverTrumpers of all stripes.

These combined forces account for the vast majority of the publicly consumed media and politically influential groups in the U.S. Their total monetary contributions to Biden, Inc. to date is somewhere north of a billion dollars. And still the race is dangerously close. What gives?

The answer is both obvious and more nuanced than you might think.

And it's not just the rage of the woke mob, or the greed of China-focused big business, or the near-religious convictions of the climate activists, or the uber-left tilt of teachers unions, or the anti-sovereignty cries of the open borders crowd, or the determination of secularists to remove religious liberty from the public domain, or the willingness of academics to suppress free speech on campus, or the desire of careerists to get "their" establishment back.

It's actually much larger than all of this—and more dangerous. It's about a subpopulation long ignored (or misconstrued) by the powers that be.

President Obama disparaged them as "clinging to guns or religion."

Hillary Clinton labeled them a "basket of deplorables."

Eminent historian Jon Meacham called them "anguished, nervous" white men with a "lizard brain."

Joe Biden just called them "chumps."

Seems just about every notable lefty has a favorite pejorative or dismissive phrase aimed at minimizing the 63 million voters who supported Donald J. Trump in 2016—and still do today.

And at the very foundation of this rhetoric is a visceral condescension toward average Americans and their values. Seems there are just too many lizard brains preoccupied with making a living, raising their kids, paying their bills, and hoping that the elites might someday make better decisions when it comes to the best interests of middle America.

It is true that a disproportionate number of these disfavored voters lack advanced degrees. Many do not possess undergraduate degrees either. But they are not dumb. They work hard. More than a few still work with their hands. And they do not appreciate condescending dismissals from the "let 'em eat cake" crowd.

And they like it when an outsider shakes things up, questions the status quo, degrades the establishment, and stands up for their slice of America.

Moreover, *les misérables* are sharp enough to see that people who have been in public office for 50 years have not one ounce of understanding as to how to run a business, make a profit, or create a single job. They have seen too many manufacturing jobs dry up and disappear—often because not enough people in Washington, D.C., thought about them.

Today, they see economically ignorant political leaders who blithely say "close the economy down" in their city, state, or country. They also stand by the blue and wonder how "defund the police" could ever gain cultural acceptance. But most of all, they hate being told whom to vote for by people who send their kids to elite schools, live in gated communities, and enjoy armed security but wish to eliminate security for their "lessers."

A quick glance at NBA, MLB, and Oscar ratings may have begun to bring the point home to the woke owners and cultural elitists along the coasts. The "flyovers" (yes, the ones you see lining the streets whenever you-know-who is in town for a rally) may yet again remind the elite that They. Do. Count.

CHAPTER 11

THE END...BUT NOT SO FAST

Post–Labor Day polling reflected a tightening race in the all-important industrial midwest states (Pennsylvania, Michigan, and Wisconsin) and sunbelt (Florida, Georgia, Arizona, and North Carolina). Joe Biden accordingly left his basement with a bit more frequency (notably reassuring union Democrats in Western Pennsylvania that despite his running mate's deep and abiding opposition he was not *really* against fracking) but otherwise entertained extraordinarily few media queries. The contrast on the other side was striking, as well-attended (and not so socially distanced) Trump events took place one after another in the battleground states. But event turnout was only one measure of base intensity, as Biden/ Democratic party fundraising outpaced Republican efforts by significant margins. This time at least, the Democrats' big business advantage would not be silent. Wall Street and Silicon Valley—otherwise known as "Big Tech"—were opening their wallets while going "all in" for Biden.

As if Election 2020 was not polarizing enough, Supreme Court Justice Ruth Bader Ginsburg died on September 20. The 87-year-old had gamely fought cancer for years. The passing of the well-respected liberal jurist was met with great angst on the left. It was their worst nightmare: yet another Trump judge on the high court. Democratic leaders threatened every imaginable delaying tactic should Mr. Trump attempt to fill the vacancy prior to the election. Speaker Pelosi went so far as to threaten another impeachment simply in order to slow the nomination process.

But the threats lacked substance. History revealed that it was indeed regular election year order to bring a Supreme Court nomination forward when the president and Senate were controlled by the same party. And no amount of Antifa or BLM protestors showing up at the homes of Senators Lindsey Graham or Mitch McConnell could stop the Senate from moving forward on the nomination of Circuit Court of Appeals Judge Amy Coney Barrett.

What was a nightmare for progressives was a home run for conservatives. The highly regarded Notre Dame law professor and mother of seven (two adopted) had been confirmed for a circuit judgeship by the Senate a mere three years earlier. It was accordingly clear that the Democrats were limited to two modes of attack: (1.) her textualism, and (2.) her Catholic faith. The former has become standard fare criticism for progressives desirous of activist courts; the latter fraught with danger as Democratic attacks on organized religion—and Catholics in particular—placed the Biden campaign in danger in strongly Catholic, working-class union households in Western Pennsylvania, Ohio, and Michigan. In the end, what began as a battle royal ended in muted resignation. Pro-choice activists mounted a couple of demonstrations at the high court (including one wherein Minority Leader Chuck Schumer warned conservative judges they will "pay the price" and release a "whirlwind" if they voted to restrict abortion access). As well, Judiciary Committee Democrats boycotted the committee vote. But Majority Leader McConnell delivered all but one of his members (Susan Collins of Maine) when Judge Barrett's nomination came to the Senate floor.

The final two weeks of the campaign witnessed two very different strategies: a largely dormant Biden campaign conducted a few poorly attended public events close to his Delaware home, while the president made well-attended mad dashes to the swing states, ending with a 16-stop, four-day barnstorming tour over the campaign's concluding weekend.

Most pundits—and pollsters—viewed Mr. Trump's fourth-quarter efforts as too little, too late. With few exceptions, the national polls supported this opinion as Biden took what was reported to be a 6- to 10-point national lead into Election Day. The same pollsters predicted Democratic gains in the House and a new Democratic Senate. Indeed, a blue wave was about to sweep the country...

But the Trump era pollsters were wrong again. No "blue wave" materialized. Election night witnessed GOP gains in the House (11 seats) and surprising Senate holds in Maine (Collins), North Carolina (Tillis), and Iowa (Ernst), and no declared winner in the main event. No House GOP incumbent lost. Just about all of the major swing states (Pennsylvania, Michigan, North Carolina, Arizona, Georgia, and Nevada) remained to be called as America went to sleep. But significant Trump leads in the "must have" states of Pennsylvania, Michigan, and Georgia began to disintegrate later that night and over the next week, leading Fox News and the Associated Press to declare a Biden victory on Saturday, November 7. Predictably, despite alleged instances of voter irregularities, the media and anti-Trump Republicans immediately began to call for the president to withdraw from recounts and cease court proceedings in contested states. This notwithstanding the fact that Mr. Biden won only 17 percent of American subdivisions (Hillary Clinton won 16 percent) but managed to receive 15 million more votes than Clinton.

A weird transition/non-transition was accordingly begun. Every day was *Groundhog Day* as additional Trump court filings were reported—including examples of fraudulent voting—but followed by increasingly fierce condemnations of a "sore loser" from an uncurious media fixated on moving on from the Trump administration.

Here, Facebook began referring to Mr. Trump as a "political candidate"—*while he was still president of the United States.* Harvard graduate students began a petition to bar Trump administration officials from teaching, speaking, or visiting the Ivy League campus. And Alexandra Ocasio Cortez (joined by fellow progressives and NeverTrumpers) called for the blacklisting of senior Trump administration officials from future employment. Not to be outdone, CNN commentator Christiane Amanpour compared "[the president's] attacks on history, facts, knowledge, and truth" with Kristallnacht ("night of broken glass")—the infamous antisemitic terror pogrom conducted by German paramilitary units on November 9 and 10, 1938. Amanpour did issue a half-hearted apology when even leftwing journalists began to criticize her hideous comparison, but only to stop the bleeding. Indeed, Nazi references had become a matter of course (and no consequence) for progressive commentators over the Trump years.

On the legal front, heavyweight attorneys Rudy Giuliani and Lyn Wood were brought in to coordinate the Trump campaign's multi-state challenges. Fireworks ensued as the Trump team alleged all kinds of election day and post–election day shenanigans: dead people "voting," non-residents voting, non-creased mail-in ballots, non-existent or commercial return addresses on mail-in ballots, historically low rejection rates for mail-in ballots (despite huge increases in mail-in voting), post-deadline mail-in ballots deemed as legal, non-matching mail-in signatures, and GOP vote-counting observers kept away from actual vote counting. One additional phenomenon was noted—a spike in African American voting in Philadelphia, Milwaukee, Atlanta, and Detroit—four major cities located within critical swing states.

The (insurmountable) problem, of course, was proving such alleged negligent/illegal actions were enough for a court to order a new election or a state legislature to refuse to choose electors. The challenge campaign was further hampered by the refusal of a hostile mainstream media to report on even clear instances of voting irregularities. In its view, Trump was done—and they were accordingly unwilling to provide credibility to questions (and evidence) about what went down in the swing states after the polls had closed on November 3.

The State of Texas upped the ante (if possible) by filing its own challenge to election results in the states of Georgia, Michigan, Pennsylvania, and Wisconsin. The suit alleged the states had relied on the COVID-19 pandemic to justify unconstitutional manipulation of state and federal election laws, thereby producing flawed results in the presidential election. Eighteen red state attorneys general and 106 GOP House members signed on in support of the challenge.

Alas, even a conservative Supreme Court held Texas lacked the legal standing required to move the matter forward. The 7–2 decision cleared the way for a Biden victory once electors met the following week in state capitols across the country.

Another GOP problem related to how the president's insistence on following through with the challenges would impact two Georgia Senate runoff races that would determine control of the upper chamber in the new term. A vexing question arose: If Georgia GOP voters were convinced that the fix was in on November 3—why would they bother to show up again in the big-stakes races two months later?

And so Georgia became the focal point of American politics in the final weeks of 2020. Interest groups from right and left pumped historic amounts of dollars into what were projected to be ultra-close races. Total spending in the two "specials" approached half a billion dollars. And all this in a state that not so long ago was considered reliably red. Yankee migration into the deep south was not doing the GOP any favors.

In the end, historic African American turnout gave Democrats Jon Ossoff and Raphael Warnock razor-thin victories. The deep south now counted two certified progressives on its roster of federal representatives. A victorious Senate (now) Majority Leader Chuck Schumer commented, "It feels like a brand new day." And what a new day it would be for a chamber that now counted Bernie Sanders and Elizabeth Warren in its leadership.

With the 2020 cycle now complete, a triumphant news media settled down to a light-touch Biden press operation—a new reality far removed from the breathless, often chaotic Trump era. Speculation turned to the future prospects of both political parties and what would become of the NeverTrumper movement now that its singular mission had been accomplished. Most analysts discerned a split into two general camps: one toward the exit sign, the other deciding to stay in order to "rebuild" a post-Trump GOP. The latter would be an exercise easier said than done. After all, their aggressively anti-Trump handiwork had helped elect a candidate who promised to be the "most progressive" president in American history. Early appointments tended to support that notion as progressive

Obama-era veterans were chosen for key posts. Those NeverTrumpers who chose to stay and continue to run under a GOP banner would have to justify their high-profile decision. Not such an easy task in a party wherein Donald J. Trump carried 94 percent of registered Republicans.

The remainder of the media's pre-inaugural attention (besides the January 6 riot at the Capitol, referenced in the Epilogue) was spent on Biden cabinet nominations and senior staff appointments. Here, the carefully scripted campaign morphed into the carefully scripted Office of the President-Elect. Cabinet slots were filled with little fanfare. Public appearances were few and far between. Early lids became the norm. No rhetorical grenades were tossed; no edgy tweets were issued. Life under Joe Biden would indeed reflect a much lower temperature. The cable news outlets and big city newspapers were beginning to learn that life without the fire starter Trump would be…boring.

12 Warnings for Trump Supporters if Biden Survives the Courts and the Recounts

Western Journal
November 13, 2020

Approximately half the country has concerns about how vote counting was conducted in a number of the most important swing states. Lack of transparency, computer glitches, and (quite possibly) some old-fashioned fraud will keep us in suspense for the next few weeks. As they say, let's hope every *legal* vote is counted.

Should Biden/Harris be certified the winner, things are going to change in a hurry—and flyover America's 72.3 million deplorables will be in for a rough ride. Accordingly, in the realm of what I was taught in law school (always prepare for the worst), here are a few warnings for the Trump army:

For Religious Conservatives

A "dark winter" awaits—and nuns forced to pay for birth control is only the half of it. Religious freedom was on the ballot, and it lost. Now, religious conviction is at serious risk as disproportionately influential secular progressives press their advantage within the progressive movement.

For Free Speech Advocates

Look for campus-style "speech codes" coming to the private sector and increased repression of speech on the grounds of our colleges and universities. The long-term trend in support of our First Amendment freedoms is not a good one. Throw in the propensity of Big Tech to tilt the (speech) playing field and the failure of traditional liberals to join the free speech campaign, and we are confronted with a real cultural crisis.

For American History Buffs

The "1619 Project" just trumped the "1776 Project." Parents must now take the initiative. Your child's education is at risk. As more parents become active in turning back the woke tide in school board politics, it is well and good to recall the wisdom of President Ronald Reagan: "We've got to teach history based on not what's in fashion but what's important. If we forget what we did, we won't know who we are." Wow.

For African American Trump Supporters

Your road just got more difficult. Expect the usual intolerance from the progressive left: "race traitor," "sellout," "token," etc. Your best defense: Donald J. Trump's record on minority empowerment. It has been outstanding. Reference it and defend it.

For Disenfranchised Young Conservatives

No warm cookies, crying sessions, group hugs, or days off for you. Your campuses are chock-full of snowflakes, those intolerant purveyors of identity politics. Time to organize, engage, and prepare for 2022.

Remember, there are plenty of freedom-based nonprofits ready, willing, and able to provide advice and protection. Be less bashful about voicing dissent. Liberal schools bank on your silent acquiescence.

For the Parents of Young Conservatives

It is long past time to rethink your annual giving contributions to schools that refuse to guarantee philosophical and ideological diversity within their faculties. Stopping the dollar spigot is about the only way to get their attention. Do it: it's easier than you think.

For Discouraged Immigrants from Socialist Countries

Time to engage with young people. Most young Americans have no idea what socialism does to the human spirit. You have done an effective job of spreading the message in South Florida and South Texas. It is now time to spread your wings to other venues—especially our college campuses.

For GOP NeverTrumpers

Congratulations—you were an essential part of the Biden coalition. Your Lincoln Project raised a reported $67 million. You accordingly have ownership of what will now unfold; no backtracking for you. Just sayin'.

For Disappointed Blue-Collar Union Workers

It is long past time to make the party switch. Your parents and grandparents will assuredly forgive you. After all, the Democratic Party left you, not the other way around. For those still on the bubble, please take a few minutes to read the Democratic Party platform for 2020. This should clear your mind.

For Dispirited Small Businesspeople

A likely GOP Senate will kill the worst inclinations of the Bernie/ Elizabeth crowd. Still, odds are that the people who will now regulate your business have never spent a day in the private sector. But, rest assured, they know what is best for you and your bottom line.

For Confused Entrepreneurs

A few of you may be wondering what happened to the long-running marriage between the GOP and the Chamber of Commerce. The short answer: Trump happened. You see, an America-first, main-street-focused populist movement was never going to be an easy fit with big business.

Multinational enterprises see big profits in China (just ask the NBA)—and the Great Disruptor was never going to let up on a regime that has made an art of stealing our intellectual property for the last 40 years—let alone unleashing a killer pandemic on the world.

For Worried Hong Kong Dissidents

The totalitarians in Beijing have regained an old ally in the China-friendly Biden. U.S. policy will now reflect that fact: John Kerry–style diplomacy is back in vogue. I suggest you continue to court traditional Republicans and human-rights Democrats to your cause. And good luck; you're gonna need it. China is not well known for contrition.

A final note: recent reports of "outing" Trump campaign lawyers and calls for a blacklist of senior staff are not all bad news. Such tactics smack of deep insecurities and desperation. How else to diagnose those who attempt to silence the loyal opposition?

The 4 Tricks Democrats Will Soon Use to Bring America to Its Knees

Western Journal
November 23, 2020

What do we do now?

What a weird convergence of media reports. On the one hand, we are told to follow an unfolding Biden transition, no questions asked. And if you dare engage serious concerns about the legitimacy of what went down on Nov. 3—especially if you refuse to recognize the former vice president as president-elect—well, you are a certified right-wing nutcase.

You are further admonished to shut up and deal with the demise of Donald J. Trump and the era of hate. "Love" won, dontcha know?

On the other hand are the discoveries concerning software "glitches," newly "found" votes, mismatched signature lines, and a big-time lack of transparency in big-city vote counting. Yet each lawsuit brought a media rejoinder that such attempts to usurp democracy are immoral and nothing more than a waste of time.

Here, then, are four serious obstacles as we seek to achieve a positive outlook on life at the very beginning of a likely Biden era.

Censorship

Right-wingers regularly suggest rereadings of *1984* and *Animal Farm*—and for good reason.

It was not so long ago that censorship of political opinion was condemned by both political parties, especially the Left.

But that was the '60s, when the ACLU had credibility and dissidents of different stripes employed First Amendment freedoms to build historic movements: civil rights, the women's movement, the anti-war movement. It would have been unfathomable for that era's rebel-lefties to indulge censorship in any way, shape, or form.

ORIGINAL, UNCONVENTIONAL & INCONVENIENT | 251

Fast-forward to today, and a new progressive Left is all in for heavy-handed censorship and thought control.

On campus? Of course—how else to control "hate speech" and all those riotous College Republicans?

On social media platforms? You betcha—how else to contain those millions of white supremacists who watch Tucker Carlson nightly while planting voter fraud conspiracy theories on the internet.

In public? Sure—just confront any suspected Trump supporter in the public square and then intimidate him or her.

In the courtroom? Why not—seems NeverTrumpers have taken to "outing" attorneys who dare represent the Trump campaign in court. No freedom of association for you, Sidney Powell!

Beware the Reset

Former Obama aide and Chicago Mayor Rahm Emmanuel is credited with the original quote, "You never want a serious crisis to go to waste," but the latest inclination is more akin to "Let's use coronavirus to achieve a cultural reset."

Just about every Democratic leader who counts has uttered the "R" word in recent months. You should accordingly expect the Biden administration will attempt to institute a steady diet of transformative policies commencing in approximately eight weeks.

Of course, there is no one definition for the promised cultural changes. But they are likely to include draconian mask mandates and/or a national lockdown.

The Davos crowd and other really smart people will also press their latest pet initiative: a turn away from market capitalism toward allegedly more equitable economic systems. Here, a reset to Obama-style multilateralism (rejoining the Paris climate accords, the Iranian nuclear deal, and UNESCO) is clearly in the cards.

Engagement on mega trade deals and rapprochement with Beijing are other important priorities. Indeed, there is no more tangible repudiation of Trump-style nationalism than the latter. Both party establishments (and especially the NBA) will breathe a sigh of relief—and who really cares about a couple million Uyghurs or those problematic dissidents in Hong Kong?

An Educational Nightmare

Educational freedom was on the November ballot—and it lost. Per Mr. Biden's promise, national teachers unions will now be firmly in control of public education. And the damage doesn't stop there. Wholesale forgiveness of student debt is now on the agenda. As is wholesale revisionism in K-12 curricula.

The losers (in chronological order): poor, mostly minority kids in successful charter schools; hardworking students who scraped and clawed their way to paying off their school debt; and truth in American history (you can forget about "The 1776 Project" replacing "The 1619 Project.")

I have long envisioned parental choice as the logical next chapter in the civil rights movement.

After all, African American women started the charter school experiment in Wisconsin in the 1980s. But I now have my doubts. School choice might poll well in minority communities, but relatively few minority legislators are willing to adopt the cause. Just too much political payback involved.

I saw it play out in Maryland 15 years ago. Things just don't change much for kids stuck in poor-performing schools. The bottom line: structural dysfunction is a multi-generational fact of life for far too many disadvantaged kids.

Shame

It's the shiny new word on the left—and it has 73 million targets.

You know the surrounding buzz phrases: "He's not us"; "We can do so much better"; and, of course, "Shame on you [for supporting Trump]."

As a matter of rhetoric, it is effective: the target is placed on defense straightaway. Recall the old rule: "When you're explaining, you're losing."

The downside is its one-sidedness. The shamed Trump supporter is somehow not supposed to examine the alternative.

In this case, a rather weak, sometimes confused 78-year-old coming to grips with the ascendant progressives in his coalition and party. Equally irrelevant are the tangible policy successes of the Trump administration—from Middle East peace to border security to a warp-speed-produced COVID vaccine. Alas, even major policy breakthroughs don't count when shaming is on the agenda.

There you have it. Four challenges for the right side of the aisle. Are you up for 'em?

Political Predictions Rarely Come True, But Here's One You Can Take to the Bank

Western Journal
December 3, 2020

Political predictions are a dime a dozen. There are typically few if any consequences for incorrect, dumb, or embarrassing prognostications made in the heat of a campaign.

Indeed, as time marches on, millions of Americans will forget how far off base the pundit class was about the 2020 election, as they do after every election. And yet here I am willing to make a prediction you can take to the bank.

I'm so sure about this vision of the future because we have heard this promise before—four years ago to be precise.

Then, as now, the Democrats pledged to listen—to rework their agenda in order to address the needs of a long-neglected, beaten-down American working class. But the commitment was quickly jettisoned by a progressive leadership intent on dismissing the last remnants of its New Deal coalition.

Henceforth, there would be no more pretending to care about all that working-class angst. And that is precisely the way it has played out. Today it's all about the coasts, all about Big Tech, all about Wall Street, all about a return to globalism (read: China).

In this world, the verdict has been rendered, and the deplorables have been found guilty of nativism, among endless other isms. And so no more best-selling testimonials (*Hillbilly Elegy*) or *New York Times* analysis pieces devoted to this easily forgotten group. They had their chance at restoration, and all they did was double down on the bad man Trump. Even worse, they grew, from 63 million to 74 million.

This unforeseen growth has been the object of much scorn by woke analysts since election night 2020. Their conclusion: Trump's base survived four years' worth of media brutality because—you guessed it—Trump voters are racists (and forget the 48 months of inspired conservative successes).

This conclusion was given added perspective in President Barack Obama's recent election analysis—a review that reads in part much like his past indictment of small-town, small-minded, dispossessed folks who "cling" to "guns or religion" or "antipathy toward people who aren't like them."

But the former president has added a new indictment reserved especially for millions of Hispanics who somehow saw fit to support the alleged racist Trump. Specifically, despite Trump's racism—"[evangelical Hispanics] think that's less important than the fact that he supports their views on gay marriage or abortion."

A new batch of deplorables is hereby branded—this time "redneck Hispanics" happily clinging to their traditional values and hating all things socialist. The circle will be complete once Hillary Clinton issues a vicious attack on this newly minted group. But one can only hope.

Back to the empty promise. Recall Democrats circa December 2016 lamenting the loss of working-class voters.

In interview after interview, they vowed to win back those same blue-collar workers who had fallen on hard times—and who had twice voted for Barack Obama in the expectation of real hope and change.

Two dozen newly elected House Democrats from purple seats echoed the commitment, and then America watched as those same politicians spent the next four years following an extreme agenda wholly at odds with working-class values—all the while pushing every anti-Trump button available to them.

Today, the old promises are especially hollow and have even less staying power. You see, facts on the ground have changed. Joe Biden (presumably) won an election without a majority of the great unwashed. Indeed, his new administration looks increasingly like Obama 2.0—and that's bad news for the deplorables.

Accordingly, Mr. Biden will jettison the "America First" rhetoric. It's just not what Wall Street wants to hear. Besides, leading from behind is so much easier—and the Europeans (and Chinese and maybe even Iran) will like us again.

So it's back to Paris, Tehran, and most of all Beijing. Americans will no longer be exposed to tales of intellectual property theft or reminded that China unleashed a virus that shut down the entire planet. The NBA has jerseys to sell, dontcha know.

You can also forget about Appalachian poverty and idle factories in Canton, Ohio, and frac sand mining in the Iron Range. Those agenda items are now officially written off as the property of 74 million deplorables of no special relevance in Joe Biden's brave new world of collectivism and internationalism.

The blue-collar covenant is now officially broken. Free agency has arrived for the working-class voter. Republicans need to close the deal.

Here's One of the Most Insightful Replies a NeverTrumper Ever Sent Me

Western Journal
December 18, 2020

On Monday, I sent the following message out on my Twitter and Parler accounts:

Recall media assurance: "Nothing there" on Hunter. Recall media prediction: Trump could not produce vaccine in

2020. Recall media prediction of November 3rd "Blue Wave." Recall media assurance that two-state solution had to predate Middle East peace. Our uncurious media BREEDS cynicism.

No new ground was broken here. I even violated at least the spirit of my usual rule: "Don't complain about things you cannot control."

And then a most insightful reply was received. It read: "Whatever. The good news is Trump will be gone."

Wow. A nine-word response that encapsulates the worldview and the singular concern of the NeverTrumpers.

The terse response served to remind me (and us) how approximately 80 million anti-Trump Americans have viewed the last four years—and specifically how they interpret and process tangible evidence of Election Day shenanigans.

To boot, it reflected how completely onboard the haters are with respect to any person—issue—thing that might possibly damage Donald J. Trump.

Never mind that "Whatever" is short-sighted; never mind that ignoring evidence of voter irregularities because the result was the desired one is inherently dangerous and a threat to our democracy; and never mind that if it worked this time, it could happen again—for the other side. Just. Never. Mind.

The original draft of my tweet was noteworthy for how much I had eclipsed the 240-character limit. You see, only a word count limit could stop me from listing the variety of offenses against journalism committed by the mainstream media over the last five years.

Off the top of my head, think of the Trump "dirty dossier" story, the Don Jr. met with a Russian spy story, the Putin helped Trump rig the voting machines in 2016 story, the Trump aides had regular contact with Russian agents story, the Mike Flynn setup, and so on. That a three-year, $32 million special counsel investigation failed to corroborate even one of these or dozens of similar CNN headlines was no big deal.

Indeed, for the NeverTrumpers, there was a huge upside. It read: whatever. The good news is Trump will (soon) be gone.

But Trump/Russia collusion was not the only phony narrative given legs over the past five years.

Recall the allegation that the president had removed the Rev. Martin Luther King Jr.'s bust from the Oval Office; that he was suffering from mental illness; that he had told Michael Cohen to lie to federal investigators; that Don Jr. had obtained stolen Wikileaks material prior to public release; that special counsel Robert Mueller had issued a subpoena to Deutsch Bank regarding the president; that Russia had hacked into the U.S. power grid; and that the CIA had been forced to remove an agent from its Moscow office because Trump could not be trusted with sensitive information.

All such items were incorrect, of course, but the attitude was (you guessed it): whatever. The good news is Trump will (soon) be gone.

Note that these Trump-inspired journalistic hit jobs were acts of commission—where the media endeavored to spin people and/or events into nefarious plotlines aimed at Trump Inc. In contrast, the Hunter/Joe Biden (non)story was an act of quiet omission—as in, "Nothing to see here"; "This story has been discredited"; and my personal favorite, "It's all Russian disinformation."

Still, whether active or passive, the common denominator toward both sins is striking: whatever. The good news is…(you know the rest).

And so the last four years were marked with endless "Trump is inept"—"Trump is crazy"—"Trump is corrupt" storylines on one side and—literally nothing on the other. Joe Biden did not campaign. He rarely left his basement. And when he did—as during the waning days of the campaign—he had to face existential questions such as, "What flavor ice cream did you order today?"

For context, it is important to recall that all Republican presidential candidates have suffered similar fates from a hostile media. Recall Sen. Harry Reid's bottom-line reply once his well-publicized claim that 2012 GOP nominee Mitt Romney had failed to pay taxes was shown to be false: "Romney didn't win, did he?"

No surprise here; the media tilts 95 percent left on its best day. And so much of the coverage directed against Ronald Reagan, both Bushes, Bob Dole, John McCain, and Romney was along the lines of, "We don't like this guy's ideas—so we're going to hurt him."

The treatment afforded to Trump has been more severe—akin to, "This guy is counterfeit—undeserving of high office—corrupt and insane—and so we will throw everything against the wall and see what sticks."

In other words, "Whatever. The good news is at least Trump will be gone."

The Media Are In for a Nasty Surprise from a Biden Presidency

Western Journal
December 28, 2020

My new favorite political word is "uncurious." The reason is that it so perfectly captures a light-touch national media's dereliction of professional duty at the very beginning of the Joe Biden era.

But before a review of all the missing-in-action failures of the press vis-à-vis Amtrak Joe, it is appropriate to examine what is always so curious for the Fourth Estate, i.e., anything detrimental to a Republican running for president.

Here, we can think back to the brutal profiles of Ronald Reagan as a lazy, dumb, "racist" warmonger; to the hostility afforded the one-time media darling John McCain for his "racist" and hate-filled ads run against that era's new media darling, Barack Obama; to the harsh treatment given to Mitt Romney because of his good looks, wealth, religion (Mormon), occupation ("corporate raider") and, of course, for his alleged failure to pay federal income taxes (a "Dirty Harry" Reid special that Reid would not admit as knowingly false until after Romney had been defeated); to the horrific coverage of George W. Bush for his wealth, "racism," and ne'er-do-well life (recall Dan Rather's infamously false report on the junior Bush's time with the Texas National Guard).

Just Google any Republican nominee over the last 60 years for additional context. It's a familiar, running horror show of hit jobs and low blows from the usual suspects.

And then there is the case of Donald J. Trump—also once a media darling while doing his man-about-town, Queens developer, casino owner, *Celebrity Apprentice* gigs.

During this time, he was also a Democrat and a contributor to Democratic campaigns. He invited the attention and accordingly generated plenty of positive coverage.

That all changed on June 6, 2015, when The Donald and his striking family rode down the escalator at Trump Tower.

This Trump was different. He was still the unapologetic self-promoter but was now an unleashed right winger—ready, willing, and able to attack liberals and their cherished institutions (and establishment Republicans when it suited his purposes).

Stunningly, and to the dismay of the media, the new Trump was pro-gun, pro-life, pro-deregulation, pro-tax cuts, and happy to take on a Chamber of Commerce that in his view had supported trade deals detrimental to America's working class.

Immediately, the media changed course. Trump 2.0 was now the enemy and so the entire media establishment became curious about anything and everything Donald J. Trump: his previous marriages, his business operations, his children, his beauty contests, his casino developments, his dealings with foreign governments, and, of course, his taxes.

What followed was five years' worth of never-ending media exposés on these and so many other issues associated with Mr. Trump and his family. It was a 24/7 nonstop full-court press devoted to damaging the Trump presidency.

Back to the media's benign attitude toward Mr. Biden and his family.

To this point at least, it is a stunningly uncurious approach despite concerning indications of Biden's cognitive decline; a serious allegation of sexual assault; an unwillingness to take positions on controversial issues such as court packing; great wealth despite lifelong employment in the public sector; a son who has profited handsomely via foreign business deals while accompanying his father on official trips; and the specter of accumulating 80 million votes, mostly by the new medium of mail, while failing to campaign.

Some of you may have read the mild objections recently raised by a handful of reporters after yet another Biden "cupcake" press availability.

There may indeed be additional such complaints in the future as even a pro-Biden mainstream media cannot continue to exist on nonresponsive "answers," invariably brief press availabilities, and noontime "lids." But you can bet the negativity will not amount to much.

The media are pleased with a Biden win but also complicit in what comes next. On the upside, they won. On the downside, there is not going to be a whole lot of action. Basements—even in the White House—just aren't that exciting.

Uncuriousness has its price.

2020 Has Taught Us That the Elite No Longer Have to Pretend to Care about "Flyover" America

Western Journal
January 15, 2021

It's always been this way, just not as blatant. But the advent of 24/7 news coverage has made it upfront—and always personal.

I refer to "the attitude"—how our elites view America's laboring class.

It is a workforce where some still punch a clock and work with their hands. Over the years, they have been stamped with many monikers—some more belittling than others. These include "the silent majority," "Reagan Democrats," "Walmart people," "irredeemable deplorables" and, most recently courtesy of CNN, "Olive Garden" and "Holiday Inn" people.

The point—or image—is impossible to miss. These are the unfortunate folks who missed the boat into the middle class. And regardless of which label is in vogue at any one time, the "really smart" people in charge of media, academia, Hollywood, social media platforms, and (more recently) corporate boardrooms have the same demographics in mind: downscale, white, blue-collar people without college degrees.

But the caricature does not stop there. Other familiar elements include gun owner, churchgoer, bowler, cop supporter, rural dweller. More recently, certain African Americans and Hispanics were added to the narrative, but always with this sort of disclaimer: "traitor to the cause."

That cause, of course, is a potent brand of secular progressivism. It is an ideology that has enjoyed considerable success on academic campuses (being taught, again, by really smart people) and along the coasts for decades.

But it is now ready to assume a more dominant role in our cultural identity. I know this because Joe Biden and Kamala Harris won the election while feeling secure enough to run on a platform far more progressive than Barack Obama's.

You see, there is a world of difference between the warmed-over, Western European, socialism-lite mush peddled in past campaigns and what now confronts America. To wit, a long-promised transformation of our cultural identity. (Some on the left have characterized it as a "reckoning.")

Indeed, the Biden/Harris team is the only ticket in memory to win the presidency while indicting the country it wishes to govern for its many alleged flaws, including countless "-isms" and "-ics." That such a critique could beat an unapologetic "America-first" agenda speaks to its wide-ranging appeal.

I am not the first observer to bemoan what this transformative time means for the beaten-down and now truly woebegone working class. Yet we can all recall that not so long ago, certain of the elitists found this subset of working people to be of some scholarly interest.

Books were written and movies made (most recently *Hillbilly Elegy*) about them. Here, a degree of condescending empathy was employed for the "bitter clingers" of religion and guns (to borrow from President Barack Obama's critique) left behind by our technological age. They were more to be pitied than pilloried. After all, they weren't especially bright—and certainly not dangerous.

But all that changed when a Queens developer spoke to them as people, not peasants. They returned the favor with 63 million and 74 million votes respectively in the next two general elections.

The "let them eat cake" members of the intelligentsia were not happy with the turn of events. They saw an empowered proletariat and didn't like it one bit. And so no more empathetic books for you, Appalachia!

It is a safe bet that not a whole lot of pundits and writers at the *New York Times*, the *Washington Post*, or CNN follow NASCAR, watch WWE, or understand deep down the importance of high school football in small-town America.

But it doesn't matter so much anymore. The circa-2016 outsized influence of the working class has been eclipsed in 2020.

In other words, there are now enough highly educated white and minority voters in Philadelphia, Detroit, Atlanta, and Milwaukee that progressives no longer need to *pretend* to care about them.

Flyover America accordingly has a very big problem. Very soon, it will no longer be a national priority. And the next opportunity to do something about it doesn't come around until 2022.

CLOSING THOUGHTS

Much of the Left's reaction to the Trump presidency was expected. A reality TV star, casino magnate, and real estate developer (and registered Democrat to boot) had unexpectedly arrived on the scene and against all odds ruined a long-planned coronation on behalf of the first female president. The president's unapologetic history of supporting both parties and fondness for over-the-top tweets only added to progressive angst. But there was another, far deeper reason for all the antagonism. You see, the progressive intelligentsia had interpreted the election of Barack Obama as a turning point in American politics—and our cultural values. The smartest folks in the room had elected—and re-elected a black, true blue progressive intent (in his own words) on "transforming" America. And to some extent, he had been successful: two uber liberal Supreme Court justices, a war on fossil fuels, a slimmed-down military, the empowerment of public sector unionism, and, of course, "Obamacare." But even this agenda was not enough to placate an ascendant progressive class. They saw Hillary I as Obama III—the time wherein truly big progressive ideas would dominate the national agenda. At that time, the sloppy Obamacare would be repealed by a single-payer system—"Medicare for All" in the new vernacular. Then, abortion-on-demand—at taxpayer expense. A new national minimum wage of $15 (or more). The fossil fuel economy would be replaced by...a "Green New Deal." Gun confiscation would finally come to fruition. Religious liberty would be unmasked as a placeholder for discrimination. And, most important for transformative purposes—permissive national borders would become the accepted status quo. Here then (would have been) the opportunity to transform an allegedly systemically racist America into a more diverse, secular, and green place—one far more interested in equality than economic growth, political correctness than truth. And it all was postponed because of one disruptor and the newly crowned deplorables that had come to champion his cause.

Four tumultuous years later, and it was over. A combination of too many controversies, too many investigations, too many self-inflicted wounds, too much negative media coverage, and too many mail-in ballots had closed the chapter on the Trump era. Relieved media, political, and academic elites cried, "HALLELUIAH." Seventy-four million disappointed deplorables claimed, "Foul," and worse. Trump himself said he would be "back in some form." A Trump-hating—but dependent—media likely interpreted the latter with mixed feelings.

Still, no tome about the Trump years would be complete without some speculation concerning the future, and the very real challenges facing a sharply divided country.

A Biden presidency literally and figuratively will look a great deal like Obama III, with many former administration officials coming back to pick up where they left off four years ago. Whether increasingly insecure and mostly silent liberals will challenge the new administration's progressive tide will be an important storyline. Nevertheless, you can take it to the bank that much of the intra-party debate will concern not whether but how far left the policy agenda will shift. Whether middle America is comfortable with its liberal-labor party tilting so hard away from the American mainstream will be determined in the 2022 midterms and, of course, in 2024.

On the other side of the aisle, a post-Trump GOP may include… Donald J. Trump, whether as a nominee for 2024 or the self-appointed leader of a "new" Republican Party. Regardless of any Trump role, it is likely that future GOP wannabes with presidential aspirations will incorporate—and articulate—a healthy dose of nationalist/populist priorities in order to energize the working-class and rural grass roots that propelled

DJT to record-setting vote totals in two presidential runs. Easier said than done, for sure. The establishment wants its party back. Engrained expectations indeed die hard. And Trump's ways certainly turned off many veteran Republicans.

But the post-2020 GOP has a different look—and feel. It is a party that (against all odds) gained ground with African Americans and Hispanics not only because "defund the police" and silence in the face of urban anarchy provided Trump with an opening—but because of a four-year campaign of "promises made, promises kept." Here, Trump and down-ticket Republicans campaigned on an agenda targeted to minority communities: *real* justice reform, *real* pardons and commutations, *real* support for historically black colleges and universities, *real* urban renewal ("opportunity zones"), and *real* increases in minority household incomes pre-pandemic.

And then there are the millions of independents and Democrats who became Trump fans but are hardly core GOP voters, having voted for Barack Obama (twice) just a few years ago. Maintenance of this blue-collar connection is essential in light of the overwhelming might brought to bear by today's increasingly aggressive and progressive Democratic Party. This wing of GOP, Inc. *can* grow—likely with a candidate who possesses enough disruptor credentials *and* the political acumen to soften rough edges and coarse language in a way Mr. Trump never cared to do. Such a candidate would be welcomed in the suburbs, where white Republican women are increasingly comfortable voting for progressive Democrats.

As articulated above, another problematic issue is the firm conviction among millions of Trump voters that the 2020 election was fraudulent. Evidence of dead people voting, computer "glitches," ballots "found" days and even weeks after an election, and lack of transparency in vote counting made millions of Americans question the integrity of the 2020 election. Plenty of "Stop the Steal" campaign signs were accordingly visible at post-election rallies in support of the president.

But an inconvenient fact followed the Trump challenges around the country: party operatives had been outmaneuvered in the days and months leading up to November 3. Coronavirus-generated procedural changes had allowed Democrats in a number of swing states to bypass their existing election statutes in favor of large-scale mail-in voting—including a Georgia consent decree that allowed for more permissive identification for mail-in as opposed to in-person voting. Dozens of post-election Trump challenges were subsequently deemed moot. Election re-dos are extremely rare, and judges from both sides of the aisle found it easy to avoid ruling on the merits where Republicans had slept on their pre-election rights.

And so a crystal clear bottom line emerged: Democrats would have nothing to do with the president's numerous legal challenges. No amount of expert testimony regarding potentially flawed software or middle of the night Biden vote surges would make them curious about irregularities or mitigate their unbridled happiness at the end result. Conversely, tens of millions of Trump supporters were not only left disappointed, but cynical. They asked: Why bother to invest all this emotional capital in "rigged" elections? The question is all the more problematic for a party dependent on heavy outer-suburban and rural turnout in order to counter Democratic machines in the cities. Suffice to say future GOP governors, secretaries of state, and state party organizations cannot afford to be out-processed the way their predecessors were in the lead-up to the election of 2020. If they continue to be so outplayed, the GOP best prepare for a long time in the desert.

EPILOGUE

I planned to complete this book once the results of the January 5 runoffs in Georgia were final. In fact, I had finished the "closing thoughts" chapter only hours prior to the Trump election challenge protest scheduled for January 6—a well-attended demonstration that devolved into a violent invasion of the U.S. Capitol. The mob scene was captured on videos that went viral. Windows were smashed, and offices were overturned. Five deaths were attributed to the resulting chaos, and dozens more suffered serious injuries.

The president's response recognized the legitimacy of the protest while requesting the intruders stand down and "go home in peace." But the response was deemed wholly inadequate by a large segment of the press corps and official Washington, including Republican members of Congress and even members of his own senior staff. The next day, Leader Schumer called for the removal of the president through the 25th Amendment, while Transportation Secretary (and wife of Republican Leader McConnell) Elaine Chao and Education Secretary Betsy DeVos resigned.

Universal condemnation of the demonstrators' criminality and the president's delayed response to the riot encouraged House Democrats to again press impeachment proceedings—this time a mere nine days prior to the end of the president's term. Accordingly, a hastily pieced together single Article of Impeachment was passed by the House on January 13, 2021, with 10 Republicans voting along with party-line Democrats in the

House. And all this with no chance of conviction in the Senate, where a two-thirds majority vote would be required.

But more ominous was Big Tech's—and Big Left's—reaction. Industry leaders Google and Twitter undemocratically locked the president out of his accounts. Similarly, Apple deleted the free-speech friendly platform Parler from their App Store. Amazon Web Services followed suit by suspending Parler from its servers. Democrats picked up the narrative of a social media–driven bunch of anarchists and white supremacists come to Washington for purposes of insurrection. A full court press against all things Trump followed, focused on the riotous actions of a small minority of instigators on January 6.

A post-election rocky road had just gotten rockier for beleaguered conservatives—and Republicans. Herein was an opening for all the progressive angst built up over the Trump years and the Left intended to take full advantage of the opportunity. Seemingly overnight, a newly popular censorship card would be played. After all, the president and his sycophantic fans had been too loose with all their election fraud talk, right? Making matters worse, there would be no cavalry racing to the rescue, as free speech liberals went distressingly silent—kowtowing to the ascendant progressives now in charge of their party.

As the Trump era dwindled down, some on the right were exhausted by a bare-knuckled, four-year fist fight. Others remained ready to oppose those who sought to persecute Trump supporters while deconstructing the America they knew and loved. No easy task here (nothing worth fighting for is) and especially difficult in light of a newly acceptable and intimidating cancel culture suddenly embraced by large segments of corporate America.

In the end, however, those who celebrated so many conservative victories over the last four years exited stage right. There will be no more midnight tweets; no more verbal altercations with Hollywood lefties; no more let-it-all-hang-out interviews; no more celebrations of a long-neglected, beaten-down working class; no more America First rallies; no more salacious material for late night comedians; no more excitement…but it sure was an unconventional—and inconvenient—four years with an original Donald J. Trump.

SPECIAL THANKS

To Greg and Chris Massoni for their diligence, support, friendship, and loyalty over the many years, and…

To Professor Rick Vatz ("Prof") for his steadfast friendship and willingness to review my work at a moment's notice, and…

To Post Hill Press for their (always) exceptional teamwork and support in transforming a transcript into this book.